THE TRUTH ABOUT CHRISTIANITY

THE TRUTH ABOUT CHRISTIANITY

The Gospel of Thomas &
The Book of Revelations,
Deciphered

Higher Connections Group

iUniverse, Inc.
New York Lincoln Shanghai

THE TRUTH ABOUT CHRISTIANITY
The Gospel of Thomas & The Book of Revelations, Deciphered

iUniverse books may be ordered through booksellers or by contacting:

iUniverse
2021 Pine Lake Road, Suite 100
Lincoln, NE 68512
www.iuniverse.com
1-800-Authors (1-800-288-4677)

Book Cover Design:

Artwork by Christine Hunter
Graphics by Freedom's Design
freedomsdesign.com

ISBN: 0-595-33043-6

Printed in the United States of America

Contents

THE GOSPEL OF THOMAS

DECIPHERED

Preface

When Moses ascended the mountain to talk to God, he went into prayer and then meditation. When Jesus wanted to talk to God, he went into the Gardens or another quiet site. When you desire to talk to God—and hear what he has to say—you go into a quiet place where you can pray (talk) and then meditate (listen). The same is true with this book. We first asked for guidance because we knew something was calling us. We prayed and then meditated on the subject, both separately and together.

Just a little biographical information about the both of us. My wife is a teacher and for many years I was a practicing CPA. We are both part Irish and my wife is also of French descent as I am also of English descent. Maybe that is why we have the gift of being able to listen and hear the words given to us, but then again we have been told repeatedly that *EVERYONE* (just like Plato and Socrates) has the ability if they would but keep *asking* and *trying*. Trust me—it works!

When we first began we were instructed to read and study "*The Course In Miracles*" published by the Foundation for Inner Peace (ISBN 0-9606388-8-1) and become versed in its contents. The basic premise of the book is: "Nothing real can be threatened. Nothing unreal exists. Herein lies the peace of God." I am here to tell you that studying that book by yourself is no easy matter. As a consequence we began studying the book and then going into meditation. Within a very short time my wife started receiving information about the studies—sometimes about the chapter, sometimes about the paragraph and later about each sentence. Needless to say we filled many tapes with the conversations.

After we finished *The Course In Miracles*, we were asked to write this book explaining the correct interpretation of the *Gospel of Thomas* and the *Book of Revelations*. We diligently met every night of the week—except on Sundays—for approximately two hours and then the next few days, I would reduce the tapes to type. The result is what you have in your hands right now. If you have any doubt about this, I still have each and every tape stored away in a safe place should reference be needed.

There were many evenings when our mouths gaped in awe over what we were hearing and, both of us having been raised as Catholic and Baptist respectfully, it was at first a little difficult to relate to. However, as we continued on the whole picture became so crystal-clear that we couldn't wait to finish. It took us over fourteen months to get this message to you. I have to admit it made us believers, and I am sure it will open your eyes and certainly give you something to seriously think about.

Please do not—in any way—take this book as a criticism of the immaculate teachings of Jesus Christ.

Enjoy and may God Bless You.

Forward by Yeshua ben Joseph—Jesus Christ

Judas ben Ezra, called Didymos Judas Thomas, was as much my brother as were my other siblings. In fact, he and my younger brother James were so close in age as well as in relationship, that they were frequently called "the twins." Didymos is Greek for twin as is Thomas Hebrew or Aramaic for twin. Thomas's father was my fathers' brother who was a widower and traveled extensively with my Uncle Joseph of Arimathea; therefore was frequently absent. We spoke Aramaic, Hebrew, Greek and Latin practically as one language due to the presence of our trading partners and also the Roman conquerors.

During the course of our travels between Egypt and Palestine, and even into India, Thomas and I used to flex our minds by encoding my sayings. Now, understand, during those times we were just as much (if not more so then you are) under the control of religious institutions and corrupt governments; therefore it was necessary that we encode the sayings to be deciphered in the future.

As we traveled around, Thomas was an ardent note taker and, because he had the bookkeeper spirit, it was important to him to get everything as right as he could; it is too bad that his gospels were not gathered together and published as you would have found them much more accurate than your current ones. He took notes that made sense to himself, but not necessarily to anybody else; however, he captured more of the meat of my sayings. In going back through the Gospel of Thomas now with everything that you know, you are going to get a better view of what those sayings are about.

Thomas, as I said, would scribble down the sayings and then go home at night and write out more about what the sayings meant. Those writing have been lost and all you have are his preliminary notes. The more thorough notebook he kept well hidden because of the nature of the people to whom he was ministering. He couldn't give them too much information at once and it would have been harmful if his notes had fallen into the wrong hands, so he protected them and they were lost down through the ages.

In providing you with the essence as well as the literal meaning of my sayings, I am about to use modern day examples and occurrences so that you will understand how these ancient sayings pertain to your times.

Keys to the Gospel of Thomas and to all the sayings of Yeshua

- God evolves, learns, and grows in wisdom from nanosecond to nanosecond.

- As part of His growth, God desires to be able to enter physical form to enjoy the fruits of his creation.

- Everything that exists was created by God and serves as a temporary repository for his Universal Soul.

- You, as part of the Universal Soul, voluntarily came to earth to inhabit an imperfect, temporary vehicle (body).

- As a piece of the God spirit you are a soul with a body, not the other way around.

- Your mission in coming to Earth is 1) to fully awaken to yourself as God in human form, 2) to enjoy the creations of God, 3) to help your brother awaken and 4) to live in harmony with your brother as, collaboratively, you continue the evolutionary process.

- You exist to love and co-create with Me and to act as a guardian for the earth.

- *Neither good nor evil exist, only fear and love exist.* Fear causes you to believe you are alone and separate from God and Man. Cast away fear and you cast away ego.

- The <u>ego</u> created heaven and hell by causing you to believe you are 'special' and thereby separate from Me, your brother and all things on the earth.

- *Satan is your own ego* and lives in the hell it creates.

- Whatever the ego loves more than Me—is *your* god.

- Whatever the ego thinks about all the time—*is* your god.

- Do not love the body, which is merely a temporary vehicle that allows you to experience earth; instead love your source (God) above all things.

- You can not awaken to your true identity until you cast ego aside and return your thoughts to God, then you shall know the truth and the truth shall set you free.

- The Ten Commandments represent the Ten Attitudes you must develop in order to awaken to your true identity and fully participate in your Godhood.

- The man-made churches of Judah, of Christ and of other cults, have turned my words 180 degrees from their original meaning. Come away from organized religion; read my words for yourself and know the truth. (For verification, read the Book of Revelation).

- God loves diversity. Earth and all the other habitations in the universe have served as temporary experimental stations where the Universal Soul has evolved various physical forms in which to live. The time of experimentation is almost over. Soon, the perfected physical form (The New Jerusalem) will be revealed and life will begin anew.

- In the perfected physical form of The New Jerusalem, God can come and go at will between physical form and spirit to experience His creations. The time of pain and suffering will be past as the Universal Soul of God continues to grow in wisdom and understanding of itself.

Gospel of Thomas

This translation of the Thomas Gospel comes from *The Ecumenical Coptic Project* (Athens) which is non-profit and non-sectarian, distributing scholarly editions of the Nag Hammadi Gospels to the academic and religious communities. Uploaded Jan.98, last revised Mar.04. This edition of the translation is not copyright, and is *updated regularly*. For further information visit: http://www.metalog.org/files/thomas.html

These are the secret sayings which the living Yeshua has spoken
and Didymos Judas Thomas inscribed.

Side note: Thomas originally wrote these sayings in Aramaic. They were later translated into several languages, included Coptic and then into English. In the process many of the shades of meaning were lost, as was the mysticism. In this commentary, I will restore the shading and the mystic thought.

1. And he says: Whoever finds the interpretation of these sayings shall not taste death.

Many of my sayings do not translate well since you do not have enough words in your language to translate the shades of meaning from my native language. Also you are neither familiar with my native culture nor with the idioms used by my people. In Aramaic, for instance, the word I used for God means "All inclusive." However you have translated it to mean that God and your environment are *separate* from you.

We had many words for love. My word used for "love thy brother" meant "come to recognition of yourself and your brother as part of Divine harmony." My words for "love Thy enemy" meant "go inside yourself and find the divine vibration that matches that of your brother so that you might bring about divine harmony."

When Constantine took over the church and completely corrupted it, he introduced Roman, Greek and Egyptian mythology and turned my words to suit his own political agenda. Therefore you have been misled by the man-made church for over 2,000 years. For instance, the concept of "original sin" was foreign to me. You might be out of touch with yourself and with your place in the universe; however your *natural* state is harmony.

By saying that whoever finds the key to interpreting my sayings will not taste death, I am telling you that you ARE God, and that when you understand my words you will understand that your soul can never die. I am also telling you that by studying my words, you will never experience spiritual death.

2. Yeshúa says: Let him who seeks not cease seeking until he finds, and when he finds he shall be troubled, and when he has been troubled he shall marvel and he shall reign over everyone and find repose.

Upon your birth on this planet, your memories of your God identity are erased temporarily as you grow from birth into maturity. During those maturing years, you wonder about who you are, the purpose for which you came and the relationship between you and the outside world. I tell you the answers to your questions lie within. First do the internal work to understand, accept and honor who and what you are, and the rest will fall into place.

At first you will be troubled because your churches and society have lied to you about your identity; you see yourself as a foreigner in a foreign land, separate from God, and separate from your brother and the environment.

You may feel guilty, intimidated and frightened to think about yourself—with all your foibles—as God. Yet the Father loves diversity. Even your idiosyncrasies and faults belong to the Father who has come to experience himself so that he might know himself better. Once you cease trying to be "perfect" as defined by the man-made Christian churches, live the Ten Commandments as positive attitudes, accept and embrace your idiosyncratic self as a part of the "All That Is," you will first marvel at the wonder of God—and then find peace.

3. Yeshúa says: If those who would lead you say to you: Behold, the Sovereignty is in the sky, then the birds of the sky would precede you. If they say to you: It is in the sea, then the fish of the sea would precede you. But the Sovereignty of God exists within you and it exists without you. Those who come to recognize themselves shall find it, and when you come to recognize yourselves then you shall know that you are the Sons of the Living Father. Yet if you do not recognize yourselves then you are impoverished and you are poverty.

The man-made church tells you that God is outside of you and that the kingdom of God is in the heavens. That is like telling a sponge that it is separate from the sea when in reality the sponge is in the sea and the sea in the sponge. Yes, you have separate bodies, which like cars carry you from place to place. But you are not the *car*. The same soul inhabits your body that inhabits that of your brother and that surrounds you in the air you breathe.

The notion of separation was foreign to me. God so loved diversity that he brought me—a wholly integrated child of unity—into the world to show you how to live in unity with the diverse aspects of the one God. Once you realize that there are many bodies, but only one soul, you will come to know that God himself forms the substance of all matter, that he lives inside you and outside you. You come from and are made up of "The All That Is"…as does the spirit and substance of all about you.

You do not know yourself therefore you remain caught up in fear and ego. Like the blind leading the blind you attempt to rule but are ruled over by limitation and poverty. You fight to own and control the dirt of the earth, when in reality all that you see and don't see are yours to share.

4. Yeshúa says: The person old in days will not hesitate to ask a little child of seven days concerning the place of life—and he shall live. For many who are first shall become last, and the last first. And they shall become a single unity.

Look upon new life and realize that you and this new life are one. You are but a tag team increasing the diversity of one united life force. The old prepare the way for the new, which in turn become the old handing off the rod of life to the new. The cycle of birth and life go on. The body dies, but the one soul is shared by all.

5. Yeshúa says: Recognize Him in front of thy face, and what is hidden from thee shall be revealed to thee. For there is nothing concealed which shall not be manifest, and nothing buried that shall not be raised.

You struggle with separation from God and your brother, and adhere to the paradigm of good versus evil, thus creating all sorts of havoc and competition for the delicacies of life. Yet right in front of you lies a Truth that requires no "mysteries," no church control, no spiritual pain. You are one with everything seen and unseen for neither good nor bad, pain nor ease exists, except that you label them such. You call forth your own destiny by what you truly believe. Therefore, first achieve harmony inside; then you will see harmony outside. When you believe it, you will see it; thus nothing shall be concealed from you.

*6. His Disciples ask him, they say to him: How do thou want us to fast, and how shall we pray? And how shall we give alms, and what diet shall we maintain? ||
Yeshúa says: Do not lie, and do not practice what you hate—for everything is revealed before the face of the sky. For there is nothing concealed that shall not be manifest, and there is nothing covered that shall remain without being exposed.*

Man loves ritual, be it ritual fasting, prayer, alms giving or diet. My disciples came to me early in our ministry wanting to know what rituals (outside behaviors) they needed to practice in order to be holy. "Forget being holy," I responded, "Instead concentrate on becoming whole." By this I meant, don't be like the Pharisees who put on a big show for the benefit of the outside world while inside they remain greedy, controlling and disconnected from themselves and their source. Rather go first to the "All That Is" and breathe in your connection to the eternal truth; then breathe out your own creativity and allow your new knowledge and creativity to come into your conscious mind. By thus becoming whole, you can not lie. Do what your heart tells you to do as opposed to the rituals you have been taught to practice. I am your teacher your mentor and your guide. Someday you will go out to teach others. Can you not see through the Pharisees? Can you not see their true nature despite their rituals? So too will those you mentor see your true nature. No amount of ritual will hide who you truly are. What you truly believe on the inside will manifest on the outside.

7. Yeshúa says: Blest be the lion which the human eats—and the lion shall become human. And accursed be the human which the lion eats—and the human shall become lion.

I told my apostles: you are a piece of the "All That Is" made manifest in human form. Before all else, unite in meditation with "The All That Is." Go inside so that you may come to know your divine nature, otherwise you are like a raging lion, an undisciplined beast. First go inside (eat the lion) so that you recognize the creative energy of your own unity and self-knowledge, rather than from divisiveness and fear (ego.) Those who do not take time in prayer and meditation to unite with "The All That Is" and to know themselves, act from fear, divisiveness and control (ego.) They are indeed eaten by the lion and become as raging beasts, destructive and out of control.

8. And he says: The Sovereignty is like a wise fisherman who cast his net into the sea. He drew it up from the sea full of small fish. Among them he found a large good fish. That wise fisherman, he threw all the small fish back into the sea, he chose the large fish without hesitation. Whoever has ears to hear, let him hear!

The small fish represent those who have not grown, i.e. they have not come to their own knowingness, have not conquered their own ego and still maintain the illusion of separation. Inasmuch as your job is to awaken (ascend) and then to awaken your brother, spend your time with those who have made an effort to grow in spirit. The rest throw back for they will take up your time without doing the work they need to do on themselves.

9. Yeshúa says: Behold, the sower came forth—he filled his hand, he threw. Some indeed fell upon the road—the birds came, they gathered them. Others fell on the bedrock—and they did not take root down into the soil, and did not sprout grain skyward. And others fell among the thorns—they choked the seed, and the worms ate them. And others fell upon the good earth—and it produced good fruit up toward the sky, it bore 60-fold and 120-fold.

Gardeners know when their soil is ready to receive seed. You do not plant tender plants in the winter; neither do you plant seeds in barren soil. However, when spring comes, you can amend the soil with fertilizer and grow even the tenderest of seed.

As my apostles grew in wisdom, they became anxious to awaken their friends and neighbors…even complete strangers. Like you, they became anxious when society rejected their teachings, made fun of them and even threw stones. Therefore, before you go out, I tell you the same as I told them: "Do not waste your time evangelizing those who are not ready to know the truth." Many of your brothers are like raging lions of self-destruction or like bottomless pits of despair waiting to be rescued. Either they will reject what you tell them or they will start to awaken, only to be overwhelmed by their peers. In other words, the Fundamentalist Christian Church is not the place to start your ministry. Those who think they are the most loving and the most holy will be among the first to murder you in my name.

Rather be at peace inside yourself. You will recognize fertile soil by the work your brother has already done on himself. Make your writings generally available, but spend your time with those who have already discovered much of the truth for themselves."

10. Yeshúa says: I have cast fire upon the world—and behold, I guard it until it is ablaze.

I have cast fire—the Truth—upon the world. Notice how a new flame needs to be kindled and fed, but how a blazing fire feeds upon itself. The Truths that I bring to you begin in your heart as you come to full awakening consciousness of who and what you are. First you call in the divine spark, "The All that Is" in order to unify with it. Starting with that spark you, in turn, breathe out your own divine creative nature and come to full awakening consciousness. From your awakened consciousness, God comes to know himself better, and that new consciousness spreads to all that God continues to create. In other words, God's consciousness ignites a living flame inside of you that, in turn, ignites the world.

I did not come to "save the world through the blood of the lamb." I came to awaken the world and to invite it to participate in unending creation. I lit the spark in my apostles and sent them out to ignite the same in others. The man-made Christian Church attempted to douse the flame and hid it under a blanket. Yet for as many as came to me actively seeking the truth, I lit the flame anew and guarded it until the present day when the Truth will grow into a bonfire over-throwing the man-made Christian Church and replacing it with my Word.

11. Yeshúa says: This sky shall pass away and the one above it shall pass away. And the dead are not alive, and the living shall not die. In the days when you consumed the dead, you transformed it to life—when you come into the Light, what will you do? On the day when you were united, you became separated—yet when you have become separated, what will you do?

This saying is much simpler than you might think. I am telling you that:

- *(This sky shall pass away and the one above it shall pass away)* I am a God of continuous growth, creativity and wisdom. I created this present universe and all contained in it. Eventually I will erase it and start anew. At that time the planet you call Earth and all your universe will disappear.

- *(And the dead are not alive)* Your body and all living matter will eventually cease to exist.

- *(and the living shall not die).* However, the creative nature of God inhabiting the body—and all things—shall not die.

- *(In the days when you consumed the dead, you transformed it to life,)* At conception, the soul came into this spiritually dead vehicle you call a body and the soul gave it spiritual life.

- *(then you come into this light, what will you do?)* Now that you have attained human-consciousness, what will you do? Will you do the internal work required to bring the dead (the un-awakened human consciousness) to life (God Consciousness)?

- *(On the day when you were together, you became separated,)* God loves diversity. He brought you together, gave you life and consciousness of yourself, and gave you a place to stay and thrive. Instead of awakening and recognizing the single soul inhabiting diverse forms, you saw yourself as separate from God, from your brother and from your environment. In fact, with the help of your churches, you told yourselves that life was a battle of God against you; God against nature and *you* against yourself.

- *(yet when you have become separated, what will you do?)* Now I have come among you to tell you who and what you are. Will you remain like the wild lion, separated, destructive and all consuming, or will you learn to do the internal work of awakening to unity?

12. The Disciples say to Yeshúa: We know that thou shall go away from us. Who is it that shall be Rabbi over us? || Yeshúa says to them: In the place that you have come, you shall go to <u>Jacob the Righteous</u>, for whose sake the sky and earth come to be.

Eventually my apostles accepted the fact that I was about to leave them and they wanted to know who would then lead them. Do you remember how Jacob was born second and not entitled to the blessings bestowed upon the first son? His brother, Esau, took the blessing for granted, not recognizing it for the power it held. Then Jacob stole the blessing away from his brother and spent years in hiding until finally they re-united in love.

In this saying, I am reminding my Apostles that the blessing of awakening and eternal life belong first to the Jews as my chosen people. However in my time, the Jewish leaders were asleep and my Word fell on sand. Therefore I instructed my Apostles, like Jacob, to assume the blessing and take on the responsibility of preaching to all nations.

Remember how Jacob worked for and was cheated by his father-in-law? My apostles and the Remnant preached the truth and worked to build the early Christian church, but their words where obfuscated by the Christian Church of Rome. So the Remnant (Jacob) returned "home" and made peace with those among the Jews who understood, accepted and were willing to find the meaning of my Word inside their selves.

In other words, I told my apostles to make peace with those of their own religious background, culture and language as the repository of my word. Among the Gentiles, many of you have heeded your souls' call to awaken and have searched night and day for the truth. You too, are truly blessed and included among the Remnant. For you, as Gentiles, have had to throw off the false teachings of the Christian Church and go deeper inside yourself to find the Truth. Many have had to search out the culture and language of my time in order to honestly translate my words.

The Remnant possesses the soul of Jacob, his strong desire, his persistence, his willingness to do the work, and his broken heart that returned to unity with his brother.

13. Yeshúa says to his Disciples: Make a comparison to me, and tell me whom I resemble. || Shimon Kefa says to him: Thou art like a righteous angel. || Matthew says to him: Thou art like a philosopher of the heart. || Thomas says to him: Teacher, my mouth will not at all be capable of saying whom thou art like! || Yeshúa says: I'm not thy teacher, now that thou have drunk, thou have become drunken from the bubbling spring which I have measured out. And he takes him, he withdraws, he speaks three words to him:

hyh) r#) hyh)
ahyh   ashr   ahyh
I-Am   Who   I-Am

Now when Thomas comes to his comrades, they inquire of him: What did Yeshúa say to thee? || Thomas says to them: If I tell you even one of the words which he spoke to me, you will take up stones to cast at me—and fire will come from the stones to consume you.

As I told you in the preface, Thomas was like a younger brother to me. He lived at our house and was as close to my brother, James, as a twin. In the beginning of my ministry I asked the others who they thought I was. They replied from their heads and hearts, but not from their awakened soul. Thomas however, had spent many years learning from me as we traveled through the various mystery schools of Europe and the Middle and Far East.

He understood about unity and about the creative nature of the divine soul. Like you, however, he realized that he had not yet reached his full awakening to the point of being able to describe, the All That Is. So when it came his turn, he said, "I can't fully describe who you are." By that he told me what I already knew about his spiritual development. I took him aside, and said to him something quite different than ahyh ashr ahyh. In fact I used two completely different words for God.

The meaning translates to this: *"I, the all inclusive creative soul and lover of all diversity, have come among you as a child of unity—a thoroughly integrated being capable of gathering all the strings of diversity and tying them together."*

What was not included in this saying was Thomas' response: "And who Lord am I?" My response to him was "You are part of the Father, as He is part of me and I am part of you." Knowing that his brothers were not yet ready to learn the

Truth, he did not try to tell them. Telling them at that point would have caused them to stone him and thus delay their own spiritual awakening.

14. Yeshúa says to them: If you fast, you shall beget transgression for yourselves. And if you pray, you shall be condemned. And if you give alms, you shall cause evil to your spirits. And, when you go into any land to travel in the regions, if they receive you then eat what they set before you and heal the sick among them. For what goes into your mouth will not defile you—but rather what comes out of your mouth that is what will defile you.

In my time, as in yours, there was no lack of people willing to publicly fast, pray and give alms. Look at your far right television ministries of today for instance. How they howl and carry on and condemn everyone who is not of one mind with them.

I told my apostles, "Don't do public acts of worship like the Pharisees. Don't become actors and showmen caught up in your own trade. All too soon you will believe your own lies and lead both yourselves and your brother astray. Rather go out to the byways, find those not caught up in religious ritual, accept their culture and their ways—in other words truly love them—before you try to heal them." My saying about it not being what goes into your mouth, but what comes out of it that defiles you, speaks for itself. In saying this I made a major break with the Jewish community of my time, which relied heavily upon ritual to control its followers.

15. Yeshúa says: When you see him who was not born of woman, prostrate yourselves upon your faces and worship him—he is your Father.

It sounds as if I am talking about myself as described by the man-made church of Christ (not born of woman.) First of all, you have to understand that "not born of woman" refers to the spiritually awakened man and has nothing to do with biological birth. Throughout mythology, the virgin birth announces a teacher. Why is someone worthy of becoming a teacher? Because he has done the work required to fully understand himself—the same with my birth. There was the birth; then there was *"THE BIRTH."* The physical birth was a physical birth. However, I came through from birth as a child of Unity, one capable of realizing my Godhood in a human body. As I grew in wisdom and knowledge AND *DID THE INTERNAL WORK REQUIRED*, I became a teacher—someone able to put the Truth into words.

The literal translation of the above saying means: "When you run across a person who has fully awakened to his spirit nature, listen to him, because he speaks from his Godhood."

16. Yeshúa says: People perhaps think that I have come to cast peace upon the world, and they do not know that I have come to cast conflicts upon the earth—fire, sword, war For there shall be five in a house—three shall be against two and two against three, the father against the son and the son against the father. And they shall stand as solitaries.

I have come to speak the truth! There are those of you who will accept it because your hearts are open. There are others whose hearts are closed and they shall reject me and my words. Much discord will result and indeed you will see father against son and son against fathers and brothers—and nations against nations. There will be wars fought in my name by the various Christian Churches, with each religious group proclaiming its own righteousness. Know that I stand for peace at all times, it is not my desire that Father and Son war—however man will turn my words to his own purpose and church members will fight to the death to proclaim the truth of that which isn't so.

17. Yeshúa says: I shall give to you what eye has not seen and what ear has not heard and what hand has not touched and what has not arisen in the mind of mankind.

Simply put, I will give to you knowledge. I tell you this: upon your acceptance of the fact that you and I—all of us—are God here on earth having an earthly experience, you will understand what the majority of mankind has never recognized before: **THAT WE *"COLLECTIVELY"* ARE GOD.**

18. The Disciples say to Yeshúa: Tell us how our end shall be. || Yeshúa says: Have you then discovered the origin, so that you inquire about the end? For at the place where the origin is, there shall be the end. Blest be he who shall stand at the origin—and he shall know the end, and he shall not taste death.

Upon discovering your source (that fact that you are spirit, a piece of "The All That Is" having an earthly experience) you will have no doubt about what will happen when your earthly mission has been accomplished. You are spirit, a fragment of God and as such you will return to the Godhead. The body may perish, but you—the spirit—will *never* perish.

19. Yeshúa says: Blest be he who was before he came into being. If you become Disciples to me and heed my sayings, these stones shall serve you. For you have five trees in paradise, which in summer are unmoved and in winter their leaves do not fall—whoever is acquainted with them shall not taste death.

I have come to tell you the truth: you existed as God before you took on human form. Once you understand what I am telling you, and assume your Godhood, even the inanimate objects of the earth will obey you. Before you come into human existence, you possess God-consciousness. In human form you have five trees (five senses) which during your lifetime (summer) help you experience and create your physical existence. In death, (winter) you re-assume your God-consciousness and continue to think, plan and create on a higher level, all of that which you call God, having grown in wisdom from your earthly journey.

20. The Disciples say to Yeshúa: Tell us what the Sovereignty of the Heavens is like. || He says to them: It resembles a mustard seed, smaller than all (other) seeds—yet when it falls on the tilled earth; it produces a great plant and becomes shelter for the birds of the sky.

I tell you that it takes but a little speck of faith to realize and understand who you truly are; that one little speck of faith, along with your request that the Father come into your heart, will cause growth, peace and understanding beyond belief. Once you have asked the "All That Is" to come within, He will never leave you and you too shall become as a shelter for your fellow human beings.

21. Mariam says to Yeshúa: Whom are thy Disciples like? || He says: They are like little children who are sojourning in a field which is not theirs. When the owners of the field come, they will say: Leave our field to us! They take off their clothing in front of them in order to yield it to them and to give back their field to them. Therefore I say, if the householder ascertains that the thief is coming, he will be alert before he arrives and will not allow him to dig thru into the house of his domain to carry away his belongings. Yet you beware of the system—gird up your loins with great strength lest the bandits find a way to reach you, for they will find the advantage which you anticipate. Let there be among you a person of awareness—when the fruit ripened, he came quickly with his sickle in his hand, he reaped it. Whoever has ears to hear, let him hear!

I responded to Mary: My disciple's hearts have become innocent like little children. When they are advised to leave a place, they open their hands and their hearts to show that they have no evil thought. They bare their souls with the truth and bless those about them; for once you have learned the truth, you will maintain it always. You will have doubters and dissidents among you, but stay with the truth, do not let them diminish your innocence. Keep your eyes open at all times, knowing that there are those who will seek to denigrate you and your words. Your words will fall on unwilling ears at times, but always be aware, there are those who will follow your example—within *them* sow your faith.

22. Yeshúa sees little children who are being suckled. He says to his Disciples: These little children who are being suckled are like those who enter the Sovereignty. || They say to him: Shall we thus by becoming little children enter the Sovereignty? || Yeshúa says to them: When you make the two one, and you make the inside as the outside and the outside as the inside and the above as the below, and if you establish the male with the female as a single unity so that the man will not be masculine and the woman not be feminine, when you establish an eye in the place of an eye and a hand in the place of a hand and a foot in the place of a foot and an image in the place of an image—then shall you enter the Sovereignty.

My friend, understand this one saying and all the rest of my sayings shall become clear to you. My Aramaic language bears shades of meaning not translatable into English. So let me begin by saying that you of the West who have learned dichotomy from your churches must first do the internal work to learn unity. This can only be done through prayer and meditation.

How do you obtain Unity? Unity comes from realizing that only one soul exists—the spirit of the "All-That-Is." As a child of the universe, the soul that resides in your body is the same soul that resides in your brother, in the trees and in the soil beneath your feet.

What is meant by Eternal Life and how do you obtain it? Eternal life in my language does not mean leaving your body and going to the happy hunting ground in the sky. Rather eternal life means resting from your labors and renewing your spirit through quiet time spent in meditation where you connect to the universal soul.

How can connecting with the universal soul result in eternal life? By coming to know and understand yourself as co-creator of the universe and rejuvenating yourself through prayer and contact with the eternal soul, you support all life; in fact all existence, including inanimate objects, and spiritual renewal throughout the universe. You support the universal soul as the ground beneath your feet supports you. In that way you continually renew the universal soul as you, the co-creator of the universe, go on and on through time. Like tapping "refresh" on your computer you continuously refresh God with new information, new creation, new Wisdom; and God refreshes you with new information, new creation and new Wisdom from the universe.

How can Unity create me inside as outside, adjusting the masculine with the feminine? Your so-called Christian Church portrays you as a sinful being, born in sin, imperfect and "saved by the blood of the lamb." Utter nonsense!

That whole creations story came from Greek/Roman mythology at the time of Constantine. The concept of man as basically sinful and flawed did not even exist in *my* vocabulary. You do **not** need me to save you. And you *CERTAINLY DO NOT NEED MEMBERSHIP IN ANY CHURCH TO "SAVE" YOU!!!*

You were born into perfection, a perfect co-creator of the universe. Your job, upon hitting planet Earth running, is to remember who you are and to act accordingly. Most humans never even try to re-discover themselves; they simply accept tribal wisdom as "Truth" and go from there. For that reason, the tribal guilt-cult of Roman-based Christianity forms a particularly pernicious blanket over human awakening. Not only does the man-made church of Christianity feed you wrong information, it prohibits you from thinking any other paradigm exists. For that reason I say: come out of your Christian Churches. If you must form alliances, do so with groups which encourage you to explore your soul, *not* with groups that dictate dogma.

Once you realize your true connection to the Universal Soul, and your role as co-creator of the universe, and once you adopt the Ten Commandments as Ten Attitudes or guardrails for sanity, your internal standards for behavior will become the same as your external behavior. Your feminine instincts will meld with your masculine instincts to prepare the soil of your soul for peace. Notice that peace in my native language refers not so much to ceasing war as to building a trench to plant the seed for new growth.

My saying printed above tells you to become one with your soul, with your brother and with the universe—and then prepare the soil for universal creativity to renew the universe.

23. *Yeshúa says: I shall choose you, one from a thousand and two from ten thousand—and they shall stand as a single unity.*

All mankind is called to awaken and fully participate in the eternal re-creation of the Universal Soul—God. The feeling that you are special and here for a specific purpose pervades the very genetic structure of all humankind. Yet few break away from their tribal wisdom in order to read my Words and do the internal work required. So I choose you as one from a thousand and two from ten thousand, because *you choose me.* The Christian church plays a large role in Western consciousness and most Christian churches have far too much to lose to ever allow you to realize you don't need them. They prey upon your comfort zone, your hope for continuous forgiveness and salvation based upon my death (and the church's authority to tell you how to benefit there from) and your comfortable belief that church membership will help you attain eternal life as defined by the happy hunting ground in the sky.

I tell you this: there is no happy hunting ground in the sky. There is only here and now and your ability to connect with the eternal Universal Soul on a nanosecond by nanosecond basis. When you understand my words, you will understand your unity with everything that is, and you shall stand as a single unity. I also tell you this: that most Christians, if they knew what I truly said, would flee from me, and most Christian churches would defile me and kill me. However, *My* way *is* the true path to peace—it is not the path to comfort and amnesia.

24. *His Disciples say: Show us thy place, for it is compulsory for us to seek it. || He says to them: Whoever has ears let him hear! Within a person of light there is light, and he illumines the entire world. When he does not shine, there is darkness.*

His disciples are asking him: explain your state of spirituality for we find you a person of peace and contentment. Within each person who has come to his own realization that he is a living piece of God, there exists a peacefulness noted by all and he indeed illumines the entire world. Realize your own being-ness and you too will banish darkness.

25. *Yeshúa says: Love thy Brother as thy soul, protect him as the pupil of thine eye.*

Once you do the work to *know* (as opposed to only believe) that your soul and your brother's soul are one, then the first part of this statement becomes clear. At that point you are no longer thinking in terms of a sappy happy good feeling towards your brother (even if he is a nerd). Rather you are recognizing the eternal contract with your brother to create an eternal repository for new creation and new beginnings.

The second part: "protect him as the pupil of thine eye" is a bit more complex. For some reason, Christianity makes no place for me as a learned man who studied the cultures of both East and West. In fact, I was quite knowledgeable about Aesop's Fables, the I Ching and also Buddhist philosophy. The Aramaic word for "protect" used here, refers to constant vigilance. How human to complete a task and then fall into complacency!

"Protect" in this verse refers to looking ahead, anticipating possible problems and preparing to overcome them before they happen. I am not talking about protecting your brother against outside catastrophes, rather I am telling you, to protect your brother against the worst catastrophe of all—your own internal judgment against him. Protect your unity, your loving relationship with your brother at all costs. See your soul connection and be on constant alert to maintain your unity and harmonious collaboration.

Why do you think terrorism arises in the first place? Why do you think that retribution is the only—or even a possible—solution? You think these things because you are blind to my words.

26. Yeshúa says: The mote which is in thy Brother's eye thou see—but the plank that is in thine own eye thou see not. When thou cast the plank out of thine own eye, then shall thou see clearly to cast the mote out of thy Brothers' eye.

On one level this saying restates: "People who live in glass houses shouldn't throw stones." I tell you this however, as long as you stand in judgment upon your brother you have not come to a true knowingness of who the two of you are and your relationship to each other. Your brother is not "guilty" of anything, any more than you can be. You are a piece of the soul of God and who can stand in judgment upon God? Your brother will always act in what he perceives as his own best interest. Ergo, his actions are a function of his understanding of himself and are correct in his eyes. Actions which cause him to injure another therefore, are due to ignorance rather than stupidity or malevolence.

What happens when you judge another person? You drive him further from you. In Aramaic, the word for peace means digging a hole and making a place for new seeds to grow. Your mission is: 1) to come to know yourself and to live the best life you know how. The Father gave you the Ten Commandments/Attitudes as guidelines for this; and, 2) to help awaken your brother. The more that you look for places of agreement between you and your brother and work towards peace from there, the more successful you will be. As you can see, my statement goes beyond "People in glass houses shouldn't throw stones," it requires you to deliberately plant peace.

27. Yeshúa says: Unless you fast from the system, you shall not find the Sovereignty of God. Unless you keep the entire week as Sabbath, you shall not behold the Father.

I've already told you that if I appeared in the streets of New York today, I would be stoned. Your Christian church doesn't want to hear or understand my message of self-discipline, peace and reverence for all people and the environment. The so-called "Christian Church" wants a romantic Jesus with blond hair, blue eyes and a sweet halo, who goes along with all the treachery committed in the name of Christ.

Your current religious system does not work, nor has it worked for the past 2,000 years. Look at the behavior of nations. Man has made immense technological advances but has not advanced one iota in wisdom, compassion or collaboration. If you must give up something, give up the Romanesque church of Christ. Read my words and keep them every day of the week…not just when they suit your agenda.

28. Yeshúa says: I stood in the midst of the world, and incarnate I appeared to them. I found them all drunk and I found none among them athirst. And my soul was grieved for the sons of men, for they are blind in their hearts and do not see that empty they have come into the world and that empty they are destined to come forth again from the world. However, now they are drunk—when they have shaken off their wine, then shall they rethink?

I came to tell you the truth about your origins, your mission and the actions required of you. Drunk in the comfort sayings of religion and society, you did not want to hear the truth. Instead of man's search for meaning, you developed a good versus evil duality supporting man's search for greed and power.

Because you choose to remain asleep and drugged with a plethora of dogmas, you come into the world without knowing the Truth about who you are—and you leave the world in the same condition. Now you follow your bloated religious leaders and corrupt politicians blindly. The time will come shortly, however, when <u>world government</u> will be installed and the *REAL* power behind the scenes will show itself. Then many will rethink, reject religion and government and turn to my words for "salvation."

29. Yeshúa says: If the flesh has come to be because of spirit, it is a marvel—yet if spirit because of the body, it would be a marvel among marvels. But I marvel at this, how this great wealth has inhabited this poverty.

What a marvel that a *thought* from the Divine Soul could create a physical body…but what an even greater marvel that the human body can create a thought that adds to the divine wisdom, knowledge and stature of God. When I said to you: "Heaven and earth shall pass away, but my words shall not pass away," this is what I was telling you. You came from wave energy into particle energy so that the All That Is could experience Himself. Everything that you experience—and think—adds to the overall growth of the Divine. Heaven and Earth shall pass away, but your contribution to Divine Consciousness shall not pass away. I truly marvel that such a lowly entity as human consciousness can add to the eternal depth of the All That Is.

30. Yeshúa says: Where there are three gods, they are godless. Where there is only one, I say that I myself am with him. Raise the stone and there you shall find me, cleave the wood and there am I.

How much more plainly could I have proclaimed the truth? There is but *one* God, *one* Soul and but *one* creation. Raise a stone and there you shall find me. Cleave the wood and there am I. God isn't *theoretically* in everything, *GOD IS EVERYTHING!* God is you! God is the air you breathe! God is the birds of the air and fish of the sea, for **ALL IS ONE!** God created everything from Himself. Everything, living and dead comes from and IS the Divine Universal Soul. God so loved diversity that he spread himself upon the face of the earth and all about the heavens in many forms; but *all* forms carry the soul of the one God.

31. Yeshúa says: No oracle is accepted in his own village, no physician heals those who know him.

This saying should give hope to those of you who lived less than stellar lives in your youth. I began my awakening process around age 12. Before that I lived a normal childhood—including stealing candy from a local merchant (and having my father bring me and the candy back to apologize.) As a young man I had the natural sexual urges and encounters with available girls about town, did you think I was asexual or attracted to men? In adulthood I settled down with the one you identify as Mary Magdalene. *(Note: Yeshua and Mary Magdalene were never married due to possible retribution by the Temple upon his ministry. They had three children, the first of which did not live past infancy. The second child was named James after his brother and affectionately called, "The Runt." The third child was named after Yeshua's Aunt Elizabeth, the mother of John the Baptist.)*

Why do you think I waited until my thirties, after I had studied and traveled, to start my ministry? It took me that long to explore life and to mature. Believe me, in a little town the size of Nazareth, everyone knew everything about everyone! How could someone as imperfect as I, Jesus, possibly be their mentor and guide?

The same holds true for you. Some of you began your life less than perfect. How many of you stole something as a child, had sexual escapades well into adult life, did things you now know break the harmony of the universe? "So now he is a saint?" those with long memories ask. I tell you this. Come into oneness with yourself. By going to the excess, you were but exploring the outer limits of who and what you are; be it an excess of sexual gratification, addiction, pretending to be what you are not, or desiring the goods of others…each piece of wholeness has its corresponding piece of separateness and excess.

When you see with your soul the limits of excess, you also see the middle ground which is ripe for peace. You are like the soil; both your internal and external beingness must be prepared for the seed in order for the seed to grow. The death of your excesses forms the fertilizer of wisdom, acceptance and compassion for all of life. When the soil of your soul is united, at peace and ready, the seed of eternal life will be sown.

As you must prepare for the seed, so must the seed prepare for you. The seed of eternal life contains the physical/spiritual genes that allow God, Allah, the

Father—The All That Is: to experience mysticism in human form. That strong desire and vision on the part of the Universal Soul must be nurtured and provided divine energy in order to come into harmony with soil you have prepared for it. In other words, God must come into divine union with you the same as a man comes into divine union with a woman, to produce both the fertilized seed and the place for the zygote to grow.

As a man produces a bastard by coming into unholy (un-wholly) union with a woman, so too do you produce chaos by coming into casual union with the Divine, for these are your flirtations with excess. As man produces a wholly unified love-child by coming into sacred union (body and soul) with a woman; so do you too produce a child of universal love by coming into intimate relationship with God to the point of orgasm and divine mutual fulfillment. Gather up your bastard children and bring them back into your loving heart so that they may be reborn as children of the universe.

I deliver three messages in one in the above statement from the Thomas notes. 1) Humans love mystery. They forever seek after the "new" healer, the "new" teacher…until they become familiar with him and see his feet of clay. 2) You remember your own shortcomings and discredit yourself as badly—maybe worse—than society, and 3) cut yourself off from what "other people" think of you. Your job is to complete your own mission, and then to help others who WANT to learn from you. It's not your job to be a perfect role model OR to evangelize. Instead, unite your soul with your God source and stay in that place, free from judgment about yourself or others. The rest will come automatically.

32. Yeshúa says: A city being built upon a high mountain and fortified cannot fall nor can it be hidden.

At first glance the meaning of this statement is simple: Belief that builds upon my words and fortified with faith can not be breached, nor can it go unnoticed. Unfortunately, the man-made church of Christ used the above idea to convince humanity to follow a doctrine built on control and greed—and to fortify that belief with blind faith. Of course that too is evident. Christianity made me into a pawn and a silent partner in greed, mass destruction and the current last-ditch effort to rule the world.

Here is what I tell you. Do the necessary internal work on yourself. Read my words and meditate upon them FOR YOURSELF—devoid of any church influence—then test me. Soon you will realize that I came from unity and will lead you back into unity.

Here is a dream: "Once there was a room full of inanimate toys. You come into the room and the toys come to life and begin fighting among themselves as other toys flood in from outside. You try to control the toys but they fight until they destroy each other."

"Once there was a room filled with inanimate toys. You come into the room and the toys come to life and begin fighting among themselves as other toys flood in from outside. You send the toys in the room your love; they awaken and start spreading love to the toys filling the room. Some of the outside toys destroy the toys in the room and the toys in the room retaliate. They fight until they destroy each other."

"Once there was a room filled with inanimate toys. You come into the room and the toys come to life and begin fighting among themselves as other toys flood in from outside. You help the toys in the room to awaken to their own love and connection to all things. Because of their love, they have no need to retaliate, and they continue to love no matter what. Some of the outside toys destroy most of the toys in the room. Retaliation is replaced by love. The example of supreme love overcomes the toys from the outside. They no longer destroy each other."

Once you know my way, you no longer feel you need to fight to the death or retaliate in order to fortify your faith—quite the opposite. After 9-11 do you believe I would have gone to war with the Taliban or Afghanistan? Do you think I would have attacked Iraq? Can you picture me flying a bomber, standing on a tank throwing flame or machine gunning anyone? Yet your churches can…and do! Do you think I would have backed big business in delaying the efficient development of energy resources in order to maintain a dependence on oil, thereby *leading* to the Iraq war?

I tell you, should I come to life today, tell my truth and then stand next to the Pope and the fundamentalist Christian Right, I would be stoned and the Pope and the Christian Right elevated. THAT is how little *you* understand about my words.

Yes, build your faith on a higher plain than human fear, greed and control. Fortify your faith through unrewarded acts of love and unity with the universe. Return only good for evil. THEN your faith can neither fall nor go unnoticed.

33. Yeshúa says: What thou shall hear in thy ear proclaim to other ears from your rooftops. For no one kindles a lamp and sets it under a basket nor puts it in a hidden place, but rather it is placed upon the lamp stand so that everyone who comes in and goes out will see its light.

Here is another statement misinterpreted and misused by your Roman war machine church of Christ. What better way to conquer the world than to <u>forcefully</u> "spread the word," to bring masses of people under fear and dread of mind control—and then put that mind control at the disposal of the politicians?

Many people are about to be misled by the confederation of church and state as the politicians ride on the back of the church to world government. All the while the masses will proclaim their "light," which grows like a hydra from the false Church of Rome.

Your job is first to awaken yourself and then enable your brother to awaken. First, understand my Words and then live them from moment to moment in your heart. Write about my words—as they truly are, and speak about them. First breathe in the wisdom of the Universal soul, and then breathe out your creativity and love. Be willing to suffer "the slings and arrows" of injustice and to transform them into tools of peace. Do not shout dogma from your mouth. Rather speak quietly as I spoke and live as I lived. THEN your words will echo from the highest mountain and your light will shine for the world.

34. *Yeshúa says: If a blind person leads a blind person, both together fall into a pit.*

Your Christian churches stumble and fall in their blindness, holding fast to the blind leadership of ancient Rome—which itself fell by the way. Their preaching good versus evil: a sinful man born into an environment of temptation saved by "the blood of the Lamb" makes me puke! Do you know why I died? Do you know why I CHOSE a publicly humiliating and painful death? It certainly wasn't to encourage you to launch the crusades in order to rape and pillage the Middle East! It wasn't to allow the money lenders to pull the wool over your eyes so you would invade Iraq! It MOST CERTAINLY WAS NOT to bribe an insane God to let you into the happy hunting grounds when you die.

I died to show you how to die with love and dignity. When I said I would give you life and give it to you more abundantly, I meant I would help you understand who and what you are so that you might live every moment of your time on earth with more pizzazz and energy. When I spoke of eternal life, I spoke of raising your energy and combining it with the everlasting energy of the Universal Soul— *WHILE YOU ARE STILL ALIVE!*

Your job on earth is to support the energy of the Universal Soul, as the ground supports you. THEN you continue as part of the living Soul long after your temporary vehicle (body) rots and returns to the earth. There is NO happy hunting ground in the sky. What exists exists in the now all around you. There exists no "later" other than the continuing evolution of the God energy that forever grows in wisdom and understanding of itself. From that expanding growth will rise "The New Jerusalem;" a physical form capable of holding God energy in diverse form as God enjoys walking among you in full recognition of the diverse aspects of itself. But even "The New Jerusalem" will evolve and pass in time.

35. *Yeshúa says: It is impossible for anyone to enter the house of the strong to take it by force, unless he binds his hands—then he will ransack his house.*

No one knew this saying better than the Emperor Constantine. A smart man, although not a man of wisdom, he saw instantly how eliminating gospels, changing and then misinterpreting my words; then introducing a "new" mandatory religion on his people could instill blind obedience to his will and a war-like fervor among his legions. He knew exactly what he was doing—binding the hands of all in his wake in order to control their minds and bodies—and then to ransack their lands.

Why in this time of technology, abundance of information and freedom to explore the truth, do so many remain blind—in fact actively militant—in my name? Your human brain evolved to the height of being able to change dog-eat-dog into a guardianship mentality. Yet you break every single one of the Ten Commandments in "The name of Jesus." Why? Because Constantine and his successors first locked up truth and then, used mind-control and brute force to throw away the key.

Like a flame, the Christian Church feeds upon itself, engulfing its followers in a guilt-cult, and then causes them to think that their salvation depends upon their poisoning the minds of their children. What fervor exists upon the face of the earth more powerful than a parent's love for his child? Lie to the child and you control the man!

When you were a child you believed as a child and you behaved as a child. Now you are a man and it is time to put away childish beliefs. Before, you saw the reason for your existence through a darkened mirror, but now it is time for you to turn on your light and throw off the darkness.

Soon the false church and its henchmen politicians will attain world government and the true faces of the silent partner merchants will become evident. At that time, many will awaken to the truth and turn away from the false church and the puppets of the money lenders and at that time, many teachers will be needed. *Wake up teachers and be prepared!*

36. *Yeshúa says: Be not anxious in the morning about the evening nor in the evening about the morning, neither for your food that you shall eat nor for your garments that you shall wear. You are much superior to the windflowers which neither comb wool nor spin thread. When you have no clothing, what do you wear? Or, who can increase your stature? He himself shall give to you your garment.*

Sooo…I am going to make you all rich, right? Are you not rich now with all the bank of the Divine Soul at your disposal? And what would you do with coins if you had them? Are not coins symbols of power and control in your society? Or maybe I'm not going to make you rich, maybe sainthood comes from living in abject poverty. Is sainthood about gathering coins or rejecting coins? I think not.

Another story: "Bruno, the fish, one day became deathly frightened that he might sink. He was experiencing problems with his float bladder and couldn't quite keep his equilibrium. So he devised a float vest and began selling them to other fish in exchange for their natural hunting grounds. Pretty soon he had more hunting territory than he could use and the other fish had none. Therefore he issued pebbles that allowed the other fish to scavenger the hunting grounds in return for labor in building warehouses and filling the warehouses with food for Bruno.

"Soon fish for miles around relied on Bruno for both their life vests AND for the privilege of working for him in order to gather food from what was once their portion of the sea. The other fish worked and worked. Some fish earned so many pebbles that they could purchase the services of other fish. Soon all of life revolved around earning and storing pebbles.

"Then one day, the littlest fish of all discovered that when he swam through the sea, the sea moved through his gills. He could go up or down at will and he needed neither the life vest nor the pebbles. The other fish resented the littlest fish because he swam about freely caring less about security or the delicacies pebbles could buy. Whenever he tried to swim out into the open sea, the fish school crowded around and pushed him back into their midst.

"One day the littlest fish hatched a scheme: 'Look,' he said, 'let me swim out into the big ocean and tell those fish about the life vests and pebbles. Then they will come join us and you will have even more fish working for you and providing for your needs.' The fish school set the littlest fish free. He swam away in perfect confidence that the ocean would support him and provide for him to meet his own needs."

The moral to the story: First adjust to the true nature of the ocean and then swim away like the little fish.

37. His Disciples say: When will thou appear to us, and when shall we behold thee? || Yeshúa says: When you take off your garments without being ashamed, and take your garments and place them under your feet to tread on them as the little children do—then [shall you behold] the Son of the Living-One, and you shall not fear.

What happens when you take off your clothes? You become fully exposed. In this saying, I was talking about the "I" within the "I." When you take off the mask you use to hide from the outer world and fully expose the depth of your inner world with no shame or guilt, then you shall connect to the breath that flows throughout the cosmos and continuously recreates new things.

The unholy Church of Rome taught you to run and hide your "sinful" selves and to clothe your true nature against outside viewing. Shameful, unripe and corrupt you came into this world and shameful, unripe and corrupt you shall leave it, the church teaches you…unless of course you join the church, come under its tutelage and rule—then enslave your children and your children's children to its guilt-cult teachings. Its' Protestant offspring have continued the chant—same song, second verse.

Yet I tell you, explore your innermost being. Gather your lost thought-children to you. Expose your inside to the same light that greets your outside until the light refreshes both your inside and outside. Those things about yourself for which you feel most shame, most likely are the same aspects that have enabled you to survive in the landscape of the guilt-cult, damnation and eternal punishment. Why would they even appear, except that you needed them to survive?

I bring you a new time, a new word. Open the doors of your internal consciousness; set the captives free. Accept your place as a piece of the same eternal soul as created the universe—the eternal soul that goes on and on. Recognize your soul connection to all Men, to the earth and to all that reside upon it. God breathes and his energy flows through you and all about you like a mighty wind. You breathe in your God energy and breathe out new creativity in harmony and collaboration with all men and with the Universe. The Universal Soul (God) expands and grows in wisdom because you have come out of your cave and fully participate in life.

Those aspects of your tender heart that lie hidden behind your mask fool no one but yourself. Like the Emperor, you pretend to wear your new clothes and others pretend to see these outer garments, but in reality they see through the clothes to the naked you. What good has the mask served except to allay your own internal anxiety that no one could love you if they knew who and what you really are?

Take off the theoretical mask and take off the theoretical clothes. Stand naked in spirit before God and Man. Ah, what energy fills your soul. No more hiding, no more excuses…no more fear of discovery. Only the real you, free at last, to express your divine creativity.

38. Yeshúa says: Many times have you yearned to hear these sayings which I speak to you and you have no one else from whom to hear them. There will be days when you will seek me but you shall not find me.

How many times thus far have you said, "I already believed these things, in my heart I knew they were true?" Of course you did and now that they are out in the open, you find yourself freed up to explore more of what you already knew.

This Gospel remained hidden until just recently in the 19th century, in order to protect it and preserve my original words as preserved by my cousin, Thomas. Over the years the translations have changed shades of meaning…which now, like a painter, I refresh them for you.

Who is going to tell you that you ARE God; that you came here to discover your identity and to work in collaboration with your brother as guardian of your planet so that God can experience Himself in form? Who would tell you that shortly an even better form (The New Jerusalem) will allow God to inhabit greatly diverse forms with the ability to come and go at will?

For a time I was with you and left my words preserved where no rot could find them. Now my words come once again to the fore; that which was predicted has now been fulfilled. But I tell you that soon, more than this will become evident to you. In the coming time of the complete corruption of your churches as whores to world government, I will come to you, and you will see through new eyes that which is hidden from you now.

39. Yeshúa says: The clergy and the theologians have received the keys of recognition but they have hidden them. They did not enter, nor did they permit those to enter who wished to. Yet you—become astute as serpents and pure as doves.

Here I speak two truths to you:

1. I, Jesus, used Aesop's fable of the dog that jumps the fence and settles into the manger for a snooze. The Ox comes to eat the food upon which the dog lies. The dog barks and growls until the Ox walks away muttering: "Some people can not benefit from what is right in front of them nor will they allow others to do so."

   Your priests and ministers are like the dogs in the manger. They sit on the bread of life, unable to consume the fruit of life and unwilling to allow any other to do so. You, in the meantime, continue your pernicious cosmic sleep, rocked in the cradle of moral self-satisfaction, seduced by the "Blood of the Lamb." What would the priests and ministers do if you did not pay their wages and provide for their comfort? You have sold yourself into slavery and don't even know it.

2.   So I tell you now, become as astute as serpents and as pure as doves. The first part, "Become astute as serpents" means snoop about, shed your skin, release anything that keeps you from connecting to your true inner wisdom as part of the divine consciousness and your true mission as co-creator of the universe. The Aramaic word for God means everything is included, nothing is excluded. Re-claim your inheritance as co-composer of the sacred song of universal unity and continuous creation.

The second part: "…as pure as doves," relates to releasing all that is rigid within you in order to receive and nurture the seed of God's call to unity. Like the birds of the air, leave your earth-bound existence behind in order to receive strength, vigor and renewable energy from ever evolving cosmos.

40. *Yeshúa says: A vine has been planted without the Father, and as it is not viable, it shall be pulled up by its roots and destroyed.*

Your churches would like you to believe this means that unless you belong to their particular brand of Christianity, you are not of the Father and will be sent to hell. Quite the opposite!

The Jewish religiosity of my time evolved into a man-made temple of power, wealth and control. The Romanesque Christian Church that followed my death fared no better. Both these rotting, stifling vines grew up to choke the tree of life—mans' inheritance as a part of Allaha: the all inclusive breath of sacred unity. Like the Pharisees before them, your priests and ministers have made my temple a den of thieves.

The prophecies of the Book of Revelation have now all been fulfilled with the exception of the true leaders of the already established One World Government showing their hand. At that point, the true nature of the Christian Church shall be revealed and will be torn up—not by me, but by an awakened mankind—to be thrown into the dung heap from whence it came.

41. *Yeshúa says: Whoever has in his hand, to him shall (more) be given. And whoever does not have, from him shall be taken even the trifle which he has.*

I brought all you needed to know in order to experience life and experience it more abundantly. Every breath you take in the here and now brings with it new vigor, new energy and new opportunities to renew your creative spirit. If anything, the true sign of your connectedness to Allah, the "All that Is," is continuous joy and energy.

I brought all you needed to experience eternal life: the divine connection to ongoing, renewable energy and life. All you need do is read my words for yourself. Even in your native tongue the truth reveals itself to you. Research the Aramaic, my native tongue, there you will find the breath and depth of my mysticism.

Unfortunately, the majority of Mankind prefers to remain dead in their dead churches. I tell you this: unless you live your life to the fullest (experiencing on behalf of the Father) you will lose your birthright. Life is for learning and experiencing; also life is for enjoyment and happiness. It is true that you may suffer difficulties and/or hardships, but even so, you are still living and creating. Do not withdraw from life regardless of your difficulties for you are experiencing for the Father.

42. *Yeshúa says: Be passers-by.*

Listen to me! Do not bury your head in the sand; you came to earth to experience your role in Divine Unity. When you visit a town as a tourist, what do you do? You look around, you enjoy, you see the sights and you pay your way. You live there for a time; however, the town is **not** your true home. Therefore you remain detached and do not take on ownership for what you see. Do the same with your earthly existence. Free yourself from judging others and avoid assigning illusionary meaning to people, places or events. Realize that nothing has meaning other than what you yourself give to it. Observe, enjoy, bless with your love, hold all in an open hand and then pass by.

I tell you now and I will tell you again: If you love your earthly life and make it your god, then you will lose your one opportunity to live the much richer, more abundant and divinely creative life intended for your soul as a passerby in this existence.

43. *His Disciples say to him: Who art thou, that thou say these things to us? ||Yeshúa says to them: From what I say to you, you do not recognize who I be, but rather you have become as the Jews—for they love the tree but hate its fruit and they love the fruit but hate the tree.*

Oh how the Christian church loves the romanticized me, but hates the literal meaning of my words. How they love the fruit of their own making (war, murder, avarice and separation) but how they hate the real Jesus from whom they take their name.

Who am I, the Christ? "I am a child of Unity. As such, I proclaim no separation between Man and God or God and nature. In fact I have come to help you find the strings of unity in vast diversity.

"I am a pacifist. Your churches may prostitute themselves in the beds of your politicians and turn a blind eye to all forms of abominations, but I do not. I tell you to return good for evil, to turn the other cheek, to forgive indefinitely, to give your brother your coat when he comes to steal your cloak.

"I am an anarchist." I tell you to be a passerby, someone who observes but does not become entrapped in the worship of politics, power and wealth; who does not get caught up in the illusion of separation, who acts as the good Samaritan but who goes on about his business.

"I am a beggar"—with no desire for wealth, nor any interest in owning things. Rather I give thanks for the temporary loan of what I have today and give no care for tomorrow. Yet I have all of God's bounty at my disposal and leave each home better than when I found it. Even your pets have a home, food and water—but I own nothing.

"I'm a socialist." I share my talents and all that comes to me with those about me.

"I'm a mystic." I prize the internal life, participate in divine creation, enjoy the company of my brother yet have no desire to become caught up in the external.

"I have everything and nothing." I live eternal life right here on earth. I fertilize the minds of men and plant new seeds where none have grown before, thereby giving Man more vigor in his current existence and the ability to enjoy eternal life by joining the Divine Breath of Life of all about him.

"I'm an anti-savior." I came to earth to show you how to live and die. Now it's up to you to find and save yourself.

Is that the Jesus *you* want? Hell no! You, like the Jews before you, want that statue hanging on a cross so you don't have to do your own internal work. You want the soft, effeminate, sexless man who arrived on earth minus (horrors!) sexual union between his parents—who floats about healing the sick and making speeches that convey sappy messages to your Christian ear, but that bore strong messages of self-responsibility to the Aramaic ears of my time.

You love the tree (the romantic Jesus) but hate the fruit (self-responsibility.) You love the man-made fruit (thousands of years of church-led war, murder, rape and pillage conducted under the guise of missionary works of love) but you hate the tree (the real Jesus.) Think about it. Do you really believe the fundamentalist televangelists would invite me on their shows…more than once?

44. *Yeshúa says: Whoever vilifies the Father, it shall be forgiven him. And whoever vilifies the Son, it shall be forgiven him. Yet whoever vilifies the Holy Spirit, it shall not be forgiven him—neither on earth nor in heaven.*

Let me ask you this: "Who and What is the Holy Spirit?" Is it a sort of wispy divine cloud that floats about speaking in tongues of nonsense and whispering sweet nothings in your ear? In some churches, doesn't the Holy Spirit just make you swoon? Well, it makes me puke! The Holy Spirit is the spirit of divine Unity, the inclusion of everything that exists in the "All That Is." You may rebuke God and you may deny me; but deny your participation in the One Universal Soul and you lose the opportunity to live an awakened life on earth and the opportunity to enter into the eternal flow and renewal of life to come.

I don't condemn you; rather you condemn yourself by allowing yourself to be ruled by fear/ego (the real Satan) and by preserving the spirit of separation that causes you to hate your brother, to hate God, to hate the environment and to hate yourself. In effect you create your own Hell and spew it out all over everyone else around you.

Does the Holy Spirit speak to you, acting as sort of a divine internet? Of course, all you have to do is open your heart to Divine Unity and receive the message already waiting inside.

45. Yeshúa says: They do not harvest grapes from thorns, nor do they gather figs from thistles—for they give no fruit. A good person brings forth goodness out of his treasure. A bad person brings forth wickedness out of his evil treasure which is in his heart and he speaks oppressively—for out of the abundance of the heart he brings forth wickedness.

On the surface, I am saying: "If you squeeze an orange, you get orange juice for that's what's inside an orange. Squeeze a lemon and you get lemon juice. Squeeze an integrated child of unity and you get love. Squeeze a separated child of fear and you get hatred." Now let's go a little deeper than that. The Aramaic word that was translated as "Good" actually means "Sacred Unity." Properly translated, the statement about the "good" person would sound like this:

"That person who searches his internal being-ness to the point of identifying and resolving his sometimes conflicted drive, becomes a fertile soil where the Divine Breath of the "I AM" can flourish, minus any separation between God, Man and the Environment. From this vessel of Sacred Breath comes only Sacred Unity and he shall be held in the Heart of the Sacred where he will know a new, higher sense of himself and others. Thus from his own re-birth into "The All That Is" he shall release the thongs that bind his brother and help his brother to full waking consciousness of Unity."

The part about the bad seed would translate like this: "That person who remains trapped in the illusion of separateness from God, his brother and the environment, shall remain as barren soil where no breath can flourish. He will grow in fear and loathing of himself, God and his brother, and will remain unable to free either himself or his brother from the nightmare that envelopes them."

46. Yeshúa says: From Adam until John the Baptist there is among those born of women none more exalted than John the Baptist—so that his eyes shall not be broken and his feelings hurt. Yet I have said that whoever among you becomes child-like shall know the Sovereignty and he shall become more exalted than John.

John was commissioned by the Father to live a life of exclusion and meditation. Because of this, he perceived himself as "separate" from other people. He clung to the Law of Moses and judged himself and others by it—which in the long run led to his undoing. Having studied and learned, he went into the world to teach and baptize other men with the purpose of opening their Godhood. He is fully honored by the Father and, having completed his goals, will be forever honored by the Father and by his fellow man.

I bring you now a new law: "Love God above all, and your brother as yourself." By this I mean that God is all inclusive. YOU come from God and are part of him…as is your brother, for you and your brother share the same soul. Once you let go of the need to judge others and begin to live the life of divine creativity, you become as a child—full of wonderment, connected to all about you. From this understanding of the oneness of all things comes an energy and enthusiasm that opens a world of new life to you. This is what I meant when I said: "I have come to bring you life and bring it more abundantly." The next step, of course is to participate fully in life and by giving life your divine energy, you enter into "eternal life," the never ending cycle of birth, death and rebirth.

47. Yeshúa says: It is impossible for a person to mount two horses or to stretch two bows, and a slave cannot serve two masters—otherwise he will honor the one and offend the other. No person drinks vintage wine and immediately desires to drink new wine; and, they do not put new (wine) into old wineskins lest they burst, and they do not put vintage wine into new wineskins lest it sour. They do not sew an old patch on a new garment because there would come a split.

Here I give a lesson: No one can hold two belief systems at the same time. Let me go deeper into this lesson with you. In my native tongue, Aramaic, God is seen to be inclusive of all things, nothing is excluded. In my teachings I speak often about preparing the soil of your internal "being-ness" to receive the seed of God, by which I mean the seed of unity. You can not believe in your separation from God, Man and the Universe and at the same time believe in your literal unity with God, Man and the Universe. Your belief in separation leads you down the road of poverty, limitation, competition and fear. In fact it leads you down the road of your current terrorism, retaliation and war…all the snares set by your rising world government.

Belief in Divine Unity, however leads in the directly *opposite* direction: abundance, collaboration, joy, and Divine creativity. Right now fear and the myth of separation control your mind, belief system and behavior. That is why your churches fail, for they teach: "come into my camp, be part of my fellowship so that we can be safe." But like old wineskins filled with new wine or old cloth patched with stronger fabric, they burst apart when faced with outside "threats."

Instead of "Love your brother as yourself" or "Turn the other cheek" or "Forgive your brother everything," they teach: "Love your brother, but only when convenient." If you belong to a church that goes along with war and retaliation and you hear and understand my word, you are indeed new wine in an old wineskin: new fabric patching worn out goods. Come out of your churches. It's OK to form groups or a fellowship to collaborate and help one another for this is the new way. But let no man or organization stand between you and the Universal Soul.

48. Yeshúa says: If two make peace with each other in this one house, they shall say to the mountain: Be moved—and it shall be moved!

I bring you the same message over and over again, but say it in different ways in hope that you will finally hear and understand the truth. Most of your churches interpret the above saying to mean: "If two or more people come together in my name and set their intention upon a miracle, that miracle shall be accomplished." Well…they get part of the meaning—but only a SMALL part.

Naturally, if human beings stop bickering among themselves and stop murdering one another, all of humankind can advance and concur. But, here we go again: God against man; man against God, God against nature and nature against man. The same old same old primitive tribal belief: unite and conquer. The Christian Church under Constantine really understood dog-eat-dog. Get together a group of people; then use fear, guilt and mind-control to rule them— then that unified society can improve the lot of itself and its leadership and can conquer other nations.

Little has changed in modern Christianity. You still get, "We just LOVE everyone in our group," but you miss MY message: "bin Laden is one with us because you and bin Laden share the same soul. It is only the illusion of separateness that pits you one against the other. Why? Because: 1) You remain bound by the old wineskin, the old paradigm of separation and good vs. evil and… 2) You do not understand the difference in the Aramaic for "Love your brother as yourself" and "Love your enemy."

The Aramaic word for "Love" in "Love your brother as yourself," roughly translates to: "Return to your source." The word for "Love your enemy," translates to: "Find that place inside yourself where you come into resonance with your brother, and start from there to return to your source."

I tell you these things: Search out and unify those parts of yourself that remain in conflict so that you may first heal yourself; soften those rigid places within yourself; unite those lost pieces of yourself in order to increase your resources and make yourself like fertile soil ready to receive the message of my words.

1) Once you bring yourself into unity and peace with yourself, release fear, doubt and retaliation. Find those places in the soul of your brother that come into rhythm with your soul.

2) See God everywhere—in everyone and everything.

3) Make creating Universal Unity of Spirit your abiding purpose.

4) When you come into unity with another, become one in spirit. Unite out of your sense of unity between God, Man and The Universe. Then join together in your abiding purpose of creating Universal Unity of Spirit as your collaborative abiding purpose.

You will know my followers by their joy in all circumstances. When you see one group unifying against another, know neither represents me. When you see nations unifying in fear to retaliate and wage war against another people, know their leadership does not represent me—even though they may come in my name. Instead, know they come from the Father and could literally work miracles with groups of people coming together **in spirit**, without a central government, to:

1) Acknowledge their common soul.

2) Acknowledge the common soul of all creation.

3) Collaborate in healing one another and their environment for the good of all.

49. Yeshúa says: Blest be the solitary and chosen—for you shall find the Sovereignty. You have come from it and unto it you shall return.

How can you be "solitary and chosen," yet come from unity and return to it? Are some people "chosen" and others damned from birth? Did I, Jesus, believe in predestination as defined by your Christian churches? Nonsense! I tell you this. You—every one of you—comes from the Universal Soul. Together, you and *all* the universe, make up the Universal Soul you call God. Although you have individual and diverse bodies, **you literally share the SAME SOUL**: the soul of God. Your bodies, like cars, boats, trains or planes, merely serve as different vehicles for God to experience life.

Discovering your identity in human form is indeed a solitary journey to which every human ever born is called. Those who answer the call (ascend) chose themselves as willing to discover their divinity…i.e. their common soul and connectivity with everything that is: *not the other way around.* You come from Divine Unity and to Divine Unity you shall return. Some of you will not return until you die simply because you do not choose to awaken. To those who do choose to awaken however, abundant life and eternal life become available in the here and now.

50. Yeshúa says: If they say to you: 'From whence do you come? Say to them: 'We have come from the Light, the place where the Light has originated thru himself.' If they say to you: 'Who are you?' Say: 'We are his Sons and we are the chosen of the Living Father.' If they ask you: 'What is the sign of your Father in you?' say to them: 'It is movement with repose.'

Herein rests the most poetic saying of all: *"God is movement in repose."* When people ask you where you come from, tell them you come from and are part of, the Universal Soul. How much more plainly could I have said it? Yet because you are steeped in the man-made paradigm of good vs evil and separation, my words fell on sand…for the most part.

For those who—through accident of birth or by deliberate choice—came out from the Christian Churches, these words fell on well aged and fertilized soil. They chose themselves as children of Unity and deliberately left the old dog-eat-dog paradigm to accept their role as part of the never ending cycle of birth, change and rebirth. They ceased struggling to be "holy separate, forever struggling to become what they are not—separate from God and each other." Instead they chose to become "wholly unified," a part of the natural cycle of ongoing Divine Creativity. They became movement in repose.

51. His Disciples say to him: When will the repose of the dead occur, and when will the New World come? || He says to them: That which you look for has already come, but you do not recognize it.

The churches like to interpret this to mean that the Messiah has arrived; that you are saved and have no responsibility for your own awakening. That is wrong. It may come as a shock to you but: "What you see is what you get." You are not going to die and go to "The Great Spa in the sky," for there is no spa in the sky. The eternal, universal soul lives **in the here and now** and from breath to breath. You live in the New World and you ARE the New World. You are part of that experience of the living God. When you shuck your body, you simply return to the eternal soul and then go on with the cycle of creation. Neither heaven nor hell exists except that *you* create them.

That being said, you have the opportunity to fully awaken and actively participate in the Divine Breath of creation while you are right here in human form. You can even plug into eternal life, right here in human form. Both require periods of repose (meditation) and activity (divine creation).

Right now you sleep and wake, but remain blind to the Divine Cycle within you. Your sleep brings no rest and your awakening time creates chaos between the many voices of creativity, fear and contradictory drives inside of you. You want to save money, but you want to purchase a car. You want to remain celibate, but your body requires sexual release…a constant war of needs and wants.

When you meditate upon my sayings until they reverberate within your body and all you want is more of the Divine, you begin integrating the various parts of yourself and forming a strong purpose for promoting Unity—within yourself and with the world. Then you see through new eyes and what has been right in front of your nose becomes plain.

52. His Disciples say to him: Twenty-four prophets proclaimed in Israel and they all spoke within thee. || He says to them: You have ignored the Living-One who is facing you and you have spoken about the dead.

In the early days of my ministry, my disciples kept looking for the Messiah…just as you keep looking for some future place called "Heaven." Some thought I was a confederation of all the prophetic knowledge. I said to them what I say to you now: "Stop looking for some future wisdom." Everything you need to know is available to you in the here and now…both in my words and in the words of Buddha, Mohammed, Gandhi and many others. You have been told the truth about who and what you are, but like sheep you follow this one and that one hoping that someone else will bring repose into your life. The truth is that the only one who can bring repose into your life is YOU.

When I spoke the above phrase to my disciples I was telling them: "I AM HERE RIGHT NOW, LISTEN TO WHAT I AM TELLING YOU!" To you I say: "YOU ARE HERE, RIGHT NOW, LISTEN TO WHAT YOU ALREADY KNOW."

The Living Truth that was in me resides within you and you have but to go inside. I never intended for you to hold on to me for dear life like a life raft. Rather I told you: "Do as I do; think as I think; say as I say." I am not personally the Way, the Truth and the Light, it is my **WAY** of thinking, searching, contemplating and behaving that is the way, the truth and the light.

53. His Disciples say to him: Is circumcision beneficial or not? || He says to them: If it were beneficial, their father would beget them circumcised from their mother. But the true spiritual circumcision has become entirely beneficial.

Notice how large a part ritual and tradition plays in your religions. On one hand, tradition united the Jews through the centuries, just as it united the Catholics, the Muslims and the Nazis. Tradition, ritual, uniforms, and flags…all these things belong to Tribal Wisdom: "*You do things in a set manner; therefore you are one of us*" as opposed to being one of "*them.*" Rituals, secret signs—all that stuff—belong to the secret sects as a way of making them "special" and set apart in a dog-eat-dog world.

I tell you, if awakening relied on circumcision, you would have been born that way. Contrariwise, you <u>were</u> born whole in spirit; then society gave you your identity. *Spiritual* circumcision—cutting yourself off from worn out beliefs, rituals and separation—not only is beneficial, but essential to realizing who you are and to coming into full awakened consciousness.

54. Yeshúa says: Blest be the poor, for the Sovereignty of the Skies is yours.

This saying has nothing to do with money or possessions. For the awakened man, riches and poverty have equal value: none. A man's readiness to receive the Truth dictates his spiritual heritance, not his wallet. The Aramaic word I used in the Thomas Gospel for "poor in spirit" translates "ripe or fertile ground ready to receive new life."

This beatitude can be translated as: "Fortunate are they who have separated themselves from the illusions of society, who have quieted their minds, and who have made their minds fertile ground for growing the seed of Truth; for they will awaken to their unity with the Sacred Breath and will inherit the ability to come into oneness with all that exists about them."

55. Yeshúa says: Whoever does not hate his father and his mother will not be able to become a Disciple to me. And whoever does not hate his brothers and his sisters and does not take up his own cross in my way, will not become worthy of me.

The Aramaic verb I used here was not "hate" as in despise, but rather "to set aside, break free of, leave behind or outgrow." I never said "take up his own cross," that's a figure of speech used in the later Gospels. The actual words I used meant: "to assume responsibility for himself, take control of his life, go his own way, become independent of others, mature."

If you heard me in Aramaic, you would have heard: "Whoever remains stuck in the comfort of tribal wisdom and does not possess the desire, drive and courage to come out from his tribe (family, church, and culture) and explore a new way of thinking, will not find his true identity."

Imagine what would happen if you say to your Roman Catholic Family: "I am not going to belong to this institution any more, it teaches the exact opposite of the words of Jesus."

Imagine what would happen if you say to your country: "I am not going to obey those national rules that require me to contribute to war or to kill other people."

Imagine what would happen if you say to your employer or parents: "I will not work in a business that requires me to cut the throat of my fellow employees or of my customers; or that denies me dignity or integrity."

Imagine what would happen if you say to society: "I care more about how we provide for and educate the children we have, than I do about a woman deciding to have an abortion," or "I care more about people loving and being faithful to each other than I do about their sexual orientation."

The reason later interpreters added in "take up your cross" came because of the penalties leveled by families and society upon those who take responsibility for their own understanding and who chose to find common ground in all people as opposed to loving who society currently loves and hating who society deems unacceptable.

I tell you that were I to walk the streets today, I would be one of the most despised men in America—or the world. So when I tell you that until you are ready to detach from the good opinion of others you are not worthy of me, I am saying that until you are ready to stand on your own truth you will not be "ripe" to follow in my footsteps. My way is easy because it is the way of Unity, Love and Acceptance. My way is difficult because it is not the way of tribal wisdom.

56. *Yeshúa says: Whoever has recognized the system has found a corpse—and whoever has found a corpse, of him the system is not worthy.*

Have you noticed that despite vast technological changes, plus world-wide spread of Christianity, that man's behavior towards his brother has actually gone *backwards* over these past two thousand years in terms of collaboration, unity and harmony? The third world countries (look at the Balkans, Afghanistan, Iran and Iraq) are as barbaric as ever and the super powers unleash their weapons of mass destruction all in the name of eliminating weapons of mass destruction. The United States uses an elephant gun on a swarm of bees and wonders why the stinging gets worse.

He, who finds the church/state federation of the coming world government, finds a spiritual wasteland built upon misinformation, hypocrisy, fear, greed and corruption.

He who hears and obeys my word, of that person, the tribal wisdom of the church/state federation is unworthy.

57. Yeshúa says: The Sovereignty of the Father is like a person who has good seed. His enemy came by night; he sowed a weed among the good seed. The man did not permit them to pull up the weed, he says to them: Lest perhaps you go forth saying: 'We shall pull up the weed' and you pull up the wheat along with it. For on the day of harvest the weeds will appear—they pull them and burn them.

Once again we come to the story of the good/bad, ripe/unripe seed. The Universal Soul, God, plants the seed of Divine Unity that eventually evolves into self-conscious beings ripe for developing into full God-conscious vehicles suitable for God to experience Himself in physical form. Then along comes organized religion which plants the weeds of fear and mis-information and these weeds block out the light.

Why not yank out the man-made Church of Rome and all the others that hold man in bondage? In doing so you would also remove those seeds which start out entwined with the church, but eventually escape the darkness and ripen to spiritual maturity. In fact, some of the ripe seed will mutate into a stronger strain because of the adversity. At the harvest, that seed that grows fruit will be harvested, the un-ripened fruit will die on the vine and be cast aside with the weeds.

This story is not about moral judgment. Weeds and unripe fruit are neither good nor bad; they simply are not suitable for harvest. This is not a parable about "Hitler is going to go to Hell and the Pope is going to heaven," this is a story about your making a fully conscious decision to live fully in the here and now…regardless of the weeds about you. The Father calls every man to awaken and some will cling to the comfort of their churches and tribes and will never ripen. Removing the weeds removes free will and the new opportunities to strengthen the good seed.

58. Yeshúa says: Blest be the person who has suffered—he has found the life.

This is another of those misunderstood statements that mistakenly foster victim-hood. The Aramaic word I used for "suffer" is a gardening term; it means: "continued to change and grow, died to its old nature and re-birthed as a new individual, took the time to wither into itself and then sprouted a new plant."

Another story: A gardener takes a potato, cuts it up into small pieces and sticks it into the darkness. There the potato proceeds to grow riper and riper and more and more rotten, until one day a new green sprout shoots up to the light as new roots grow deeper into the fertile soil. The old potato is no more, for a new plant comes forth. Eventually the potato bursts into bloom, a sign that below ground the roots have developed ten fold the number of seed potatoes. The plant has returned to its roots, strong and ready to start again.

In my parables I speak not so much about suffering pain as about welcoming change and growth for until a man is ready to change and grow, he is not ready to throw off his old skin, assume a new spiritual life and then return to his root in the All-That-Is.

59. *Yeshúa says: Behold the Living-One while you are alive, lest you die and seek to perceive him and be unable to see.*

Let's go back to the potato. When does the potato grow? When it is cut up and placed in the blackness of fertile soil. If it tries to hold on to its old self, what happens? It becomes food for worms, unable to sustain the chain of eternal life.

You are like that potato. Grow and change while you are alive. Throw off your old ways of thinking. Rise to the light—the Truth of my words—so that you may enjoy life abundantly. Put down roots that tap into the eternal cycle of renewable life. Once planted, you either grow or die.

60. *They see a Samaritan carrying a lamb, entering Judea. Yeshúa says to them: Why does he take the lamb with him? || They say to him: So that he may kill it and eat it. || He says to them: While it is alive he will not eat it, but only after he kills it and it becomes a corpse. || They say: Otherwise he will not be able to do it. || He says to them: You yourselves—seek a place for yourselves in repose, lest you become corpses and be eaten.*

This saying pertains to the evolution of the man-made Christian Church that after my death was transformed from a Jewish/Essenes mystical belief system into a pagan political organization.

The Samaritans (Gentiles) join our ranks and after my death, they carry what they under-stand of my sayings out into the world. This becomes the first Church of the Book of Revelation. Eventually Gentile politics and mythology take over the church and it becomes a corpse. I tell my disciples: remain centered in my teachings, stay out of the politics of organized religion lest you become spiritually dead and the words you speak become incorporated into the man-made Church of Rome.

In the end, most of my disciples did lose sight of the true meaning of my words. Rome, under Constantine, took over the mystical school I established; killed my message and then it was later eaten by the church it created. Only the Remnant (those who held fast to my words, or who awoke on their own, studied my words and lived them) remains to this day in repose, glowing with the light of internal truth, but safe from the limelight and political control.

61a. Yeshúa says: Two will rest on a bed—the one shall die, the other shall live. 61b. Salome says: Who art thou, man? As if sent by someone, thou laid upon my bed and thou ate from my table. || Yeshúa says to her: I-Am he who is from equality; To me have been given from the things of my Father. || Salome says: I'm thy Disciple. || Yeshúa says to her: Thus I say that whenever someone equalizes he shall be filled with light, yet whenever he differentiates he shall be filled with darkness.

Simplistic explanation: Two people may exist in one household and despite having the same opportunities, one will awaken and join in the dance of eternal life; the other will not. How would you like having me as a houseguest…interesting conversations around the breakfast table, no? Neither one of us would know what the other was talking about…well at least *one of* us might not….

First of all, who was Salome? She was the mother of the sons of Zebedee (James and John) mentioned in Mathew 20:20 and also one of the women present at my crucifixion:

Mat 20:20 Then the mother of the sons of Zebedee came to him with her sons, kneeling and asking a certain thing of him.

20:21 He said to her, "What do you want?" She said to him, "Command that these, my two sons, may sit, one on your right hand, and one on your left hand in your Kingdom."

20:22 But Jesus answered, "You don't know what you are asking. Are you able to drink the cup that I am about to drink and be baptized with the baptism that I am baptized with?" They said to him, "We are able."

20:23 He said to them, "You will indeed drink my cup and be baptized with the baptism that I am baptized with, but to sit on my right hand and on my left hand is not mine to give; but it is for whom it has been prepared by my Father."

20:24 When the ten heard it, they were indignant with the two brothers.

20:25 But Jesus summoned them and said, "You know that the rulers of the nations lord it over them and their great ones exercise authority over them.

20:26 It shall not be so among you, but whoever desires to become great among you shall be your servant. 20:27 Whoever desires to be first among you shall be your bondservant, 20:28 even as the Son of Man came not to be served but to serve and to give his life as a ransom for many."

Do you have friends who you dearly love and for whom you would do anything, yet who drive you crazy? That was Salome; although she was a very loving and caring woman, she was also quite pretentious. Anyway, I would stay at the home of Zebedee and Salome quite often as a young man and later as a teacher. Salome, try as hard as she might, could never quite "Get it." She came from a middle class family and married Zebedee who, by income was middle class, but who came by background from an upper-class Jewish family. How John, James and I would laugh at Salome's antics in making me into a "Prize" when showing me off to her neighbors.

In this conversation she asked me who I was. I told her that I came from the word; which in Aramaic means: "Nothing is excluded and everything is included" and that I brought with me the gift of the Aramaic word for eternal life: connection to the Divine Breath. She immediately replied: "Well *I* am your disciple." In her paradigm that meant, "I am this man's disciple and *you* are not."

I could hardly keep a straight face. "Well Salome," I replied, "At those times when you include everybody in your heart, you walk with me; when you think in terms of separation, you walk in darkness." It was just one of those days and Thomas loved to parody the story over the campfire whenever we were alone.

The two stories above (the two people resting in the same bed and of Salome) represent the fact that everyone is called to fully awaken to the reality of the one shared sacred soul. Some are able to go into the hardness of their hearts, soften those places that are ridged and then join in the joyous dance of unified existence. Others choose not to. Notice that Salome was one of the women present at my crucifixion and death. In the long run, her love overcame her need for exaltation.

62. *Yeshúa says: I tell my mysteries to those who are worthy of my mysteries. What thy right hand shall do, let not thy left hand ascertain what it does.*

The word defined here as "worthy of" really meant "ripe for" in Aramaic. Often times those of evangelistic leanings insist on converting everyone to their way of thinking—whether the other person wants to be converted or not. That is not my way. If I lived among you now, I'd turn off the television the moment some of those preachers started in. Pretentiousness offended me then and continues to do so. To my disciples I said: "Listen, remain low key, be yourself. When you come into someone's house, first come into rhythm with them and your heart before you start to heal them. If they receive you, bless them and bring them into unity; if they don't, then simply leave."

One of the hardest lessons of all is that of humility. How easy it is to tell everyone everything you know—even when they are not ready to hear it. Learn to keep your mouth shut. When someone asks you a question, and they are receptive to your response, then share what you know. Otherwise keep your own truth lest you offend someone with your bragging, or make an enemy through competition.

63. Yeshúa says: There was a wealthy person who possessed much money and he said: I shall utilize my money so that I may sow and reap and replant, to fill my storehouses with fruit so that I lack nothing. This is what he thought in his heart—and that night he died. Whoever has ears, let him hear!

I have talked to you before about the ripe and unripe soul: the ripe soul represents the person who has reached a point in time when he is ready to receive new information, new grace. His heart is open and fertile and ready to nurture new understanding. The unripe soul may hold the potential for ripeness but, like winter ground, has not yet reached the right time to foster new growth.

Once there was a man who, in his thoughts of separateness, possessed great wealth and talent. Because he was not ripe in his heart to the idea of sharing his wealth and skills with his brother, he decided to increase his material gain in order to be secure in his old age. He continued along the road of separateness until he became even more wealthy and distinguished. Then he died in his youth and had no use for his material gain.

The story of the wealthy man who dies in his sleep has nothing to do with being rich or poor in the material sense. It has to do with awakening while you still can and then using your abundance of love and understanding to awaken your brother. This man is the prodigal son who never returned home. He spent his spiritual inheritance trying to make himself secure when all the time he was welcome back in his father's house.

Heaven isn't some place to be enjoyed at a later date. Heaven and eternal life are in you and around you right now. You can not buy heaven, but you can indeed miss the opportunity to recognize it and participate in it when you become distracted with piling up toys you will never live to enjoy.

64a. Yeshúa says: A person had houseguests, and when he had prepared the banquet he sent his slave to invite the guests. He went to the first, he says to him: My master invites thee. He replied: I have some business with some merchants, they are coming to me in the evening, I shall go to place my orders with them—I beg to be excused from the banquet. He went to another, he says to him: My master has invited thee. He replied to him: I have bought a house and they require me for a day, I shall have no leisure time. He came to another, he says to him: My master invites thee. He replied to him: My comrade is to be married and I must arrange a feast, I shall not be able to come—I beg to be excused from the banquet. He went to another, he says to him: My master invites thee. He replied to him: I have bought a villa, I go to receive the rent, I shall not be able to come—I beg to be excused. The slave came, he said to his master: Those whom thou have invited to the banquet have excused themselves. The master said to his slave: Go out to the roads, bring those whom thou shall find so that they may feast.

God, the Father, created Earth to be the Garden of Eden where He could come, take on human form and live with the people He had created. Here we find that the ones He had originally selected to dwell with Him were so caught up in their own egos (self-interests) that they did not want to be bothered. Therefore he sent me, Jesus, to awaken those who would listen to the Truth—and to let those who are so caught up in their own egos, go their own ways.

64b…and he says: Tradesmen and merchants shall not enter the places of my Father.

My Uncle Joseph of Arimathea was a tin merchant and tradesman. I used to travel with him from time to time and help him with his camel train. Was I condemning him in the above statement? Am I telling you that you can not earn your living as a salesman? Not at all! Uncle Joseph was first and foremost a mystic, a man of Unity. Then he filled his time doing the work he loved. Whether or not you can do the same depends upon your understanding of unity and Divine Breath (the energy that flows through all things.) You have a right to make a living, however, you have an obligation to recognize and respect the unity that exists between you and your brother. You can not worship wealth, separation, integrity and unity at the same time.

By tradesmen and merchants, I meant those unripe hearts that make their way in life through deceit, treachery and separation—they win—you lose. Among many of the Jewish merchants, cheating people was a game—particularly if they could cheat a Gentile.

65. He says: A kind person had a vineyard. He gave it out to tenants so that they would work it and he would receive its fruit from them. He sent his slave so that the tenants would give to him the fruit of the vineyard. They seized his slave, they beat him—a little longer and they would have killed him. The slave went, he told it to his master. His master said: Perhaps they did not recognize him. He sent another slave—the tenants beat him also. Then the owner sent his son. He said:

Perhaps they will respect my son. Since those tenants knew that he was the heir of the vineyard, they seized him, they killed him. Whoever has ears, let him hear!

In this story I talk of a kind person (God, the Father) who created a vineyard—Earth, His choice of locations—to experience Himself. He sent many messengers to ascertain if the inhabitants had achieved sufficient maturity to accept Him. The un-awakened mistreated each one of the messengers until God sent me, Jesus, to inform, heal and awaken them to the soul they share with the "All That Is." Instead of putting down their plowshares and welcoming me, they killed me.

Your politicians, televangelists and church leaders couldn't afford to have me around today any more than the Pharisees could 2,000 years ago. A difference exists however, between today and yesterday. In my time, the power mongers were able to scoop me up, *try* me and be done with it, with no accountability. Today, putting me on trial would be much too public and dangerous; they would have to arrange for me to be murdered. I wonder what spin your leaders would put on that. If you don't believe me, imagine what I would say to the terrorists about the World Trade Tower and what I would say to the US politicians about invading Iraq and using the never ending "War on Terrorism" to line their pockets and break down democracy.

66. Yeshúa says: Show me the stone which the builders have rejected—it is the cornerstone.

Once more you see another highly misinterpreted saying. Your churches tell you that I am the cornerstone that the builders rejected. Well…yes and no. I came to teach you about the cornerstone, but I am not myself that stone. I came to tell you about a highly creative, joyous God who rejects no one and no thing. He is the wave of light you see, those particles of light examined by scientists. He is the Sacred Breath that blows through the universe that is a part of Him and which He created. He is the one and only Universal Soul from which all men come and to which they return. You are one of the many physical forms in which God experiences himself as He grows in wisdom and knowledge. You and I are one. You and your brother are one. You and God are one—no separation; no good or evil and certainly no need for organized religion.

It wasn't me that the church builders rejected; it was the Truth that I brought to this planet. This truth—the Divine Unity of all things—is the cornerstone of all existence. It is the cornerstone of the Remnant who will prepare the way for the New Jerusalem predicted in Revelations. It is anathema to the man-made Christian Church.

67. *Yeshúa says: Whoever knows everything but himself lacks everything.*

At the end of the day, all we truly possess is our divine breath of life. Find your connection to the Divine Breath, and that is all you need to know. I, Jesus, mourn that over the years my message has been twisted, misrepresented and misunderstood. In my name, pagan theologies of good versus evil and doctrines of separation and punishment have sprung up to support and nurture man-made "Christian" political institutions who, for the most part, provide you mandatory pat answers and which *exclude* you from searching your own internal environment.

Let me tell you this: everything you need to know **already lies inside of you.** I did not come as a "savior" in the sense of saving you from some outside force. I came to save you from yourself, from your ego and fear. I came to set you free from institutional control and to open you to your divine consciousness.

Against my wishes and my teachings, Paul led the man-made movement to establish the so-called Christian Church. Being a lawyer and a Jew, he understood the power of rules in connection with institution-building. He also understood the power of hope in attracting a following. An opportunist by nature, he saw the advantage of incorporating the gentiles. Unfortunately he used seat-of-the-pants rules to keep them in the fold, versus spending sufficient time teaching them the true meaning of my words.

Led by spiritual zeal and ego, Paul single handedly built one of the most powerful churches on earth…making and breaking rules as he went along. In doing so, he used my name, but did not follow my teachings. He built the Church of Paul which later would be co-opted by Constantine to become the state church of Rome; which would in turn be co-opted to take over regional government, which ultimately will become a federation of church/state government prior to the apocalypse.

If you really believe that I am the one and only son of God, do you think I could not have built a strong religious institution on my own—especially if you believed in my resurrection? Why would I need Paul—particularly when he preached the exact opposite of my sayings? Have these thoughts never crossed your mind? Wake up! He may have kept my name in front of mankind all these years, but look what it is taking to reclaim my true identity. Indeed, anyone who seeks me in the modern era DOES have to be reborn to a whole new way of understanding man's place in the universe.

Here is the truth: I did not come to establish a political institution, rather I came as one committed to teaching YOU how to access the information inside of you that ties you to the Eternal Soul. Your spiritual journey is yours and yours alone, for no one else can save you. Only you can find the one divine strand that ties you to The All That Is.

68. *Yeshúa says: Blest be you when you are hated and persecuted and find no place there where you have been persecuted.*

What do you talk to yourself about? What do you say to yourself when you come under stress or when you make a mistake? Do you tell yourself you are stupid and no good, or do you remain in repose knowing you are God? I am telling you a very simple yet profound truth. Each of us becomes an adult—mentally and spiritually—when we consistently respect ourselves even in the midst of persecution and chaos.

69a. *Yeshúa says: Blest be those who have been persecuted in their heart—these are they who have recognized the Father in truth.*
69b. *Yeshúa says: Blest be the hungry, for the stomach of him who desires shall be filled.*

Hopefully by now you are beginning to see the pattern in my teachings. First let's define some terms. "Persecuted in their heart:" unsettled, unfulfilled, yearning for their divine connection, longing to know the truth and longing to reunite with their soul. "Blest be the hungry:" hungry for something bread alone can not fulfill; longing for knowledge of their divine connection, an ever searching, insatiable desire for spiritual fulfillment.

How would you know something was missing in your life unless you felt emptiness, a longing, a need for fulfillment? First comes the pain of withdrawal from your natural wholly (holy) spiritual state, then comes the longing and searching. Blest is he who feels the pain, acknowledges it and then sets aside everything he has to go in search of that which is lost and which is his to reclaim.

70. *Yeshúa says: When you bring forth that which is within you, this that which is within you shall save you. If you do not have that which is within you, this which you do not have within you will kill you.*

I tell you again: all the drive, knowledge and conviction you need to live an abundant life here on earth and to achieve eternal life, already lies within you. Seek the truth about yourself and your connection to the "All That Is" now, while you have life and can find it. For once you die you will not be able to claim your heritage. If what lies within you is a love of God, then you will find God and within God, you will find your connection to life and to eternal life. If what lies within you is ego, then you will find separation and death.

71. *Yeshúa says: I shall destroy this house and no one will be able to rebuild it.*

This saying has a double meaning: "House" meaning dwelling or body, the vehicle in which your spirit resides; and "House" meaning your belief system, organization or church. I will destroy this body and no one will be able to bring it back to life. I will destroy this person called Jesus and no one will be able to use me as an icon to control the minds of men. I will destroy this false Christian Church and no one will be able to rebuild it.

It will not be until the time of world government during the apocalypse that the true world rulers will show their faces, thus causing man to turn from organized religion to seek his true identity. In three stages, I will destroy my body, my icon, and the church built in my name—and *no* man will be able to bring these back to life.

72. *Someone says to him: Tell my brothers to divide the possessions of my father with me. || He says to him: Oh man, who made me a divider? || He turned to his Disciples, he says to them: I'm not a divider am I?*

By now I hope you understand the truth: there is nothing to divide. You *are* the Father; the Father is *you*. You are your brother; your brother is you. You own everything in common and nothing separately. I have not come to preach the Christian guilt-cult of separation, sin and eternal damnation. Nor have I come to preach pre-determination or eternal salvation. I have come to give you the tools to awaken to who and what you truly are: unending universal consciousness temporarily inhabiting an illusion of a body.

73. *Yeshúa says: The harvest is indeed plentiful, but the workers are few. Yet beseech the Lord that he sends workers into the harvest.*

There are many yet to be enlightened about their own Godhood, but few teachers to spread the word; pray that the "All That Is" sends more teachers to help with the enlightenment of all mankind.

74. *He says: Lord, there are many around the reservoir, yet no one in the reservoir.*

Let me define reservoir: "tank, pool, basin, lake, place of deep unconscious understanding;" in other words me, the Christ. Your Christian church builds me as an icon upon which the wealthy get wealthier while mankind stands on the outside, separate and apart from me waiting for "salvation" and "enlightenment." I tell you, the truth about yourself lies inside your own consciousness. I am NOT separate from you; in truth, I AM you, as you are me, and the Father is you.

75. Yeshúa says: There are many standing at the door, but the solitary are those who shall enter the Bridal-Chamber.

Sounds like: "Many are called, but few are chosen" does it not? Nope, just a bad translation of my teaching. The Bridal-Chamber represents unity with "The All That Is." In my world and in my teachings, nothing exists but unity. The Divine Breath of creation created all things from its unified self. As different aspects of the same soul we each act both as a receiver of Divine Love and as a transmitter of the same. In fact, we only receive to the degree that we transmit.

This saying reminds me of a meatloaf where all the separate elements of the meatloaf lie on the counter. To become a meatloaf however, they lose their separate identities and enter into the new identity called "Meatloaf." Just as many separate bodies stand at the door; but to achieve full awakened spiritual consciousness, all must recognize their place as part of the one divine soul.

76. Yeshúa says: The Sovereignty of the Father is like a merchant possessing a fortune who found a pearl. That merchant was shrewd—he sold the fortune, he bought the one pearl for himself. You yourselves, seek for the treasure of his face, which perishes not, which endures—the place where no moth comes near to devour nor worm ravages.

Giving up everything you believe you have in order to find God is the last and most difficult lesson of all. You come into this life with amnesia and then society tells you: 1) That you are sinful and separate from God, your brother and the environment. 2) That abundance is limited. 3) That death exists. 4) That power and control can save you.

The fact that the merchant bought the one pearl indicates he was seeking to find himself and his own Godhood. He sold his fortune—he gave up his old life of fear—and fully accepted his own Godhood. Finding the pearl signifies that indeed he has come to the realization that he is one with God. Finding God is like coming to a theoretical cliff, looking behind you and seeing there is no going back; then throwing yourself off the cliff into the hands of the unknown.

Salvation does not lie in blind faith in other people/institutions or even faith in yourself. Salvation comes from journeying into the wild and secluded places within your soul, welcoming home the incongruent piece of your divided self, recognizing that you and your brother share the same soul, and then taking on the responsibility of fully living every moment of your life as an act of love with the divine consciousness.

77. Yeshúa says: I-Am the Light who is above them all, I-Am the All. All came forth from me and all return to me. Cleave wood, there am I. Lift up the stone and there you shall find me.

I am God! I am with you always because you are God—as is everything! If you were to go out into the churches today you would get quite an argument since they associate God with the body and with mental activity. However, everything that you can see, touch, smell, hear or taste has arisen from God.

God did not create something outside of Himself, but He did create in many different forms. Should you worship a tree? No, for you are God and there is no point in worshiping it, but you should respect the tree for what it is because it is the same as I am—and as you are.

When you come into that recognition then the way that you associate with anything becomes different, for everything desires respect. Even the animals that you kill for food deserve respect. As you will recall, the American Indian when hunting for food would give thanks and prayers of gratitude to the animal for surrendering himself for their benefit and that is the way it should be. Your society has gotten so far away from this premise that in effect you are worshiping idols.

78. Yeshúa says: Why did you come out to the wilderness—to see a reed shaken by the wind? And to see a person dressed in plush garments? Behold, your rulers and your dignitaries are those who are clad in plush garments, and they shall not be able to recognize the truth.

Once again, let me define my terms. "Wilderness:" The wild and unexplored places within the soul. Did you seek inside yourself for no reason? Did you expect to find a spiritually frail individual lacking substance and shaking with fear or did you search your soul to find a corporate giant complete with wealth and power? Behold, your dignitaries and rulers have illusionary wealth and power, but they do not have what you have.

Those who welcome the pain of separation to go into the wilderness of their souls and do the spiritual work of awakening, shall find unity and wisdom. Contrariwise, those who value worldly power and riches have no hunger for truth. Their stomachs are filled with their own egos.

79. A woman from the multitude says to him: Blest be the womb which bore thee, and the breasts which nursed thee! || He says to her: Blest be those who have heard the meaning of the Father and have kept it in truth. For there shall be days when you will say: Blest be the womb which has not conceived and the breasts which have not nursed.

I'd like you to picture this: I, Jesus, stand in a crowd of people trying to provide the tools needed for each person in the crowd to awaken to their divine unity. Then this woman cries out: "What a lucky woman is your mother, who produced such a gifted son." What is it about unity that this woman does not understand?

I look her in the eye and respond: "Lady, stop making an icon of me. Rather recognize the truth that you and I are one; we share the same soul; the same mission and the same responsibility. Right now you see everything through the two-dimensional eyes of separation, but the time is coming when you will recognize the truth and proclaim: 'Blessed are they who see no separation between themselves and The All That Is.' As long as you see separation, you see only sorrow."

80. *Yeshúa says: Whoever has recognized the system has found the body—and whoever has found the body, of him the system is not worthy.*

The "system" represents the earthly values developed by the ego that define who and what you are and why you are here. Once you recognize your connection to the universal soul, you outgrow the illusions of the ego and outgrow the "system."

81. *Yeshúa says: Let whoever is enriched become sovereign, and let whoever has power renounce it.*

Do not flaunt your ability and—whoever has power, must relinquish it. There is a saying about how power corrupts and absolute power corrupts absolutely. You can see in your current day how so many are flaunting their ministry out of ego. If you will remember, even in my ministry I kept escaping into the crowds. Be content with what you know and be content in knowing more. As you put down what you know in writing, do so for the love of it rather than for the power.

82. *Yeshúa says: Whoever is close to me is close to the fire and whoever is far from me is far from the Sovereignty.*

"Fire:" heat, light and divine energy. Whoever draws close to me and emulates my life draws to him the light and energy of Truth and Unity. Whoever is caught up in his own ego and the illusion of separation is far from my teachings and far from understanding the truth about himself.

83. *Yeshúa says: The images are manifest to mankind and the Light which is within them is hidden. (Th 19) He shall reveal himself in the imagery of the Light of the Father—and yet his image is concealed by his Light.*

I tell you this: Two types of light energy exist: wave energy and particle energy. Both are God. The particle energy represents the physical manifestation of God, while the wave energy represents the breath and mind of God. When you see solid objects in your environment, you see only the particle light that forms their physical God structure, but not the God energy between the particles that conforms to the laws of the unity within the Universe. I, Jesus, come to you as a man who lives according to the laws of the Father. Yet you see me as an icon and worship the man-made image created by your churches, while the mind and breath of God in me and in you, remains hidden from you.

84. Yeshúa says: When you see your reflection, you rejoice.[1] Yet when you perceive your images which have come into being in your presence—which neither die nor manifest—to what extent will they depend upon you.

"Reflection:"…the illusions of our body's physical form, that part of ourselves which our senses can see, feel, hear, touch and smell. "Your images which have come into being in your presence—which can neither neither die nor manifest:"…our subconscious, that part of our being-ness hidden from us that create our personality, character and skills.

You see your body in the mirror and you believe that body is you. It's not. Behind that body lays a mind and soul that creates your personality, your character and your belief about who and what you can become. To what extent does your belief system about (yourself) depend upon you? If you act out of fear and ego, the image projected to other people becomes one of darkness and limited abilities. If you act from love and self-knowledge, the image becomes one of light and unbounded abilities.

No matter how well you know yourself however, a part of you remains hidden in the ever-changing face of God that increases and emerges constantly. To what degree does this ever-changing manifestation of your abilities depend upon you? Only to the degree to which you are willing to let go of preconceived ideas and rely on the Father.

85. Yeshúa says: Adam came into existence from a great power and a great wealth and yet he did not become worthy of you; for if he had been worthy, he would not have tasted death.

Adam—the *metaphor* for all life preceding modern man—came as a piece of the Divine Soul seeking to experience itself in new ways. All of creation therefore represents aspects of God. Until modern man however, nature remained unable to awaken to who and what it really was—or the purpose for its existence. Upon the creation of modern-day man however, humankind arrived at a place capable of examining itself. Self-examination and acceptance of your place in the universe—as God in human form—allows you to live life abundantly and to choose to go on as part of eternal life.

86. Yeshúa says: The foxes have their dens and the birds have their nests, yet the Son of Mankind has no place to lay his head for rest.

I chose to be an itinerate teacher, so naturally by choice I had no permanent earthly home. At face value it appears by this saying that I am playing martyr; and the complete giving of myself as having no place to live plays right into the "savior" myth. However, I want you to think deeper, more out-of-the-box than your churches do in order that you might understand my true message.

At the time of this saying, I had people who, caught up in the moment, wanted to be my disciples. "Listen," I said to them: "You have your organized Churches and Synagogues which preach separation from God and your brother, while drawing you together under their tent and under their rule. If you follow me, be prepared to leave the Churches, Synagogues and Priests behind. You too will have no organized spiritual institution in which to lay your head or relinquish your spirit.

"I am NOT about buildings, power or riches. I have NOT come to tell you that you need priests ruling over you so that you can continue sleeping in the cozy dens of spiritual lepers who, on the outside, appear clean while on the inside lay rotting.

"Rather I have come to tell you that *you* ARE God; that you need to journey into the wilderness within in order to welcome home all the wild and beautiful 'prodigal sons' within you. Then when you are whole, you will become wholly part of the brotherhood of man and God.

"When you know the Truth (that you and your brother are one; that your brother and God are one, and that you and the Universe are one) then you will set yourself free to think and behave as the Universal Creator with no need for a place to lay your head."

Man was not ready to receive my message back then and is even less ready in the present day. It will not be until the church/state federations complete their unification at the time of world government that the truth about the churches will be widely known. At that point a mass wakening will occur as the last prophecies are fulfilled.

87. Yeshúa says: Wretched be the body which depends upon another body; and wretched be the soul which depends upon their being together.

By this time you must realize that the job of helping you to separate yourself from your lifelong masters has not been easy. I told you it was easier for a camel to pass through the eye of a needle than for a rich man to enter heaven. Now I tell you, it is easier for a completely debauched sinner who has never crossed the doorstep of a church to learn the truth than for the most reverent of church followers. The ruined sinner has hope; the church follower has only *false hope and fear.* This is why I've have caused "Gnosis" to be published as a small book capable of fitting in a back pocket, and giving it to convicts in prison.

"The body:"…a mere vehicle for transporting the soul. Without knowledge of its soul, the body becomes ruled by fear and by its ego—which attempts to take control in order to maintain power over both your body and over the body of its brother. The body running amok is like a mad dog that seeks to slay itself and everything else in its path.

"The soul:"…the one and only soul that exists in the universe, the living Breath of God shared by all creations of God: animate and inanimate. The soul deliberately chooses to enter the body upon conception in order to experience the world created by itself. By splitting itself into many united pieces inhabiting many independent bodies, the soul seeks both to receive light from its source and to shed new light on its source.

God created man in His image and likeness; then man created the church in the image and likeness of man: desperate, separated, fearful, and lonely—and in need of the "salvation" dispensed by religions ruled by equally desperate, separated, fearful, lonely and blind men.

As long as you remain dependent upon a man-made church to dispense light and happiness for your soul, you will wander wretchedly in an everlasting morass of lies and separation from your source.

Only you can separate yourself from the stranglehold of the churches in order to heal your broken connection to God and your brother. Yet how can you do that without leaving behind the "brotherly love" and coffee klatches of organized religion? Who will be your friend when the churches despise you for following the Christ light and exposing the truth?

88. Yeshúa says: The Angels and the Oracles shall come to you and they shall bestow upon you what is yours. And you yourselves give to them what is in your hands and say among yourselves: On what day will they come to receive what is theirs?

One eternal truth: you come into this world as a vessel worthy of receiving the divine breath of life. God can not help but give you this gift of love, support and knowledge. Giving creative breath is so much the essence of God that should

He cease to give, He would cease to be. On the other hand, your role as a vessel is first to receive all that God has to provide: abundant and eternal lives; to take what you receive, add your unique creative gifts and then to share the fullness that is within you with your brother, with God and with the Universe. When you separate yourself from God, your brother and the Universe, the creative energy within you finds no release and begins to end your existence—thus dis-ease.

Do you experience illness of mind and/or body? Look to that part of you that feels the pain, then know that in that area resides trapped creative energy that cries out for your attention, recognition and love. Like the good Shepherd, find that missing piece of yourself and welcome it home as the most prized of all your flock; then welcome God and your brother back into your life to rejoice with you in your healing.

The Angels and the Oracles give you knowledge and creativity. As the Holy Ghost comes to you just as your guides, your angels and your oracles come to you, they reveal to you the truth and they help you to the extent that they know. However all that the *past* knows is that which has happened in the *past*. Now is YOUR time, for the angels and oracles deal with the past. As a living being *you* create what happens in the future and what is happening now—therefore the future is under *your* control.

You are a part of the Divine creation and everyone, from their time of birth, participates in the Divine creation. You are able to manifest exactly what you intend; but if you are too conflicted, some wants will cancel out other desires. You become part of the Godhood when your mind and your spirit are clear and there is nothing that you will want for since you will be able to manifest whatever you need.

During your lifetime you create the new universe and you give this knowledge, this creativity back to the Godhead for it is what you came here to do. As you create and participate fully in your Godhood, you give your Angels and Oracles the new information *they* desperately crave and need to continue along their own creative path.

89. Yeshúa says: Why do you wash the outside of the chalice? Do you not mind that He who creates the inside is also He who creates the outside?

"Chalice:"…container, receptacle, trophy, prize. If you were to take water, freeze it in the form of a chalice then fill it with water, you would have a metaphor for body and soul. God took a state of his energy-self, transformed it into particulate energy in the shape of a physical body and then filled it with the wave-energy state of Himself…which you call life. Both the particulate energy and the wave energy come from the unified soul-energy of God that flows through all things.

On one level the above saying asks: "why do you curl your hair, do your nails and put on fine clothes—but neglect your internal life?" On a more profound level it asks: why do you give yourself body and soul to a man-made church in order to appease a schizophrenic idol, when the One God who made you cries out for your recognition and acceptance of His gifts; for your willingness to create and give back love, grace and refreshment to the Universe.

The churches tell you that your body is bad and needs to be punished purified and limited through fasting, public prayer and alms giving; all of which adds to their advertising and coffers of course. That is not why the Father shared himself with you. Your human form serves as a *receptacle* of God's love, grace and abundance. Your body is God's gift to *you*, it needs no improvement. Enjoy it and use it; be thankful for all the gifts poured into it by the Universe.

The churches tell you that your internal consciousness is their territory to terrorize and legislate. I, Jesus, tell you that your internal consciousness is a loaned piece of THE LIVING GOD for YOU to explore, develop and use as a tool to give back grace, abundance and love to the Universe.

I tell you that the churches are not worthy of you. I tell you also that those of you who surrender yourselves to the churches are not worthy of God.

90. Yeshúa says: Come unto me, for my yoga is natural and my lordship is gentle—and you shall find repose for yourselves.

"Yoga:"…complete abstraction from all worldly objects, by which you obtain union with the universal spirit and acquire "superhuman" faculties. When I, Jesus, tell you that my yoga is natural, I mean that I have come to share with you the Truth about who and what you are and about your mission on earth. When you understand my words and are willing to do the internal work necessary to discover the truth about yourself, you will no longer need priests or anyone else to create "mysteries" to explain what is perfectly natural. The way of the Father is that of creativity in repose; neither struggle nor worry, simply "be" and all things will come to and flow from you.

91. (They) say to him: Tell us who thou art, so that we may believe in thee. || He says to them: You scrutinize the face of the sky and of the earth—yet you do not recognize Him who is facing you, and you do not know to inquire of Him at this moment.

"Jesus, who are you?" This daily question fills much space in the gospels—and in the hearts of men today. So why did Thomas record yet another question and answer on this topic? Well, this one was a little different. Often people asked why they came into this world without any memory of their identity. I tell them that by the nature of their creation they separated from the creator to become a chalice composed of God-particulate energy. In human form, they are God in repose filled with the never ending God in motion wave-energy (see above). These two energies seek to return to their original state: as one united Godhead. This irresistible drive for man to return to his creator generates the power and force for man to live fully, to create and to "give back" energy to his creator.

Those people coming to me have invited in the God energy. They gave God permission to tell them who they are. But what happened? Immediate uncertainty! They grew up used to turning the "God-seeking" part of their consciousness over to their society, their churches and their synagogues. Now here I am doing and saying things they do not understand and like deer in the headlights, they freeze. "Who are you? Tell us so we don't have to think it out for ourselves."

But God isn't like that. If I just told the Truth to them, they would hear it with their ears, but would not find it with their hearts. It would stick like ice cream rather than like bubblegum to the wall. They have to go through their own journey into the wilderness, willing to face uncertainty and the challenge of their hidden Divinity.

I tell them: "*Because* you look at the earth and sky and still do not see their connection to you; you are not ripe to understand your relationship to me. You don't even know what questions to ask yet. Go home and continue to ripen. Open your eyes to the new chaos that enters your life as a result of your conferring on the Father the opportunity to make Him known to you. Stop reacting to adversity. Watch what is going on. Think about the synchronicities and then proactively take action to compare my words to what you are experiencing."

These sayings, which sound so strange in your society and language, made sense to the people of my time. That is why I am taking time now to explain them fully to you. Whereas in the past you settled for pat answers from your religious leaders, now you have ripened enough to stop, think about what lies right before your eyes and then take whatever action necessary to bring understanding into your reality.

92. Yeshúa says: Seek and you shall find. But those things which you asked me in those days, I did not tell you then. Now I wish to tell them, and you do not inquire about them.

This is one of many "Seek and you shall find" statements. On the surface it looks like I am using the Socratic Method: where you ask me a question and I ask you one in return until you answer your own questions. Your churches tell you: "Just keep asking enough questions and wanting the answers badly enough and you will be told."

I wish it were that simple. First of all, there is nothing for me to tell. Everything you need to know is already laid out before your eyes. But not only are you blind, you have no wish to see, so how do I describe the color green to one who can not see color?

You ask me who I am, who you are, who God is, what life is about, how to be happy, how and when the end times will occur and what you must do to become whole. Back in my time I could have told you all these things, since all these things were contained in the Kabbalah. But you did not wish to seek nor could you have understood without changing your mind, your attitude and your self.

All that has happened from my time to the present I could have foretold—and did—in the Book of Revelation. But you wanted easy answers and did not understand what was right in front of you all along. Had you sought the Truth anytime from my coming until the modern age, and had you sought to address world peace, your results could have been exponentially easier than they are now.

Even now I wish for you to know the Truth, but you are so full of yourselves and of your religious dogma, that you don't even know what questions to ask, so I tell you: You and I are one. You and God are one. Only one soul exists—the wave energy of God shared by all things. You have come to experience life in form so that God can grow in wisdom and knowledge.

No "Satan" exists, other than the chaos required to help you grow in knowledge and wisdom. Chaos is completely impersonal and you call it into your life the moment you wish to change and grow. Without chaos you are a Ping Pong player with no opposition—a Ping without a Pong.

With chaos you create an opponent, a helper, to move you to the next spiritual, intellectual, physical level. You are a vessel made up of God Energy and filled with God Energy. These two energies, left on their own, return to chaos and eventually to the Universal Soul. In order for you to maintain your physical form you must contribute to God, per your agreement. The correct way to do this is:

- **Ask to grow in wisdom.** Stop; observe the chaos that comes into your life resulting from the growth desire. The clearer the desire, the easier to observe and analyze the chaos.

- **Think.** Detach from the chaos. Look at it as an outsider knowing that life is an illusion and that you continually create your next experience.

- **Pro-act with love.** Ask: "How would Love" handle this problem?" Each time you choose love you plant another seed that will produce peace in your life. Each time you choose fear and hatred, you plant a seed that will bring more pain and chaos into your life until you change your behavior and learn the wisdom of love. Chaos is good. It's how you *respond* to chaos that causes pain and dis-ease in your life.

What is love? How does one respond with love? The Apostle Paul didn't get much right, but his definition of love (written for him by one of his disciples) in First Corinthians correctly defines the term. [4]Love is patient and is kind; love doesn't envy. Love doesn't brag, is not proud, [5]doesn't behave itself inappropriately, doesn't seek its own way, is not provoked, takes no account of evil; [6]doesn't rejoice in unrighteousness, but rejoices with the truth; [7]bears all things, believes all things, hopes all things, endures all things. [8]Love never fails. But where there are prophecies, they will be done away with. Where there are various languages, they will cease. Where there is knowledge, it will be done away with. [9]For we know in part, and we prophesy in part; [10]but when that which is complete has come, then that which is partial will be done away with. [11]When I was a child, I spoke as a child, I felt as a child, I thought as a child. Now that I have become a man, I have put away childish things. [12]For now we see in a mirror, dimly, but then face to face. Now I know in part, but then I will know fully, even as I was also fully known. [13]But now faith, hope, and love remain—these three. The greatest of these is love.[1]

You ask. How should we handle terrorism? Should we love those who fly our own planes into our office buildings? I tell you: "yes—absolutely yes!" You want to solve the mass consciousness of terrorism by creating your own terror. I tell you that FIRST you must learn to take control of *your own individual attitudes and actions.*

When you learn to ask for world harmony, chaos will appear. The correct response is to stop, think, and respond pro-actively with love. Had that been done on the individual level, the chaos would not have been elevated to mass consciousness. But because you could not love your brother one-on-one in earlier years, because your nation (the United States and the hidden world government) acted through greed and prejudice, you yourselves provoked hatred and retaliation.

Would ceasing to fight and changing to my way bring about world peace? No, not right away for your nation has created far too much hatred and mistrust for

---

1 World English Bible, 1 Corinthians 13, vs 4-13, accessed 4/11/04 from http://ebible.org/

that. Your politicians and moneylenders unleashed a juggernaut of hatred—both before and after the World Trade Towers incident.

I tell you this: the only way to complete your individual mission is for each of you to put down your arms; stop; think and pro-act with love. In this, many "innocent" will be injured as chaos expends its wrath, but in the long run, God Wisdom shall prevail. Had I told you these things before you experienced chaos, would you have listened to me? No! Now when there is still time and I wish to tell you who and what you are and how to live correctly on this earth you do not ask. Why?…because the answers are too hard!

93. *Yeshúa says: Give not what is sacred to the dogs, lest they throw it on the dung heap. Cast not the pearls to the swine, lest they cause it to become…*

As with all my sayings, this statement encompasses many levels of thought. If you share your wisdom with those who are unripe and resistant what happens?

Level 1: They ignore it.

Level 2: They don't get it, downplay your words and discredit your reputation.

Level 3: They do get it but are fearful and downplay your words and discredit your reputation.

Level 4: They ingest your wisdom, find ways of altering the information to meet their needs and take credit for your ideas.

Level 5: They ingest your wisdom, find ways of altering the information to meet their needs, find ways of altering your reputation to meet their needs, and then make you the front man while they reap the benefit of selling you to the public.

When you think about it, "Cast not your pearls before swine" is the antithesis of "Seek and ye shall find." What happens when you tell people the end of the story before they finish the book? In a way you steal from them the opportunity to pit themselves against the writer—their reason for reading the book in the first place. Telling people the truth before they have had an opportunity to seek out the truth on their own steals their journey towards the light.

When do you want the answers to an open book test? Is it before or after you have had an opportunity to pit your intelligence and insights against the questions? If the test is not scored by anyone, then what payoff exists for you to take the test? The very process of researching the answers, learning new material and enjoying your ability to manipulate the material, rewards you as you mentally experience and overcome a challenge. In other words, "Seek and ye shall find, but don't reveal the end of the book to those who have not yet read the first page."

94. *Yeshúa says: Whoever seeks shall find. And whoever knocks, it shall be opened to him.*

The simpleminded response: "Keep on asking God for wisdom and He will give you the answers." Unfortunately, if you belong to a religious sect, those answers had better comply with church doctrine, otherwise the church's response to my saying becomes "…find another answer."

I'm playing with you. Listen to me: The first question is: "What is it you are seeking?" The second question is: "Does an answer already exist?"

Picture this: You are an avid golfer. Nothing in the world matters more than golf. One day you are out on the course and—bam—a hole in one! Or, you write the most beautiful poetic book of wisdom in the world. The phone rings. You won the Pulitzer.

What if your mother had put a magnet into your golf ball in order to "fix" the result? You would hit a hole in one, but your efforts would have had nothing to do with your success. And, what if your husband or wife bought the Pulitzer for you, bypassing better written books than yours to make you think you had accomplished what you had not? Would you feel differently if say, YOU had put the magnet in the ball or YOU had purchased the Pulitzer? See where I am going with this? Does it matter whether success comes from your efforts (even your dishonest efforts) as opposed to experiencing success with no creative effort on your part?

You are a part of the Divine Soul. Those Divine genes, so to speak, make up your character. The Divine creates, changes, grows, learns, receives and gives— and all of those attributes are in you as well…on a smaller scale. You remember them because you experienced them before the "the big boom." Yet the joy in the hole in one doesn't come from knowing you are God and can't miss. The joy in winning comes from knowing that *you* are a splinter of God contained in a human body capable of developing coordinated muscular skills, but the possibility exists *that you might NOT win.* Earning the right to win has a sort of magic to it. You expend creative energy and obtain the desired result. In other words, *you teach yourself how to be God in human form—then you experience Godhood.*

I tell you this: The more you know yourself and focus your creative energies, the higher the high when you produce something that did not exist before you; in other words when you experience your Godhood.

In the past you may have presumed that "seek and you shall find" implied that you were wandering around in the dark trying to pin the tail on the donkey. No my friend, you are not born a victim whimpering in the dark: "Oh God, please help me, please lead me to the Truth." The Father is NOT going to turn on a divine light bulb in your head and give you everything you need to know to float around on a cloud happily playing a harp.

The very nature of your search will eventually turn up the heat in your soul enough to overcome the resistance of victim hood and allow *you* to BECOME the light. I came to show you how to operate your computer and I can educate you about the computer codes and how they are written. However you must develop and download your "God" software for yourself.

95. Yeshúa says: If you have copper-coins, do not lend at interest—but rather give them to those from whom you will not be repaid.

What are copper coins but the energy exchange for the realm? The actual copper in the coins is good for what? Serving as a water pipe, making tools? What? Such a little bit of copper won't serve for much other than a symbol of purchasing power. And why did we need purchasing power? Because we ceased to be nomadic tribes and settled in settlements under the rule of Rome, where we couldn't produce all our own food and take care of our own needs—*the same trap in which you find yourselves in modern time.* Here again, my saying can be interpreted on many levels:

Level 1: This wealth represents value only to the extent that Rome's economy prospers, but it won't buy the fulfillment you seek, so give it away to those who can use it. Whatever you do, don't do anything that will bring more of it into your possession. Why would you want to hold a garage sale to get rid of unneeded objects only to receive more of the same?

Level 2: If, through your efforts, you produce a product of value, give it away without expectation of return; this ties into the "Seek and you shall find" statement. Develop your talent. Give it to the universe as the gift of your Godhood without expectation of return. If you give away a bushel of apples, do you want a bushel and a half in return when you already have an orchard turning out more apples than you can use? Train yourself to allow the act of giving to be reward in itself.

96. Yeshúa says: The Sovereignty of the Father is like a woman, she has taken a little yeast, she has hidden it in dough, she produced large loaves of it. Whoever has ears, let him hear!

Sovereignty: dominion, rule, control, power, autonomy, self-government, nature, unity." Each of us leaves the Godhead as a small, but intact piece of our Source. Like seeds scattered before the winds of the universe, we settle on good or poor soil. Within us resides all the wisdom, knowledge, timing and creative urge of the Godhead. Depending upon where we land, each of us opens and expands into a new plant, a new piece of the divine spirit hidden in the human body.

We are like a roll-size piece of flour and water into which God infuses a piece of yeast. The yeast ferments and transforms the flour and water causing it to expand with air and light. From a small beginning comes much product…each piece filled with the power and spirit of God.

97. Yeshúa says: The Sovereignty of the Father is like a woman who was carrying a jar full of grain. While she was walking on a distant road, the handle of the jar broke, the grain streamed out behind her onto the road. She did not know it, she had noticed no accident. When she arrived in her house, she set the jar down—she found it empty.

The jar full of grain is equivalent to a jar full of knowledge, i.e. seeds that can grow. The jar breaking is tantamount to spreading the information and that this information will be spread regardless of what *you* have to say because when the word gets out, it is like a seed that will grow. The fact that the jar is empty indicates the knowledge has been spread. Therefore, she arrives home (which is symbolic of returning to Heaven) having done her work—since her job was to spread the information.

98. Yeshúa says: The Sovereignty of the Father is like someone who wishes to slay a prominent person. He drew forth his sword in his house; he thrust it into the wall in order to ascertain whether his hand would prevail. Then he slew the prominent person.

WEll…practice makes perfect. "Prominent man: a well-engrained personal habit; a prevailing belief system; a prevailing religious or political system; mass consciousness—the ego." If you wish to overcome a prevailing thought system, start with yourself. First overcome your own ego, your own self-destructive habits; then overcome the mass ego.

99. His Disciples say to him: Thy brethren and thy mother are standing outside. || He says to them: Those here who practice the desires of my Father—these are my Brethren and my Mother. It is they who shall enter the Sovereignty of my Father.

Many of you grew up in churches which taught that I was the product of a virgin birth; that my mother knew I was God; that Mary never had sex with Joseph and that I had no siblings. Well, I did have brothers and sisters; the virgin birth was a metaphor; and I myself had children…so much for myths! Now, about this saying: My Mother was a good person, however like any mother she could see where my ministry was taking me and was very concerned about the danger facing me, my younger brother James and my cousin Thomas. That night she showed up at the house of John, along with several of my brothers to dissuade me from angering the authorities further. Imagine that you were about to speak out against your churches and your government in a time when you could be murdered for doing so. Would you wish to endanger your family members?

My disciples came to me and said, "Your family is outside." I said to them, "You are my family now." By that I meant that our feet were set upon the path of teaching a new paradigm to mankind so that by *your* modern age, everyone would have an opportunity to hear and learn from my words. In order to do that, I had to leave my blood family behind since they were not part of my teaching ministry and would be in great danger by associating with me.

100. They show Yeshúa a gold-coin and they say to him: The agents of Caesar extort tribute from us. || He says to them: Give the things of Caesar to Caesar, give the things of God to God and give to me what is mine.

Let's take a closer look at this saying from my culture and perspective. This saying represents a triplet:

1. Give Caesar what is Caesar's,

2. Give God what is God's,

3. Give me what is mine.

1. <u>Give Caesar what is Caesar's:</u>

The Jews of my time were a conquered nation forced to pay taxes to the Roman Empire. One day a group of those who considered themselves my enemy came to me with a question about taxes. If I said they should pay taxes I would be condemned. If I said they shouldn't pay taxes, I'd be condemned. So I looked at the picture of Caesar on the coin; asked, "Who is this" and then told them to give Caesar what was his; pretty straightforward…on the surface.

Each age faces its overlords and tax collectors. It is the nature of man to desire pleasure and comfort, therefore each age faces its bills. Caesar's coin represents those taxes, bills and fees paid to obtain necessities and to meet the needs of the ego. By telling you to give Caesar the things that belong to Caesar, I tell you that life has its joys and sorrows—live it anyway. Participate fully in life so that you might fulfill your mission in coming to Earth.

2. <u>Give God what is God's:</u>

What does God need? In my time we understood that by his basic nature God needs to:

1. Be the root cause of all that happens.

2. Eternally create new objectives and experiences in order to know Himself.

3. Be in control.

4. Share his love with his creations.

These teachings dated back to Abraham with "The Book of Formation," the predecessor to the Kabbalah. So what belongs to God? Everything! Yes, all things originated with God and belong to Him. We owe Him our love, our obedience, our willingness to participate as co-creators of the universe. God desires to know Himself. Because of that desire, the entire universe, humans included, came into existence. He was the cause; man was the effect.

3. <u>Give to me what is mine.</u>

So here I, Jesus, stand. What is mine? Well, I came into this life the byproduct of the Father to enlighten mankind about the truth so that you could know your ultimate purpose in life; the reason you came, the meaning of your life, how to return "home" (to God) and what that is all about—the path to fulfillment and how to earn it. Oh yes, "and how to EARN your existence."

The biggest lie ever told by your churches was that you were "saved by the blood of the lamb" and that I earned your birthright for you. What a crock! Can you imagine doing that to YOUR son? "Son, I am giving you my factory. Every mistake you ever make will be forgiven and fixed for you." What an emasculating experience! What would God learn from that? He'd go from running his factory, to running his factory with no learning or growth in between. He discovered that in Genesis. That is what the Garden of Eden code is all about: correcting God's first big creation mistake.

Adam (the code word for the first masculine influence) and Eve (the code word for the feminine aspects of life) realized that they were mini-Gods. But instead of coming in with God-like attributes they came in as:

1. The Effect of God's creation.

2. The Created Entity.

3. Being under the Control of God.

4. Receiving God's love and dole.

So they said, in effect, "Hey Divine Source, this isn't working for us! We experience being your creatures, but we don't experience being ourselves. How can you have new experiences if everything we do, you decide for us beforehand?" So God replied: "Okay, let's do it a NEW way." With that God allowed man to come into life so that man could learn to:

1. Be the Cause.

2. Be the Creator.

3. Be in Control.

4. Share with the universe.

No punishment, blame, shame or guilt was involved in creation. The Father gave mankind the greatest gift of all—freewill. Not freewill to go to heaven or hell, but free will to make decisions, to fail or succeed, and to find "his own" Godhood while still on earth. The biggest fools of all are those who take the Bible code *literally*, for yes, the Bible **is** a code.

Now what about my asking that you give me what is mine? Well, what IS mine? I have already told you that my mission was to teach mankind the truth about who he really is; the purpose of his life, the path of endless fulfillment and the path "home." You give me what is mine by reading, understanding and following my words.

101. Yeshúa says: Whoever does not hate his father and his mother in my way shall not be able to become a Disciple to me. And whoever does not love his Father and his Mother in my way, shall not be able to become a Disciple to me. For my mother bore me, yet my true Mother gave me the life.

Some of the Aramaic words do not translate correctly into English. For example the words I used for this saying meant this:

"Hate: put aside, turn from, out-grow, aloofness."

"Love: embrace, hold close, treasure, breathe into yourself."

I most definitely did not come to despise Mary or Joseph. My mother, Mary, was a kind and gentle person, raised by her mother and other members of the Essenes to bring forth the Messiah. The term "Virgin Birth" meant "First Birth" or "First born to a *Temple* Virgin."

The Temple Virgins were betrothed to their counterparts, men from the White Brotherhood, a group of highly schooled men knowledgeable in the mystic religions. To be born of a virgin indicated I was to be a teacher. Mother and Father were betrothed for three years prior to their marriage. Under our sect, if a pregnancy occurred during the period of betrothal, then a second marriage would occur after the third month of pregnancy. That may clear up some of the "virgin birth" mythology.

Mother and I were close when I was a child. However as I grew into manhood my path took me away from her in terms of distance and understanding. Mother understood I was "special," but in her heart she just wanted me to remain her little boy. She feared for my safety as a mother would fear for the safety of her son.

I feared for her safety in being perceived as one of my followers, therefore I removed myself from her gradually over the years. I suspect in some ways she resented the Essenes the way a wife of a fireman or policeman might resent the organization that took away her man. I saw her cry from time to time when I accompanied Joseph for my initiation lessons. Later into my adulthood, she would seek to get one of my brothers to accompany her as she tried to turn me from my path.

My father, Joseph, and I were very close. He was a member of the White Brotherhood and principally responsible for my extensive schooling in the mystic religions. As an elder in the White Brotherhood, Joseph understood the process of awakening, i.e. undergoing spiritual development from son of Man to son of God. He died before I started my public ministry. However he lived fully aware and accepting of the meaning, responsibility and earthly result of this ministry.

Through schooling in the mystic religions I became initiated into the Essenes at around age twelve. By tradition, at the time of initiation the child becomes a man. He puts aside his birth family in order to become a member of a group of seekers entirely dedicated to serving God.

Initiation into the Essenes served as a rite of passage. In the theology of my sect, by accepting full responsibility for my religious growth, I changed from the effect of creation to the cause of creation, from created to creator, from controlled to controller, from receiving all to sharing all with the universe. I deliberately chose to change my life. I became the adult, the creator of his own destiny. I took full responsibility and control of my actions. And…I went from one who receives to one who gives of his talents and time.

This is what is meant by being "born again." I tell you this because the process of spiritual rebirth is the direct opposite of what the churches tell you, "about being saved by the blood of the lamb," thereby laying down playing dead, giving up control of your life and receiving grace from me.

Therefore in this saying recorded by Thomas, I was stating that only those who went through the initiation process of recognizing their own Godhood and taking charge of their adult lives could be my disciples. Upon initiation into the Essenes, I still loved my parents, but I was no longer a child in their house nor was I under their authority. I lived separately from them and walked a different path.

Mary gave birth to me, but the feminine spiritual energy of God re-birthed me and gave me dominion over how I would live my own life and fulfill my own purpose.

102. Yeshúa says: Woe unto them, the clergy—for they are like a dog sleeping in the manger of oxen. For neither does he eat, nor does he allow the oxen to eat.

My intent was never to start yet another church with more clergy seeking to control the population for their own power, wealth and glory. The clergy in my time were like dogs sleeping in the manger—they do not eat nor do they allow anyone else to eat. Clergy in fact, act as an obstacle between God and man. In the beginning they set up rules and regulations which supposedly keep mankind from straying from the Ten Commandments and the Father. In the long run, however, the church becomes a means unto itself and the clergy become fat dogs that eat off the bones of their flock.

My "church" was meant to be a school in which you gradually became aware of whom you are as sons of God. Instead, the clergy have made you slaves of 'the system.' Instead of teaching their flock how to think for themselves, they make them captive and that creates a situation where they make money and have power at the expense of my people.

Some will argue that they kept the religion going through all those years where it would have died out: but the truth never dies! I have already told everyone that the sun and moon will pass away—but my words *will not* pass away. What I wanted was for everyone to become enlightened. Instead the clergy has kept mankind in the dark by misinterpreting my sayings and establishing a guilt cult. God is in Me and I am in you, how much more plainly can I say it?

But that wasn't for the churches advantage and they changed things around so that my sayings have been hidden all these years. Those that did understand through all the centuries did not speak up because of the fear of by thinking any-thing different than what the churches did—they would have been burned at the stake in my name. My sayings are so plain that once you understand them from the viewpoint that you ARE a piece of the Father, there will be no missing my meaning.

103. Yeshúa says: Blest be the person who knows in which part the bandits may invade, so that he shall arise and collect his things and gird up his loins before they enter.

How many times have I told you to know yourself? By that I mean take off the mask of who you *pretend* to be and get to know and accept yourself for whom and what you *really* are. Know your strengths and weaknesses so that you may face adversity using the techniques of the Kabbalists: Stop, think about what is going on, cease to react and instead take positive, loving corrective action. Observe those areas in your life that come under constant chaos, and through prayer, meditation and kindly observation get to the root of the problem. What weaknesses exist in your character? Learn to spot them, accept them as part of you and then go about changing them gently through positive action.

In the above statement I tell you to know yourself. Know your weaknesses and be prepared to be tested on them until you turn your weaknesses into strengths.

104. They say to him: Come let us pray today and let us fast. || Yeshúa says: Which then is the transgression that I have committed, or in what have I been vanquished? But when the Bridegroom comes forth from the Bridal-Chamber, then let them fast and let them pray.

My cousin, John the Baptist and his followers used to pray and fast often as part of their religious ritual. Some of his followers came to my disciples and asked why we did not do likewise. I answered: "The rite of prayer and fasting in order to become holy is the old way. I am here now and this is the time for rejoicing. In time, like the bridegroom leaving the party, I will leave you. Then you can pray and fast and mourn."

By this saying I set a new way to do things. Praying, almsgiving, fasting…all the ritualistic practices of the Pharisees…did more to honor themselves than to honor God. Don't go about wearing hair shirts, beating yourselves with whips and all those flashy rites. Instead learn to know yourself, accept your Godhood and act with love and compassion as you share your goods with the universe.

105. Yeshúa says: Whoever acknowledges father and mother shall be called the son of a harlot.

This saying would have been better understood in my time. The Babylonians used "Holy Virgin" as a title for the harlot-priestesses of Ishtar (and) Asherah. The title "Virgin" meant "unmarried." Ishtar was the Babylonian goddess of fertility and the children of these priestesses were known to the Jews as children of the harlot.

I explained earlier that as a child I nursed at my mother's breast and called her "Mother." But as a man I went through the rite of passage and accepted my spiritual rebirth as the son of God. My mother and father were still my earthly progenitors; but my spiritual understanding surpassed my earthly existence. As the Son of God I accepted God as my father/mother and was in charge of my life and responsible for assuming my heavenly heritage. Those who never go through the rite of passage and remain earthbound in their thinking shall be called the sons of harlots for they have rejected their inheritance as sons of God.

106. Yeshúa says: When you make the two one, you shall become Sons of Mankind—and when you say to the mountain: Be moved!, it shall be moved.

This is a multi-layered saying for removing all separation:

Layer 1: Know that you and your brother share the same universal soul. The two are one.

Layer 2: Know that you and God share the same universal soul. The two are one.

Layer 3: Accept the rite of passage. Become both the cause and the effect, the creator and created, the controller and controlled, the giver and receiver. The two are one.

In this saying I tell you to put aside what you have been taught about the separation between man, God and the Environment. Everything originated with the Father's desire to know himself. Although a screen exists between you and the Father when you start your journey—your job, your mission—is to discover who and what you are: a piece of the universal soul experiencing life on this planet so that the Father may grow in wisdom and knowledge.

Once you know that, your next step is to take charge of your own journey. Make things happen. Accept responsibility as being the cause of your experiences. Focus and control your experiences by stopping, thinking and acting proactively in all situations. Share your wealth with the universe.

107. Yeshúa says: The Sovereignty is like a shepherd who has 100 sheep. One of them went astray, which was the largest. He left the 99; he sought for the one until he found it. Having wearied himself, he said to that sheep: I desire thee more than 99.

"Sovereignty: Dominion, control, self-regulation, unity, nature of the Father."
"Shepherd: One, who marshals, controls, drives, or protects."
"Sheep: Follower, conventionalists, one who is led, one who is protected."

The spiritual nature of the Father is like a person who is responsible for the welfare of many followers. Here, one follower, the one who has advanced most in spiritual knowledge, goes astray. The leader leaves the 99, who pretty much stick together like a bunch of sheep, and seeks day and night until he finds the one who went astray. He says to that one, I desire you most of all because you have taken responsibility for yourself.

Look at my flock within the churches. They do good deeds and do what they are told by their pastors. They go on believing in the separation of Man, God and the Universe—and tremble in fear of retaliations should they "go astray." Then one sheep, the wisest of the bunch, starts thinking on his own and leaves the churches behind to find Truth. I leave the church-intimidated sheep behind and go in search of this one independent being who has listened to my words instead of the words of the false Christian Church. Truly I love this one courageous being the most because he has the integrity to act on what he knows to be true.

108. *Yeshúa says: Whoever drinks from my mouth shall become like me. I myself shall become him, and the secrets shall be manifest to him.*

Drinks from my mouth: listens to, analyzes, understands, accepts and teaches my words. I have told you repeatedly who I am and who you are. Once you understand my teachings you will realize that no separation exists between us. You and I are one and *we* are one with the Father. Knowing that makes all things manifest. Don't take my word for it, test my sayings for yourself.

109. *Yeshúa says: The Sovereignty is like a person who has a treasure hidden in his field without knowing it. And after he died, he bequeathed it to his son. The son did not know about it, he accepted that field, he sold it. And he came who purchased it—he plowed it, he found the treasure. He began to lend money at interest to whomever he wishes.*

You are told when living on this planet, that the Kingdom of God lies all around you, but you do not see it. Well, He *is* on this planet and the Kingdom of Heaven *is* all around you, but *you* don't *know* it. Knowledge gets passed down through the ages and all this time you have been thinking that you are going to die and *go* to Heaven because that is what you have been taught.

The son sold the field—and isn't that what happens when you do not examine your life? You accept the field—you accept that the kingdom of heaven is all around you, but you sell it to whomever you decide to follow as your God. You may sell it to your preacher, you may sell it for money or you may sell it for many things; but you don't take any advantage of it because you don't know what you have. As it says, the son took the field and then he sold it (and did not learn anything either) but along comes someone like yourself, who starts asking questions—then *you* begin to work the land.

How do you think the person who purchased it found the treasure? He had to work the land didn't he? Once he knew who he was and he knew what the earth was about, he was able to manifest and that is the position that you are in now. When you know that we are all God, then *you* are now the new steward of the land.

As you move on in the ascension, the wheat will be separated from the chaff. All who have not discovered the treasure will be gone and the land (knowledge) will be inherited by those who have listened and understood what I have told them—and they will reap the treasure. They will then be able to pass the knowledge on to anyone who is receptive and will receive grace in return.

It is impossible to lift anyone up who has not been awakened. For four thousand years, dating back to the time of Abraham, this information has been passed along and many people have not even known what they had in their hands. They were under this heavy yoke of the religions, who kept them buried with the entire ego that controlled them from fear, greed, etc. Fortunately, you are in this day now where the ascension is upon you and people are beginning to learn. It is a hard thing to open the door to people who keep slamming it shut out of fear. They don't understand what they have, but you have been willing to look for it. Notice how long it took and look at how much effort you have put into it—and still have not stopped looking.

You have never put anything else in front of your desire to learn who you were and what your place was in the Kingdom, it has been your top priority day after day—and that is what it takes. Do you see the difference between those who have been taught to take God for granted and those who continue to search? Who is your God?

I tell you that you have more understanding right now than all the Apostles did. They understood as much as they could within their culture and it seemed like an enormous learning to them, but they couldn't reach where you are now—and yet you can reach even further.

110. Yeshúa says: Whoever has found the system and been enriched, let him renounce the system.

System: Prevailing belief, the idea of separation, the idea of being a victim, created by a schizophrenic God, controlled by fear, caught up in the illusion of lack and of—get yours first! Whoever acts through fear and ego to discover the system of separating himself from God and his brother in order to gain wealth through control of his brother, let him renounce the system, the prevailing belief.

111. Yeshúa says: The sky and the earth shall be rolled up in your presence. And he who lives from within the Living-One shall see neither death nor fear—for Yeshúa says: Whoever finds himself, of him the world is not worthy.

The time will come when those who are ripe to receiving my word will realize that during their life they are the creator of their own experiences and that it is up to them to control their behavior so that they always act through love; in doing this they live fearlessly "and live more abundantly." Those who understand my words also know that because they are a piece of the Universal soul, they can never die, they simply return to the Father to be sent out again to experience yet another aspect of their Godhood. Whoever discovers the truth about his existence, of him the world is not worthy.

112. Yeshúa says: Woe to the flesh which depends upon the soul, woe to the soul which depends upon the flesh.

The flesh is just your vehicle, therefore woe to the soul that depends upon the ego, for if your soul gets caught up in your ego, the flesh will dictate to the body. The soul may wish to go one way; however the body may wish to go in a different direction.

Woe to the flesh which depends upon the soul indicates that the soul, once it realizes who it is, will dictate the direction the flesh is to take. This passage merely indicates that the soul and the body are not the same thing and is another justification for staying centered.

113. His Disciples say to him: When will the Sovereignty come? || Yeshúa says: It shall not come by expectation. They will not say: Behold here! or: Behold there! But the Sovereignty of the Father is spread upon the earth, and humans do not perceive it.

This is the most important of all of the sayings in the Gospel of Thomas. However the clergy and lay leaders eliminated it from the "accepted" bibles because: 1) some did not understand its meaning and 2) the power brokers *did* understand it and saw the threat it posed to their power and greed. In this verse, I tell you that we *are* God—as is everything around us. However, because we have been taught that God and our brother are separate from us, we live in our egos and do not see the truth.

Heaven is not a *place* we go to when we die. Heaven *exists right here and now in our consciousness.* The ascension is not about us rising up into the sky; it is the growing knowingness of our true identity as aspects of God. We are to God as limbs are to a tree. We are individualized, and yet all one. We come to earth to love God above all things and our brothers as ourselves. Our destiny is to awaken to our true identity as God and then work with all the various aspects of our self to co-create earth and serve as its guardian.

I never intended to be "worshiped." I did not see myself as above or different from my brothers. As I awakened to my true identity I realized the destiny of all mankind; but mankind was not ready. My contemporaries thought they died and (hopefully) went to heaven. They were wrong. The ascension is ongoing and it exists all around us as more and more people awaken to our Godhood.

I never intended to found a "church," rather I intended to leave a *"school." I* said: "I am the way." By that I meant: "I am the pathway for you to follow. Hear my words. Live as I live, and then the Kingdom of Heaven will be open to you."

Instead the religious leaders allowed control and greed to intercede and thus the church was born. Instead of encouraging men to awaken to their true identity and love God above all things, the clergy continued the Jewish tradition of separation between God and Man and Man and his Brother. Instead of teaching men to find their own divinity, the church "interpreted" scripture and condemned those who tried to find their way on their own.

So how do you awaken? I told you: "Ask and ye shall receive. Knock and it shall be opened unto you." The Kingdom of Heaven *is* all around us. The way there does not come from our minds or a trip we take with our bodies; rather it comes through prayer and meditation. First ask and then surrender. Adopt the Ten Commandments/Attitudes. Love God above all things. Be happy in the moment. Cooperate, coordinate and share with others so that everyone shares in the abundance. That is my Path.

114. Shimon Kefa says to them: Let Mariam depart from among us, for women are not worthy of the life. || Yeshúa says: Behold, I shall entice her so that I make her male, in order that she herself shall become a living spirit like you males. For every female who becomes male shall enter the Sovereignty of the Heavens.

I was talking about Mary Magdalene. My disciples were jealous because Mary and I were so close and she was often referred to as the thirteenth Apostle. The men could not understand why I would share information with her—sometimes even more than I shared with them. However, Mary, being of the female spirit, would take my sayings and interpret them in a way that was both loving and nurturing.

Over time, each Gospel writer put his own twist on my sayings, depending upon what they were trying to prove. That is very evident in Matthew. He was trying to prove that I was fulfilling the scriptures, so he was always saying: "…and this fulfilled this scripture or that scripture."

But Mary had nothing of her own that she was trying to prove by any of this and she understood the concept that we are all God—and she also understood the concept of forgiveness. It was in her nature as a woman to understand forgiveness and nurturing, and this quite upset the Apostles. When talking about women not being worthy, they were referring to the culture of the time; also they were maddened and confused because she could take anything that I said and interpret it with love.

In reading the verse again, you can tell that I was pulling their tails a little bit and what I was referring to wasn't that she was going to become a man, but rather that as I talked to her and she grew in wisdom and understanding—that she would have as much understanding as any man and, in my estimation, she had more. It is too bad that the things she wrote and said have been hidden, but in time her understandings will come out.

The church would not allow women to be priests since they were Jews and adhered to the old Jewish tradition; they were caught in their own paradigm. In being men, their understanding tended to be legalized into black and white. There were few of my Apostles that could put a feminine slant on the commandments or on my sayings. But Mary understood in her heart and thank goodness that she did for she was able to teach our children.

As times goes by, now that you are in the midst of the ascension/self-realization, it will be those who are able to soften their approach and take on the caretaker role normally assigned to women that will go with me and who will abide with me in the New Age. You can see from all we have said before that only those prototypes that can live in peace and can accept diversity will be chosen; only those *prototypes* since I am *not* talking about spirit. You will not have the competition, the jealousy, the envy, the greed—but you will have those things that give you the most joy. No, Mary was not about to be cast out of our midst.

There was a predominately male viewpoint that the woman was always to be relegated to the spot of being subservient and of less consequence than the male. Of course a lot of that carries over to this day into many cultures on this earth; but it is the compassion, the love, the understanding that females give that are all part and parcel of what God is; so it is a little bit of a head-scratcher that people can't seem to understand. They say: "well God is this and God is that" yet you get this (what the Apostles got a lot of) is that God is a *male* God: not a female God. But God is *both* and to sit there and say that women can do this and cannot do that is foolishness.

The war of the sex's goes on and on, but that will change in time. Can you imagine what the Apostles would have thought if I had said to them: "I will raise you to the level of the woman." Of course the fixation in their mind was that the male is supreme.

Amen.

THE LORD'S PRAYER

Our Father, which art in Heaven, Hallowed
be Thy name.

Thy kingdom come, thy will be done
on Earth as it is in Heaven.

Give us this day our daily bread
and forgive us our trespasses as we forgive
those who trespass against us.

Lead us not into temptation
but deliver us from evil

For Thine is the Kingdom, the power and the glory forever.

Amen.

"The Lords Prayer" discussed with the Apostle Thomas

Let's talk about how to pray. We gave you the formula so let's go over it a little bit. It starts out with, *"Our Father."* Your understanding of the Father is what?

"God: The All That Is."

The all that is—the source—and you are a piece of that source. So you are not praying to some old man in the sky, you are really addressing your own source, but you are addressing the full force. You are a piece of it and you are going back to the source.

"Our Father Who art in Heaven," refers to being in the spirit realm because there is no such thing as Heaven. Our Father—the source that is in the spirit realm.

"Hallowed be Thy Name." Now what do you make of that?

"Admire and respect."

And what is God's name?

"The All That Is."

Yes, the All That Is. *"Hallowed"* is referring to the respect that is due to the All That Is, in recognition that all is one. If you were to say if differently it would be *"Hallowed be thy essence."*

"Thy Kingdom Come?"

That refers to the rejoining.

Of course—and this is in progress. It has always been happening to some extent because people, human beings, are coming and going—but we are coming closer to the time now when the enlightened will know and become one; you will move together as a cohort into the next dimension. To each person, depending on their own understanding, "Thy Kingdom Come" will be something different; but for your cohort it really is the movement into the fourth dimension.

Thy Will Be Done on Earth as it is in Heaven. What do you make of that?

"Here as it is there, we are really being united with the All That Is."

You have hit it right on the head, but let's also put just a little different spin on that. "Here as it is there" means that you create in the spirit realm. What you create in spirit and what you create in the spirit realm really manifests in the earth plane; it is what you call "Manifesting." Remember you are a part of God and so what you think about the most, what you want and what you pray for—is what you manifest. The clearer that you can be in your mind about what it is that you would like to have occur—and the more focused that you can stay on it—the more apt it is to appear rapidly.

You are aware of the fact that you make things happen in your own world. Well, the things you *hear* about, you also bring into existence. When talking about: *"Thy will be done on earth as it is in heaven,"* you are really talking about the Divine Creator's desire to create; and your desire, as part of the Divine Creator, is to create your piece of the play—the puzzle.

"I have been reading that you must "pretend" to be God. Isn't that analogist to what you are just saying; because if *you* are God, we *all* are! If we pretend to be God, we will *become* God here."

That is correct, because you are erasing the doubt. Your sub-conscious doesn't know the difference between what is true and what isn't true; and whatever is repeated to it enough times, it comes to believe. If you want to increase your awareness of your own Godlike abilities, then you pretend to be God: "You fake it until you make it."

"That makes sense to me, although I have to admit everybody saying "Pretend to be God," well, woo woo. Otherwise—the way I help myself most is looking in the mirror and saying, "I AM." It covers a whole lot of my problems by just doing that and they go away."

Just the "I AM" is fine. Now, how do you think you create something on the spirit realm?

"By setting your intent and thinking about it."

Yes, by your intent; that is correct and if not that, then in prayer, because when you pray, you are setting your intent *into* the spirit realm. When you are saying in your prayer: "Thy Will Be Done on Earth as it is in Heaven," you are really saying: "Listen Divine Source, now that we have manifested this in the spirit realm, let it also be manifested on the earth plane." You are asking for your prayers to be answered and that is what *"Give us this day our daily bread."* is about.

"Give us this day our daily bread…" take care of us, feed us. A lot of that goes back to your own prayers and, if in your prayers—in absolute confidence—you believe that you will be taken care of by doing the work, then that is how it will be. So much of it depends on *your own* belief system. If you believe that you have to strive to survive, then "Thy Will Be Done on Earth as it is in Heaven" becomes true and at that point: "Give us this day our daily bread," becomes okay. You thought that you had to strive, then "So be it, we will give you some jobs to do." Do you see how these two things interact?

The All That Is does not just give to you out of hand, it is all in your intent and some of it takes place over time. Obviously you and your wife have worked hard all of your lives and now you have pensions and that helps out greatly. As you need extra funds, along it comes—in any format that you want it to come in. If you or your wife want to work, whatever it is that you want to do, will appear and, there are alternatives to that.

Being *"one"* you don't know what the possibilities are. That is a part of what meditation is about, so when you are praying and are saying: "that is my intent God, that I will be taken care of and here is my preferred way of having it done," then you begin to manifest how you will receive your daily bread. It works quickly for light workers because you have gotten rid of the garbage and you are coming into the point of being able to believe, to understand that you create all of this yourselves.

So, *"Give Us This Day Our Daily Bread"*…you get it however you see it. If you want it to appear differently, then you need to ask for it differently. The interesting thing is that you are asking that some of your daily bread be produced through your own efforts of growing your own food and working with us too. That will reach the point where it will become manifest, so this year you will learn to can and to freeze, to do those things; but it is all part of "Give Us This

Day Our Daily Bread." It is more complicated than just having money fall from Heaven. So what is next?

"And Lead Us Not Into Temptation, but deliver us from evil."

How could God possibly lead you into temptation?

"I believe that that implies: 'let us not lead ourselves into temptation'."

You've got it; wherever your weaknesses are. There is no such thing as good or evil, there is just what there is. So lead us not into temptation, but deliver us from evil means, that if you stay tuned to the Divine Will, then you will be able to spot your own peccadillo's and overcome them. Your spouse is somewhat obsessive compulsive and that costs money because whenever she is off on her latest tangent; it is going to cost money—whether it is buying flowers or computers— whatever it is. Learning to let go of that need to obsess and to control everything is what you are praying for when you are saying: *"Lead Us Not Into Temptation, But Deliver Us From Evil."* What you are really saying is: "Deliver us from the over activity of the mind, because the mind is always trying to create."

With your friend his latest thing is the sales gimmick that he has going. But he is so tied up in it that it *is* his life, it *is* his God. Here's a question for you. When you are not actively thinking about something, where does your mind go back to: what do you think about most of the day? Wherever your mind goes back to most frequently is the obsession of the moment.

"Yes, but only of the moment. Does it not, in reading and studying, reach a point where you plateau and then wait for a while until you find another item or point?"

Yes, because the mind has to stay busy—it thinks. That is why we are urging you into meditation—so that you can get a handle on it and make it stop doing that. Your wife's mind (when she is not actively thinking about something) will drift back to her garden, her teaching or her concerns about making sure that she has enough money. That is her obsession, which is how her mind runs.

When you are thinking those kinds of thoughts, you are not opening up to other possibilities. *"Lead Us Not Into Temptation, but Deliver Us From Evil,"* really is asking that your mind be cleared from all obsessions and all compulsions: that it needs to be distracted. Evil, in the sense of a prayer, really refers to anything that separates you from your highest good. In the Christian or the western tradition, your highest good is self-denial and becoming saintly. But that is *not* what this prayer is about.

Your "Highest Good" truly is your connectivity to your own higher self and realizing who you are and what you are capable of. If you spend your own capability because you believe you are less than you are—take for instance your daughter who is continually being led into temptation and into evil in the sense that she keeps getting further and further away from her true self.

Temptations almost always come right down to what you are talking about—fear. Ones temptation is to operate out of fear instead of out of love and when you are working from fear, you are limiting the possibilities. When you work from love—the possibilities become unlimited. So, "Deliver Us From Temptation" really means: *"Deliver us from Evil, lead us not into Temptation"*

"For THINE is the Kingdom, The Power and The Glory for Ever and Ever. Amen."

What does that say to you in context with the rest of the prayer?

"We are all one."

Yes—and everything is available to you right now—in the moment. So, *"Our Father,* (Divine Creator, the All That Is,) *which Art in Heaven,"* (which operates on the spirit realm.*) Hallowed Be Thy Name,"* really means: "Glory be to the Essence of who you are and who we are: The Oneness."

"Thy Kingdom Come, Thy Will Be Done on Earth as it is in Heaven," really means, that whatever is manifested in the spirit realm, is to be manifest in the human realm.

"Give Us This Day Our Daily Bread," refers back to whatever it is that you feel you need for essence, for survival—whatever your prayer has been. "Give us this day our daily bread"—you have asked for something in prayer and now you are saying, please give it to me.

"Forgive Us Our Trespasses As We Forgive Those Who Trespass Against Us." What does that mean to you?

"It means that something we do that should not be done and causes us to fall away from the Essence That Is. Just like somebody who offends us, we are offending the All That Is; so forgive us for our offense, just as we forgive others for offending us."

"...and Lead Us Not Into Temptation. Deliver Us From Evil," refers to—please take us out of the mental mind; which leads us to evil, only in the sense that the

mental minds takes us further and further away from our natural selves: "evil" being the separation from our own true selves.

"For Thine Is The Kingdom, The Power and The Glory for Ever and Ever, Amen."

Why would we want to be in the mental mind when the All That Is, the Heavenly Father (whatever you want to call it) has all power for always, for ever and ever, and—you are part of it. The Lord's Prayer really is a request to operate in the spirit realm. Does this make sense?

"It does now and thank you for the explanation. After years and years of religious training, with the separation between the All That Is and us—because we are 'sinners': sometimes it is hard to overcome and it is truly a grand and glorious awakening since we have had 'being sinners' so ingrained."

Well that is what a week of continuous meditation is all about; it is about separating more and more from the mental mind and allowing you to operate in the spirit mind. When you then read something that pertains to your prayer, it will enlighten you a little more. Then, in your meditation, you can then expand on it and use the information that you have read to further your prayers. Your prayers are like a breath that is sent out. You take the strands of that breath and start weaving it into the pattern and the picture that you want to manifest; so if you get some extra information then go ahead and do that. Talk also, for being able to talk about what you are meditating on will bring it more into reality for you. It will also give you some ideas or plans of what to do, what actions to take next.

"I like that, to meditate on the Lord's Prayer; having never looked at it in that light before (because it has always been thought of as being presumptuous to do such things) it resonates with me."

Well, if anybody has the right to be presumptuous it is you. Be presumptuous for you are very close to us and you are very close to your own essence now. Your willingness to do as you are told speaks more than your words.

"When asking for teaching, if you don't practice what's being taught, then what is the point if you want to learn?"

What have you learned in the book that you have been reading?

"More about the fourth dimension, the transition, although you get an awful lot of…shall we say different approaches and static along the line? But the thread is there and that is what I am following: the thread. Everybody has their own opinion and it comes through a little differently with each reading. A lot of the side issues come through in fear. You see it and you see that they have a point, but I can't buy into that fear."

There is no longer any need for fear. The more that you open and love, the better things are and you see examples of that all around you. Look at your next-door neighbor who operates out of fear. She controls her own situation since she is forever throwing a party but nobody comes. And yet your other neighbor comes with flowers, stops, talks and shares your Kitty with you and he bridges it. But that openness, that lack of fear opens up other possibilities since you are also willing to cooperate with them.

Love opens all doors and you don't know what it will open the doors to until you try. You don't have to have a lot of money, but then you don't have to own everything. If you have friends, they come with pieces of what they have, they share with you and you share with them; there is enough for all, which is how it works. But, when fear starts to operate you think you have to hoard everything that you have—then others don't share with you and all you get is the result of your own work. You only have 24 hours a day, so that is as far as you can go. But when everybody shares with everyone else, then you have all of their time in terms of *"Give Us This Day Our Daily Bread,"* and everyone benefits.

So yes, operate out of love and whenever you meet anything that is in fear, realize that it is not coming from the All That Is; the fear is coming from the mind of the person who wrote the work. I am glad that you are able to pick that out, not everybody does.

We are enjoying your wife's comments today that in just watching nature, she was realizing the length of time that it takes for things to happen—that nature is very patient—most of the time. You plant the seed and you wait and you wait and then all of a sudden the plant comes up. It is the germination time that is the longest period. Once the seed starts to grow, it grows rapidly. That is how it is also with your own manifestation; the germination time is the longest. If you are praying for rain (depending on how good you are at it) it takes time to get the clouds together and do those things that need to be done to produce the rain. But once it happens, it happens rapidly.

Keep that in mind: that when you are praying, the seed needs to germinate, it needs to be protected and it needs to be watered—just exactly the same as every-thing in nature. You don't want to uncover it too soon and you don't want to keep digging it up to see whether it is growing or not. There has to be a certain amount of faith that what you prayed for is indeed happening, but it is happening in the time that it is meant to happen. Now, why do you have to pray for anything? Why doesn't the Divine just know and do it?

"Well, I think it is for our experience here is it not?"

Who is the Divine?

"We are, when I said 'our,' I was including Him."

Just to let you pick out the nuance that I am throwing out to you, why do you have to pray, why doesn't God just know automatically what to do?

"Well, why are we here?"

Who is God?

"We are."

So when does God know what to do?

"When God asks himself for it."

And who is God?

"We are."

Solves that one. You see, the All That Is put you here to create; The All That Is doesn't care, so you can create whatever you want. On this plain, because you are in a body and you have a mind, you can make decisions about which direction your creation will take. It's like you have been gifted to be a painter, now you are painting the picture. He has given you the gift—so go and do it.

Your prayer is really recognition of the Divine creation that you want to have occurred. You are not petitioning God: "God, please fix this." What you are doing is that you are bringing awareness into the universe, such as your intent for your daughter to awaken to who she is, (and that *intention* is very powerful.) When you say, *"Give us This Day Our Daily Bread,"* you are saying, "please grant me the intention that I have sent out." Then you become a co-creator with God.

That will give you something to meditate on tomorrow: if you're a part in the Divine Creation, that you take the time from all that you know to set an intent; then as part of that prayer, what I would recommend is that you say: "If it is in the best interest of my daughter, son, wife, neighbor—and of the Universe," then you are broadening the intent. It is the same as what you talk about in terms of getting a Ford. Well, I had really intended to give you a Cadillac, but since you want a Ford…!

But if what you are saying is: please give me a vehicle that will get me from here to there (and here are some of the things that I would like to have that vehicle do that is in my best interest and in the interest of the Universe) then God is free to give you a Cadillac. Everything is possible! Everything is possible—and you don't know who you are going to meet tomorrow. There are people who have more money then they could ever spend, and it all depends on how you happen to hit them and how their fancy happens to be at the moment.

Don't limit yourself to just what you can buy or what you can do—keep it open to the Universe. What you two are doing…we told you about preparing your own foods, to be prepared to store your own food. Realizing your children might have to learn some things with you, you may have to share this with your family and your friends—and you are doing it. When you are doing what is in the best interests of the Universe, don't you think the whole Universe will come to your aid?

"It is a mindset to get over. When you spend half of your life struggling and all of a sudden so much opens up to you, you are a little timid. But I sure like what you are telling us, I am opening more and more."

Tomorrow meditate on the Lords Prayer and we will talk again. Thomas, would you like to close this for us please?

"I am delighted, for you are seeing now the essence of what this is all about. We have a ways to go yet, there is more that we haven't explained to you or brought out, but trust us (and we know you do) this is just the first step. You will see that in understanding the Lord's Prayer and all of its ramifications, which if you will pay attention and be open to it, the next part is going to be easier yet. Believe me, it is something to look forward to. And with that I too will say Goodnight."

Amen.

BEATITUDES

Beatitudes

Mathew 5:

Beatitudes

Mathew 5:

A discussion between Jesus Christ and His Apostle Thomas

Mathew was a bit pedantic. He had a lawyers mind and you will notice when reading through the Bible that he tries to match everything to the scriptures because he wants to prove that I am God and that I am fulfilling the various scriptures; therefore he gets his own interpretations into things. He was a good man who saw everything in black and white: a very highly judgmental individual, but not a particularly loving or merciful person.

Remember, he was a tax collector so he had that kind of mentality: that there was justice to be meted out. He did not necessarily understand everything, even though he tried to interpret it. Then, because his interpretations did not sit well with the church and its' need for power, some of the things he said were later changed.

His best work tended to be in those things that he did not understand, because those he tended to translate and copy down correctly. You will find that whenever there were passages about mercy that they were copied correctly. With that in mind, I want to go through the attitudes with you.

Blessed are the humble for theirs is the kingdom of heaven

(Humble: Modest, not proud or haughty; not pretentious)

The kingdom of heaven is given to the humble man. Now, what does humble mean? Often humble is equated with self-effacement and that is not at all what I was talking about. Have you noticed yourself as you have awakened that you have become more humble? Not in the sense of being self-effacing, but in the sense of starting to lose judgment of other people (recognizing that you are God and that they are God also) and not seeking recognition, because recognition of the world means nothing to you. Do you see that? That was my definition of humble. It is those who have come to the Father and said: "Father, I want to serve you—I don't know who I am and I don't know what I am here for, but if you will teach me I will follow you."

Some are awakened and some are not and some are right on the spot…but all have the heart of gentleness and they seek to learn from me and of the way that I behaved with other people. Theirs is the Kingdom of Heaven because if you will remember from the Course of Miracles, Heaven is inside of you. Heaven *is* the awakening, it *is* the atonement; it is coming to know that you are God and becoming to be completely non-judgmental of any other person.

Those that are seeking the Kingdom of Heaven (and assume the willingness to be taught, which is another definition of humility) are already in the Kingdom of Heaven for they are at peace. They are no longer struggling against outer forces but rather are centered in God.

It is almost impossible to insult the humble person for they feel secure within themselves; they do not need your judgment and neither do they judge you. If anything they send you love. Now, why is the Kingdom of Heaven the right of the humble?

"I would say because that is what God, the Father, really enjoys and it is not people who are going to be so full of angst that they wreck havoc."

That is very well stated. The humble person knows his place so to speak. His place is at his Fathers throne, at the foot of God, for he is a piece—not all of God—but a piece of God. Now, can you enjoy Heaven on Earth—certainly!

Notice what this says: "Blessed are the humble for theirs is the kingdom of heaven." It does not mean that they are going to die and go to heaven because they are humble: it means because they are teachable and because they are willing to see things in a different light from how they always thought things were. Greatness, in the sense of the human term, means nothing to them for they are already in heaven—they have already reached it. As long as you remain in the perfect knowingness of who you are; are willing to listen to other people and to consider what they are telling you, your happiness remains complete.

No one can change you from the ways of God once you understand what the Ten Commandments/Attitudes really are: but they might give you new insight. Have you noticed how you have stopped competing? Usually in the early days of awakening, those on the path proceed to compete; that *they* know the right way, that it is the only way and *you* are mistaken if you think differently. However, those who are humble are not seeking for their ego is diminished and one of the definitions for being humble would be that they have a greatly diminished ego. The ego is no longer in charge of their life.

The opposite of humble is arrogance, for when you are looking at a sliding scale between arrogance and humble, you are looking at arrogance as being of very high ego—a lot of fear. People are arrogant when they are afraid and that is an offensive way of dealing with the world. However, if you move that sliding scale along towards humbleness, you are moving towards love. Ego demands that you are separate, that you are better and that you have the power to crush everybody who thinks differently.

Humble realizes that true happiness comes from not being different, not being separate and of forgiving everyone. When you forgive you not only release the other person to go do whatever they want to do, but you also release your own thought processes. You do not have to go over and over the least slight and build up a wall between yourself and someone else. It does not matter anymore since you see the God in them and that is all that you see. The person who sees that God (and has let go of ego) instead of pushing people away says: "Welcome to my World."

We will talk again about there being a difference between humble and meek. You might want to look up the word meek in the dictionary so that you can see some of the differences between the two. Nevertheless, of course the kingdom of heaven belongs to the humble, for the humble are without ego. You can understand that based on the book "A Course in Miracles."

It is so freeing, it allows you to sit back and enjoy others as opposed to feeling as if you have to correct them. You see them as where they are and sometimes you get information from them. These lectures may be short, but they are very powerful.

Amen.

Blessed are the meek for they shall inherit the earth.

(Meek: Characterized by patience; mild; long-suffering; moderate)
*(Centered: Concentrated; a place to fix: to gather at a center; the point at which an
activity concentrates or originates)*

This description of "meek" is right on, although I hate to think of it in terms
of long-suffering. I would rather think of it as patience: patient, kind and gentle.
Not everything happens at a snap of a finger…sometimes your job as a Savior
(one who helps others to awaken) is to wait until the other person is ready to
come around. Sometimes that happens in times of hardship, so when things seem
difficult, you must remain centered.

You will find that "meek" and "centered" are very similar. When you are centered, nothing bothers you. Being meek does not mean being milk-toast, it means
that you know yourself well enough and your place in the universe as the Savior,
to know that everything comes to him who waits. When you cultivate both the
spirit of being humble and meek, of not feeling that you need to be at the head of
the table, but by being perfectly willing to sit anywhere because it is more important to be next to people who need you than it is to be in a place where you are
getting other peoples respect.

To be meek, if you are sitting at the foot of the table and all the praise, everything, seems to be going to the people at the head of the table, then it does not
bother you since you are willing to wait. You do not need human acclaim; you are
waiting for your opportunity to minister to those who need you.

A person who is meek is going to be turning his eyes towards God as opposed
to turning them to the world. When you are meek, you know that there is no
such thing as time anyway. What difference does it make if it happens today or if
it happens tomorrow (sometimes it will never happen at all) for your eyes are on
God and your eyes are on your brother in terms of where you can be of the most
help.

So far, with the Beatitudes, are we not describing an awakened person? Do you
see how I could not have said that back in my time? So I said it in parables (riddles) but now you have the key and once you have the key you can open all the
riddles. You will find that if you now go back through all of my sayings, as you
will be doing when you go through the Gospel of Thomas; they are going to have
a slightly different twist. Things that I told you before would not have been
understood then, but are now at your beck and call.

What people liked about me, especially in the legends of the Christ, was my attitude. Beatitudes are beautiful attitudes—see it? I was not concerned with pushing
myself forward; if anything I kept melting through the crowd and disappearing. I

did not want to be a King, I simply wanted to get the message out and I needed to be able to reach across the centuries so that you could have it. The unfortunate thing is that the Apostles, especially Paul (who knew how to write better than the other apostles and was a very prolific writer) tended to be officious. They took the message and pushed it down people's throats and they continued the "guilt cult." At least the message did come down through the centuries, although often times used to guarantee the power of Kings and people who were in a position where they could change the message.

However, you "get it" since you were selected to get it. Part of the reason that you were selected to realize your Godhood and realize that you are the savior of this century (along with a goodly number of other saviors) is because of your attitude. Whereas at a younger age you might have been arrogant and impatient—although as you have grown older you have mellowed—it is like a rosebud opening up. I have watched it happen and I have watched you come into your own. I have to admit that when we were together, you were neither meek nor humble (laughter).

You were not arrogant, just the accountant type person who was very concerned that everything balanced out at the end of the month, (which was good I guess) but, you were always very loving. Now, in your old age of this lifetime, as in your old age previously—you have softened, for how else can you win the confidence of the people who need you other then to soften? If you are harsh, you will have people who will follow you because they are looking for direction; the problem with that is they will expect you to forever take responsibility for them.

People, who are looking to take responsibility for themselves respond better to a gentle touch. They do not want to be told what they have to do; they want to be listened to. They want to be given information when the time is right and they want to be free to make their own decisions. Those who are awakening fall into that category and they are the ones you will be working with. If you put on a front and a charade, then the person talking to you feels that he too must put on a front; he too must be tough, impatient and arrogant. It is not until he finds that there is nothing pushing him back that he is able to simply melt and become who he is.

Continue to practice these two attitudes and keep them always in mind, knowing that whenever you are tempted to strike back that you are acting out of ego, for only ego needs to prove itself right. You have nothing that you need to prove anymore, and I would think that would be good news.

Amen.

Blessed are they that mourn for they shall be comforted.

(Mourn: to feel or express sorrow for something regrettable)

Sounds like a strange statement, does it not? Why would you mourn anyone when you know that they are God and they simply return to their realm? So, what do you think it is all about?

"Because you are seeking to know God and you are not physically touching; the more you ask, the more you will be comforted. When you get out of your ego you mourn, for you feel that you have lost something. It is that you want to praise God and yet you feel a loss of a loved one and you want to mourn; or a loss of certain circumstances that causes you to want to mourn and you want to go to God. When you do, in return He will comfort you, be it through the Holy Ghost or through you Jesus—God does comfort you."

Well, you certainly get a gold star since you have hit this very important phrase right on the head. In order to awaken you first have to know that you are God and that your brother is God. You know that when it is somebody or something for mourning, since it is not just about losing a person; it is any kind of a loss. It could be a loss of a job, a home—anything that causes you to feel as though you have suffered a loss.

The first thing that you are going to do if you are awakened, is to realize that the feeling of loss is very human and it comes from the ego that would like to control things…that wants things back to where they were when you felt comfortable. However, it is as you said: Those who mourn and who turn to the Father for comfort will receive it. Notice that it does not say: "Blessed are they who mourn for theirs is the Kingdom of Heaven."

The promise of this is that God is there for all storms. To mourn is normal; to be awakened and to realize that you really need nothing, that you have lost nothing, takes things to a much higher step. Because you are in a human body and you are used to having your mate or, you are used to having a job and now you do not—you are afraid. You no longer have the comfort level that you had and you do not know what lies in the future.

Blessed are they who mourn goes even beyond just sadness. When you have a great loss in your life and you are left at a place where you are on slippery ice; when you have nothing familiar to hold on to: then in that situation turn to God. Willingly accept the fact that everything happens exactly right, that God does not make mistakes. Realize that whatever has occurred was in the best interest of the other people in your life and also in your best interest. Moreover, for a while you are going to have to improvise since your life is going to be very different. You may be alone, maybe your income has decreased and you are worried about how you are going to survive. Maybe you have plenty of income, but you wonder if your life is worse now that the other person is gone.

Turning to God and continuing on—in recognizing that you came here as the Savior and that you are the Savior—you will come to an understanding after awhile that whatever has gone out of your life has, number one: completed its mission in your life and number two: has opened up new opportunities for you. That may sound strange and maybe it sounds horrible to somebody who has just lost a loved one, but it is indeed the truth. Those you have had in your life were under a contract that they made with you before they even got here. Their contract is now complete and they are free to return home; your contract now is to move on.

Now, how does one mourn: initially you cry and you vent feelings. I am telling you that if you will spend your time in meditation, completely emptying your mind and waiting…well remember the first two Beatitudes: blessed are the humble and blessed are the meek. The meek are able to withstand the storm; they know that there is a light at the end of the tunnel; they have that faith.

When you mourn, by allowing your body to express its grief; by not denying, but going past the grief and then coming into meditation and allowing yourself to be touched by the Holy Ghost; you will reach a state of understanding. You will have the courage to walk across that void knowing that you do not need to have control since control is in the hands of the Father. No matter what it is that you are mourning, on the other side of the grief will come strength to do your job.

What is your job? As the Savior, your job is to help others to awaken. If you have no grief in your life, how can you understand others? How would you know what it is that they need when they have lost their mate, their job—what would give you the credibility to be the helper? It is not that you need to go tell them about all of your experience, it is that you need to have the good sense to simply sit with them and allow the peace that you have gained in your life to surround them like a cloak.

Your ability to give up everything is the way to what you call Heaven. To find you are holding on to anything (even him or her) that you feel you need—then you have not surrendered completely and you have not understood who you are. When you come to that point of trust, that point of inner peace where no matter what happens (and it really does not affect your equilibrium) then you will be very close to the transition. I have told you that you can reach Heaven right here on earth since it is not a place in the sky; it is an *internal* attitude and understanding of your closeness with the Father.

Whenever you mourn, recognize that you have stepped into a new learning process. The biggest thing in mourning is the change. You have lost something that was very comfortable to you and now you are going into a very uncomfortable situation—that is all that it is. The person that you lost is like losing your favorite car, but you have not lost the driver since the spirit that was in the person is still available.

Now, I do not want you to have the picture that if you have lost a loved one, that that person is walking around in a body, but you cannot see it. That is not it: for that person has returned to the Godhead and is accessible to you in meditation—for *God's entire kingdom is accessible in meditation.* When you have lost someone and you go into meditation, that someone (who of course has not gone anywhere) is still available to you. Then your comfort comes from knowing that that spirit is still there, stronger and clearer even than when you knew him or her on earth.

I am not saying that ascended people have become saints for I have already told you that is not the case: they simply go back into the Godhead. As you go to God for comfort, that comfort is coming from the very person that you are mourning, the spirit of that person. Can you understand that?

Blessed are they who mourn for when you mourn, you show that you have developed a sense of oneness and, oneness can be with a person or a pet. I have already told you that all things are God—it is not just human beings. Your pets are God, your furniture is God, your trees are God (you do not worship them since you do not need to) and *you* are God; you simply develop an awareness of the Godliness of all things, about the love of all things.

In a way, your mourning is a tribute to whatever it is that you lost, it is a recognition that they have served you well. If they had not served you well, you would be saying: "hurray it is gone" right? I would like you to view mourning as a sacred ritual in human existence. Raise it up! Go to the Father! Know that what you have lost you really have found again in another form and that your courage to succeed has become strengthened through meditation when you ask for assistance.

Mourning focuses your attention razor sharp on that person or *thing* that has been in your life. In your meditation you will come to see where your loss has been turned into a gain. That is different for different people, so I cannot tell you specifically what type of a gain it will be for you—just trust that it **will be** a gain for you.

Anything that stands still dies, and in order to go on living you must change continuously, since all things *must* change continuously. Some things change more noticeably than others because they show their age in a time frame visible to all humans. Rocks age as do mountains as does everything, it just happens more slowly. You will change throughout your lifetime; not only in body, but also in spirit, for as you grow in spirit you grow in understanding.

We feel this more about love for love is not about needing the other person and it is not about sacrificing for the other person: it is recognizing that you are whole and the other person is whole—but that you have come together for a brief period of time to learn and help each other.

Because you are human you are subject to rituals. Since a ritual is a passage, and recognizes that the body cannot change all that quickly since it has evolved over eons and it does not change rapidly. Therefore, a ritual of passage does not give a period of grief, a period of mourning. As I said to you so long ago, do not hide your light under a bushel basket. Your light comes from all of your combined experiences that you have had through the ages as you take your journey towards awakening.

You will find that each person, each thing who comes into your life, and that you truly learn to love, has brought with them a precious gift—a lesson, something that you needed on your pathway towards growth. As you mourn, you begin to let that gift come through with great clarity for you—with the help of the Holy Ghost. When you see clearly that other person—someone or something in your life (even a pet with a role in your life) you can bless them for you can grow from it and there will come a time when you will get back out into the world again.

Blessed are those who come to the Father, express their grief, express their realization of who they are, express their realization that everything was created by God and that they are a piece of God—and for the time being (the time that is necessary) put their hand in God's and allow healing to occur...when they mourn, they will be comforted.

I told you a long time ago that you would know the truth and the truth will set you free. Sometimes in fear, the truth becomes obfuscated for a while; you do not think clearly and you are not thinking straight. The time that you spend in meditation allows you to heal so that you can come back to knowing what you already know and, as I said before, recognize the lesson that has been brought to you by whatever it is that you mourn.

I too mourned. I missed my father Joseph, when he died. I knew where he was just as I knew who he was when he was alive, but I missed having the person that I learned so much from and to whom I could talk. I know what it feels like such as when Lazarus died and oh, how Mary Magdalene felt—and I brought him back to life.

Mourning doesn't come from the spirit; it comes from the body—the spirit couldn't possibly mourn because it could not mourn for what it lost, for now it is in pure spirit—out of form and into spirit. Nevertheless, the body misses the familiar.

I am always here for you. Bring your grief to me; trust that I will use my powers, my abilities to bring you to a depth of understanding and happiness that are greater than anything you have ever known in the past. In the past when you mourned, you simply cried, carried on and felt sorry for yourself. However, upon awakening and realizing what I am talking about—these attitudes—you are going to realize that mourning is just an attitude, it is not an act.

When you are in the attitude of learning, you truly will be in an attitude of prayer and surrender as all of these attitudes go together. You can see where people who are meek are going to surrender to God. A person who is humble is also willing to surrender to God and mourning is yet another aspect of all that. The story about Abraham and Isaac is an example of mourning. He was going to sacrifice his son—he was to the point where he was completely obedient to what he thought God was saying to him since a permanent loss requires obedience, a faith in God.

All of these Beatitudes are spirit-based and they can be completely mis-read if you take them from a human viewpoint of what you know in your culture. If you understand the truth of who you are, then you truly grasp the nature of letting go of things and of people. Being thankful of their being in your life; being thankful of whatever they brought you: the lessons, the happiness, the laughter, the struggle and the sorrow. Not thinking of them as being in a better place—that they came here and now it is all awful, they suffered and then they died and they are now saints flying around in Heaven. It is not like that at all.

They came here voluntarily. They experienced what they needed to experience to get as close to you as they could get. They came here to help you awaken just as you came here to help them awaken…and what they have gone back into is the Godhead. It is a very difference concept, which is why I am belaboring it a bit since I do not want to have you put the normal spin on mourning. I want you to see mourning as that process of turning everything over to God, of ceasing to judge that person or that thing (however named in the life) other than of helping you to awaken and of you helping in theirs.

It is not that a person who you loved is worth ten points and the people that you kind of liked being worth two points—it does not work that way at all. Humans tend to attach a meaning to your perception of everything and your perceptions are very limited. (I am also telling you that your perceptions as a human being are usually completely off base.)

Am I getting across the preciousness of mourning to you, for that is what I am trying to do? Mourning is a spiritual act of relinquishment: from that comes freedom and great joy. For people who have been on the spiritual path of awakening, their mourning is going to be much easier because they have already relinquished their notions about many things. They have already relinquished a lot of their ego and their fears; have come to love and have come to know the Father in a different way.

When you reach the point that you know that anything that has left you and (as you call "died,") is as close to you as I am now, you will understand. Sometimes people mourn because a loved one leaves and goes off somewhere else and stays on the earth plane—just not in theirs. Again, this is a matter of taking it immediately to the Holy Ghost and taking as long as you need in the mourning process. From a bodily point of view, or from a "mind" point of view, you may need some counseling; but if you are well on your path to awakening you can do it yourself through meditation.

Realize that if a person has gone out of your life, if they have left the earth plane or have simply left, it is because they have already taught you what they needed to teach you—you do not need them there any more—release them! God Bless them and let them go: God Bless them and say thank you—just go on.

The mourning process is that grid in time between your loss and your ability to go on. Moreover, that can be as long or short as you care to make it. As long as you keep trying to hold on to that that is gone, you will continue to mourn. When you are able to completely let go of it, realizing that you could not possibly lose anything in the first place, then you will heal much faster and you will be able to get back on the path, to get back to your work of being the Savior.

Amen.

Blessed are the peacemakers for they shall be called the children of God.

(Peacemaker: one who settles an argument or stops a fight; brings peace))

In the study of the "Course of Miracles," what is it that you are told repeatedly and that which you must do as far as your brother is concerned? Love and forgive, right? The whole Course in Miracles is about you coming to your realization that you are the savior and that your purpose in life is that of awakening your brother. How do you do that? By forgiveness! By overlooking anything that you may think that he has done wrong and to see him as pure God. In other words, becoming a peacemaker.

Your whole calling in life is to set aside anything that you have ever learned about good and evil and about judgment, particularly pertaining to yourself and other people; instead of looking towards judgment, to look towards love. Further, to help your neighbor face who he is and erasing his fear of you and of God. By doing that, you are bringing him to a fully awakened realization of his own Godhood and his own responsibilities of being God: to realizing his own responsibility to be a Savior for his brother and of entirely letting go of ego: and walking completely in love. In other words, you generate the peacemakers who generate peacemakers.

When the process is finished, eventually we will have a whole world of people who are peacemakers. Those who are really ready to awaken, to live by the Ten Commandments/Attitudes, who are willing to come to God in meditation and who are willing to develop the attitudes required by the "The Beatitudes," will develop peacemakers. So, why are "peacemakers" called the children of God?

"Because God loves peace."

Are you God's son? Is Christ God's son…is everyone God's son?

"Of course."

When do you realize that?

"You realize when you "know." When you center yourself and have meditated sufficiently—then it dawns on you from all the work and the study you have done, that there could be no other person or entity that you could be since God is *all* things—period."

The minute you know that and you put your entire trust in God—have you not found great peace? Who is going to inherit the earth?

"The meek."

Of course: now can you see how being a peacemaker fits in with being meek? Those who are the peacemakers are the ones who, as children of God, will continue with the planet when the time comes. Only the children of God, for there will be no room for anyone else once the transition is made, except those who are capable and willing to learn to live with God in peace. It is as simple as that. Everything that you have studied in the "Course of Miracles" is about the Beatitudes. Would you care to add anything to that?

"Only the satisfaction that comes to me (and I assume to other people) that when you realize these things, put them into focus and understand them, then you see that it could be nothing else."

Nothing else—for all of this is God! There is *no* Satan and there is *no* Heaven or Hell, it is only God. What you see as Satan is merely your own ego. It is not another being, it is your *own* beingness and, to the extent that you are centered, you are walking in your Godhood. If you get off center, then you become what you call evil—*you* have the choice. Your awful punishment for what you call evil is that sense of being separated from God—that feeling of knowing that things are not quite right.

But, when you know that you have done no harm to anyone; that you have only done well and you know that you love everyone; that you know you are stepping out of judgment and accepting people exactly the way that they are—and you are spending the majority of your time with the Father—than there is peace. Instead of trying to control the situations you run into, you merely let them happen.

Mankind spends so much time trying to control the situation and make it right according to his perception, that he wastes a great deal of energy and causes a great deal of turmoil and angst. If you would simply step back and let go, it would happen and no matter what the situation, live in a meditative state—than there *will* be peace.

What else causes war but an ego that has gone out of control? What could possibly bring peace to warring nations other than a transformation of mind, a transformation of thinking? People need to stop obsessing about judgment and of what has happened in the past, and what other people have done to them.

Instead, they need to center on God and to center on trying to live their own life as peacefully as possible—and with others as peacefully as possible.

The verse is true: Blessed are the Peacemakers, for they shall be called the children of God. I say, "Blessed are the children of God, for they shall be called Peacemakers."

Amen,

Blessed are those who hunger and thirst for righteousness for they shall be satisfied.

(Righteous: acting or being in accordance with what is just; honorable; free from guilt; virtuous; noble; moral; ethical.)

I am watching you struggle with all of this, but it is so simple. Blessed are those who strive for righteousness has two meanings. The first meaning that people attribute to it is: "Blessed are those who search to be ethical." Being ethical and moral is nice and if you look and try to live that way, you become that way. That is the path of the head definition of this. The other interpretation is: "You have got to want to."

Let us look at what you studied in the Course of Miracles, for you were studying the hardest lesson that anyone can learn: the lesson of guiltlessness. It is something that you must obtain before you can forgive yourself or forgive others. Is not this what the course says: that those who hunger and thirst to achieve that state, will become non-judgmental of others?

The churches love guilt and want complete control; but I have told you already that there is no such thing as guilt. Are there people who behave in such a way that they are destructive and disrupt everything? Of course there are. That is what the upcoming awakening is about and what the atonement is about.

I said that there will come a time for separating the wheat from the chaff and that will be done. In the perfect world—a place you would call Heaven—there is no strife; there is abundance where each person has what he or she wants and all live in peace. You cannot have that when you have a world that has individuals who are not able to awaken since they are not so genetically engineered. Those who come into my kingdom will be those who are capable of awakening; that instead of running away from guilt will run *towards* God, *towards* the Father.

Blessed are those who understand the Ten Commandments and those who hunger and thirst to be obedient to these guidelines that were set forth for an ancient people, an ignorant people. Guidelines, which at that time had a very different meaning than they have now—and were so, intended to be.

Your next study should be of the Ten Commandments/Attitudes as you go back over the ones that I have given you. You must set those Commandments, those ways of thinking, deeply into your mind. You must hunger and thirst day and night to act in accordance with the Ten Commandments. To help others to understand them and to do likewise; for that is part of the awakening and that is from where perfect peace comes. Once again:

"Blessed are those who hunger and thirst for righteousness for they shall be satisfied."

You see there is some work involved here. You must have that attitude of hungering and thirsting after God and of knowing who your God is. It is important to simplify your life as much as possible, for if you are going to take on something new, what are you going to give up since you only have a certain amount of time? Unless the majority of your time is spent in meditation, spent with the Father in learning who you are and learning what is expected of one who is awakened—you are not doing the right thing.

Gradually over time, it calls for giving up many of the things that you do. Do you understand your lesson? In other words, again: "you have got to want to." It has to be your top priority for when you *want* to, everything will open for you. Not only will your search be satisfied, but all the good things that come with that search will be satisfied as well.

Amen.

Blessed are the merciful for they shall obtain mercy.

(Merciful: having or showing mercy; compassion shown to an offender)

On the surface, it seems self-evident does it not? If you are kind to people and you recognize them: they look upon you with favor and they are kind in return. On the surface that is what it is about, but let me give you another twist on it.

When you are awakened, do you not look upon other people and see that in fact they are God, so how could you be anything but merciful? They have done nothing wrong and they may even need your help; they may have gotten themselves into a predicament that is beyond their ability to rectify, so you show mercy and kindness.

When you continue to love someone, even though their behavior does not seem to warrant it, you have no idea the effect you are having on them. People who have low self-esteem will test you, test you and test you since they cannot possibly believe that you love them, yet your continued love despite anything they do—and that does not mean that you enable them, that you encourage them to continue with their bad behavior—it means that you withdraw your judgment.

When you do that, you are putting yourself at peace and you are showing mercy to yourself are you not? Before the enlightenment occurs, when anyone does something to you, you are taught to immediately retaliate and if you are unable to retaliate, it just simmers inside until it destroys you does it not? It just builds and builds until you just do something; in fact, you can think of nothing else.

Those that are merciful to themselves simply do not play that game. The first thing then, when somebody has offended you, is to say: "just let it go, just step away from it." The *world* tells you that if you do that that they are just going to do it more. However, I tell you to turn the other cheek. If a man wants your shirt, give him your robe as well, because *you* are not playing by the same rules.

The basic difference between what I am telling you and what you normally get from Christianity is that you are to be *completely* non-judgmental. Stop thinking: "well, they will get theirs in the end"…or any of that nonsense. The judgment day is not about punishment, it is about taking out those members of the species who are genetically capable of amping up—and those of your species who simply are not: there is no punishment involved. The spirit that inhabits that latter body simply goes back into the Godhead. It certainly does not go to hell for what spirit would want to come into a body then be sent to hell (even if there were such a place?) That does not make any sense.

No! The judgment day is *not* about separating "good from evil," it is about picking out those characteristics of the species that can go on and serve as bodies for spirits that want to live in peace.

Have mercy—since you are really having mercy on yourself. That statement: "Do not judge lest you be judged," is really getting down to: "…if you cannot let go of judgment, then you are not suitable for the coming kingdom." It has nothing to do with your spirit, it has to do with: can that *body*, the way that that *mind* works, the way that it is set up—is it able to release judgment. Do not judge, because you want to bring your present body up to as high an energy level as you can—you are just testing this vehicle, this prototype. Do you understand what I am saying?

"Yes, although it seems a little incongruent, since we are all human, but are you not talking of the *mental* makeup?"

Yes, you are simply test-driving this vehicle, and can this vehicle be ampted up to the point where it can live in peace with other vehicles: where it can give up judgment?

"Now, for clarification, are you talking physical vehicle or overall vehicle?"

Overall vehicle, although it does not mean that you are going to come back looking as you look now. It pertains to whether it has to develop in the brain—in the mind—so that we can use that prototype with the new ones. You see the new children being born now, do you not? Well, they are the result of testing different vehicles, picking the best out of what we have done so far and working on developing a new model, so to speak. You should not worry about going back in the same body, because that body will disintegrate; you will simply be put into the new model that has all the improvements.

Do not judge lest you be judged. The more that you can be pure love, no matter what anybody does to you, the more at peace—the more attuned you will be and the more innocent you become in the sense of being a pure spirit. On the other side of this is the person who is receiving your actions.

Say you had been thrown into a concentration camp; look at the awful things that could happen there. If you do not hate the people who are doing them, you do not know the effect you will have on them. People who have lived in hate and then suddenly come into love simply do not know what to make of it. They are going to really test it and then they are probably going to be nastier for a while. It is not up to you to judge them; it is up to you to love them. That is the test of your body; the test of your makeup—and of *you*. Despite anything, give up judgment and just love. The test of their makeup is: "what do they do with that instead of hate?"

Does that mean that you do not correct your children? Of course not, you must teach your children right from wrong, yet you do it by the way that you love and the way that you take care of them. There is a difference between children and adults since children need guardrails. Therefore, unless you rebuke the adult; unless you have set down rules that the adult knows about and has these guidelines to follow, then there is no point to it.

If someone came to live in your house and you gave them guidelines about how things are in your house and you rebuke them because they broke the guideline—that is not the same thing as what we are talking about here. We are talking about people who infringe on your rights; that have not been invited in. We are also talking, in another dimension, about people who have fallen on hard times and who need mercy, people that have not necessarily done anything to you.

The Good Samaritan took care of the person he found on the side of the road and that had nothing to do with another person hurting him. It had to do with love and of not making judgment about that injured person: such as about what race or what religious belief he had—not taking any of that into consideration. Instead, just showing pure love and giving the person the help needed. Showing mercy can also mean sharing what you have with people who are in need: your goods, your love, your abilities and your skills.

These attitudes are not difficult to understand, they are just difficult to implement for those who still stand in judgment. As you can see, the keys to the kingdom, the keys to happiness and to doing the best job you can of test driving the model that you are in—is to step completely out of judgment.

Amen.

Blessed are the pure in heart for they shall see God.

(Pure: free from anything that adulterates or taints; faultless; virtuous; pure in thought; blameless)

When you are centered you know that you are God. People keep talking about bringing information into consciousness and it is actually very simple. If you wrote a book on this, nobody would understand it. It is not until you know in your *heart,* not just your in *head,* that you are God, since it is not: "you *and* God…it is *God*—period, for you *are* God, not a *piece* of God." You are the manifestation of God!

It is like an Octopus: you are the tentacle, not the Octopus—except this is a little stronger for you also have the mind of God. The fact that you do not believe you can manifest (even though you have had plenty of examples) is because you have not allowed the clarity to come in. It is absolute knowingness, of living in the consciousness—not in the form. Now, you ask if you are a piece of God. As long as you are stuck in thinking that you are this body, then you *are* a piece of God in your mind—but in reality when you go to your center, you go directly to God.

"When we get out of our mind, we are a piece of God—period."

Yes, in fact, you *are* God—period. You are me and I am no greater than you. On Earth, I was considered a great teacher, but that is because Earth has this hierarchy, but God has no hierarchy. Moses was not better than you; Moses was God just as you are God. There is nothing that anyone can do or achieve on your earth plane that is any greater than what you are doing—and you will realize that once you *know* that you are God.

"The problem that we have is that we are taught that God is so big and so powerful and that we are so lowly and insignificant—old attitudes die hard."

Get over it. (Laughter) When you meditate and you try to go up, out or some place else, you cannot reach God because you are putting God as some place separate from you. Stay centered, be at peace and *know* that you *are* God. When you can hold that center of peace, you will be taught; you will awaken and you will remember. Do not try to force yourself to go some place else. Do not try so hard: when you reach the point you have, you no longer have to strive—just be; that is all that you have to do. The truth of the matter is you do not have to do anything.

Enjoy each day and when the time comes that you are needed to take action, you will be well prepared.

"I suppose that I have. Sometimes in my meditations, things come up that I have not thought of in years and years—then it goes away. I appreciate that."

Thank yourself.

"Okay, thank you God."

Amen.

> ***Blessed are those who are persecuted for righteousness sake***
> ***for theirs is the kingdom of heaven.***
>
> *(Persecute: to pursue in such a way as to injure, afflict or distress)*

What do you make of this?

"I think it is a test of your will, of your knowingness. If you are persecuted for righteousness sake, it means that you know within yourself who you are and that you will stand up for whom you are; that you do not have to lie down and disavow anything. By standing up, the outcome could be a little more difficult than you anticipated, but—you still have your integrity and if you have your integrity (which is your righteousness) than I think you are in pretty good shape."

Can you think of a good example of something that happened to you recently? Look at when the Doctor told you that you had cancer; was that not what this is talking about?

"Yes, because it had to do with my faith. I was told to let it go; however, I could have the operation if I wanted to but I could also forgo it if I wanted too—that if I decided that I did not have the cancer, that I wouldn't. There was no argument over that: I let it go."

Now, your wife can look at what happened with her computer: she really wanted a new computer (and had a good reason for wanting it) but she told herself that you could not do it—you did not have the money and were too far in debt; but now you are getting your new computer because in your heart, that is what you wanted. You really have to have faith that everything will be provided.

Back in the days of the early Christians, it came across with a different meaning. You realize at that time the Christians were persecuted because they held a completely different belief—and what I was saying to them then was that they needed to hold steady; to realize that they were right. In the modern day, you are not persecuted for being what they call a "new ager," (although that term is not correct either) yet your faith is put to the test anytime anything goes wrong. Who is your God? Your computer fails, and there is the source of your entire livelihood, so: Who Is Your God?

"The Computer!"

That is right. Anytime you are told anything—such as when you had cancer—who is your God? You do not have that many things that go wrong so you are seldom challenged: do you see that? If you can keep your faith and you act with dignity in the face of anything that happens, (because nothing can affect you) you know that nothing means anything anyway.

Other people will look upon you the same way that they did upon the early Christians who had enough faith to be eaten by the lions for their beliefs. Well, the lions are not eating you, but you are standing up to the same hardships as everybody else. When the things happen to you that happen to other people and you face them with equanimity, other people will look to you and ask: "How do you do that?" In the saying of "how do you do that" comes their belief.

Blessed are those who are persecuted for righteousness sake
for theirs is the kingdom of heaven.

Can you see where you already are in the kingdom of heaven? What I mean is that you cannot be persecuted if you do not already have a strong faith. What they are *actually* saying is: Blessed are those who have awakened and who in the face of difficulty can hold on to their faith and go through those difficulties without losing faith in themselves and in God. That test is what tells you that you have already accessed the kingdom of heaven. It is a truth for you.

Blessed are those who inhabit the kingdom of heaven for they will endure persecution for righteousness sake. This does not mean that you run out and become a martyr. Unfortunately that is the meaning that the martyrs gave to it and it gives the truth to the saying that that is why they were martyrs. We are not asking you to go out, flaunt yourself and try to be a martyr. All we ask of you is that you hold onto your belief—no matter what.

Amen.

THE SERMON ON THE MOUNT

As Explained by Jesus Christ

The Sermon on the Mount

As Explained by Jesus Christ

"Blessed are the poor in spirit, for theirs is the kingdom of heaven."

The Kingdom of God, which you have been so long expecting, is not an empire of war and conquest, nor is it of the Jews to be exercised over foreign nations. It belongs to the humble, the quiet and the contented. It does not come as a cure for outward misfortunes, for political evils, or for the relief of proud hearts rankling under oppression, but it speaks of comfort to those who are bowed down under the sorrows of life. But, I say unto you:

"Blessed are they who mourn, for they shall be comforted."

You expect the Messiah to vindicate the weak against the strong, to repel injury, to revenge insult—that he will set up His Empire with the sword and defend it by the sword. But I say unto you:

"Blessed are the Meek, for they shall inherit the earth."

The gentle are those who are to flourish in the days of the Messiah. They shall delight themselves in the abundance of peace. You come to me expecting a sign from heaven, to be fed with manna from the skies as your fathers were in the desert. I can promise you nothing of the kind. The blessings of my kingdom belong to those only who hunger and thirst after righteousness, for they shall be filled. You expect under the Messiah a reign of bitterness and vengeance; that he will rule with a rod of iron and dash his enemies into pieces of a potter's vessel. But I come to pronounce blessings on those that are merciful; I assure them that they shall find mercy from their eternal Judge. You who observe the laws of Moses submit to innumerable ceremonial ablutions and therefore imagine yourselves pure and prepared for the kingdom of God. I assure you that no such purification will be of any avail in that kingdom. But I say unto you:

"Blessed are the pure in heart, for they shall see God."

The remedies, which you propose for mortal ills are essentially defective. You imagine that they can be cured by violence and resentment, that evil may be remedied by evil instead of being overcome with good. But I say unto you:

"Blessed are the peace-makers, for they shall be called the children of God."

They shall share the blessings of the new dispensation, not those who are vindictive and resentful. But I say unto you:

"Blessed are those who are persecuted for righteousness' sake."

Amen

THE BOOK OF REVELATIONS

DECIPHERED

Preface by Jesus

Until now, the Book of Revelation stood out as the most difficult and misunderstood segment of the Bible; however, in the light of my real mission and teachings, the Book of Revelation becomes a book of universal hope easily understood by all who wish to search its pages. Written around 96 AD and ascribed to John, the Elder (not the apostle John), the book has mistakenly been viewed as prophecy. Although it incorporates prophecy, Revelation is an *allegory*, a *parable* built in four dimensions: 1) Prophecy, 2) Parody, 3) Process, and 4) Progression. Its purpose is to radically change the world's view of Jesus Christ and why I came, as well as the understanding of ourselves and why we exist. Let me explain.

1. Revelation is a **_prophecy_** because it does indeed tell the story of an *evolution* and eventual *revolution* in spiritual thought. The allegory was written in the ancient apostolic style, popular at the time. Some of it was very obvious, such as the Seven Hills of Rome. For those caught up in the guilt-cult of the churches and for latter-day cryptologists, solving the puzzle becomes an end in itself as they connect the clues to various historical events. Like a Chinese box, however, the mind opens one box only to find another inside. On the outside, Revelation is a story about historical events and the battle between good and evil. Inside it is a story about something quite different—awakening to the truth. Revelation can not be solved using the paradigm of good vs evil, sin, guilt and sacrifice. Read my words in the Bible and in the Gospel of Thomas, then you will understand what I *truly* said—you will *then* hold the key.

2. Taken as a **prophecy,** Revelation becomes a story: 1) Things past, 2) Things present, and 3) Things to come—reminiscent of Dickens' "A Christmas Carol" in structure. John starts out by describing how and where he received the message; then he goes on to talk about ways in which the church—beginning in his time—has corrupted my message in various ways. He then builds on the earlier prophecies of Daniel to describe the coming end of time with its "Great Tribulation" and my coming to rule forever and ever.

3. Revelation is a **_parody_** because it uses exaggerated metaphors to poke fun at 1) the churches which, for their own purposes, deliberately delude the masses with misinformation, using guilt to enforce mind control, and 2) at the political structures that ride on the back of the churches to enforce physical control.

4. Revelation is a **_process_** because understanding takes time. He who understands revelations understands the truth about contemporary theology: that Man is *not* born in sin and I did *not* die for your sins, for "Sin" does not exist. You are God. I am God. The trees and the earth are God. Everything that is, is a manifestation of Divine co-creation. You created Satan (evil) not I. You created it from your own fear and with your own ideas of separation from one another. To defeat "Satan" defeat your own ego, your own need to be *special*, separate from your brother and in control.

   Once you understand the true meaning of the Ten Commandments of Moses you will understand the process of living in complete peace and trust. The churches (the beast of the sea) will no longer have dominion over your mind, nor the politicians (the beast of the land) over your body.

5. Revelation is a **_progression_** because it ignites a one-hundred-and-eighty-degree turn in mass consciousness. Good and evil, crime and punishment disappear. Humanity rises to its rightful place as co-habitants of the earth and as wise and gentle guardians of Earths resources. Churches and organizations of control take their place among the dinosaurs as our God-nature becomes the teachers and mentors of our young; helping them to accept the authority and responsibility in their place as sowers of love. In their place collaboration, not competition, becomes the key to fulfilling your divine destiny.

I, Jesus, want you to realize that when I gave this message to John, I wanted the revelations to remain hidden from the masses in order to allow each individual time to exert free will in terms of interpreting and following my teachings. Those who did so were set free during their lifetimes. Those who did not bore witness—and even to this day—continue to bear witness to the predictions in Revelation. Even the disciples did not have the knowledge that you are about to receive because it was all encrypted.

Don't be too concerned with the seven "this's" and the seven "that's," for that cryptology was popular at the time and had enough mysticism to keep the prophecy alive. In order to keep the message hidden it had to be very obscure; the same as my parables have been and as the prophecies of Daniel before me. (Notice for instance the number and layers making up the walls of the New Jerusalem as compared to the layers in the forgotten dream of Nebuchadnezzar.)

One day, this person, who called himself John, was meditating and he received the calling that we were going to write the Book of Revelations, just as the authors of this book did. Being a bit dramatic, not only does he hear drama, he also expressed it. Part of it was his own personality and part of it was the need to impress the importance of this information on the churches he was sending it to, since the churches were young then and already headed off in a wrong direction.

We needed to have some way of preserving my words so that when the time came you would be able to look back in time and see that what I told you was true. I am going to give it to you plainly and I am going to tell you that this is not about gloom and doom. Your world is well passed the end of "what is," and has almost completed "what will be," therefore it is time that everyone understands what they need to do—what their part is.

John himself did not understand the truth; he believed that I had literally died for *his sins and the sins of mankind.* He didn't recognize that my *real* mission was the overcoming of ego, or that my death was the ultimate triumph over my own ego.

I was and am God—just as you are. You have grown in spiritual understanding and *you* are at the spot I was just prior to my ministry. Your ability to understand has been greatly heightened over John's and I will bring that out many times, for in this way Revelation becomes the road to your spiritual awakening.

While I am Christ—the central figure in the book—all of the events move toward one consummation: the spiritual revolution of the mass consciousness as one by one each of *you* acknowledges *your own* Godhood and mankind collaborates to bring forth a new era where all live according to the Ten Commandments of Moses.

The Revelation of John, The Elder AD 96

The World English Bible
http://ebible.org (HTML)

Chapter 1
Part 1, verses 1–20

This is the Revelation of Jesus Christ, which God gave him to show to his servants the things which must happen soon, which he sent and made known by his angel to his servant, John, 2who testified to God's word and of the testimony of Jesus Christ about everything that he saw.

3Blessed is he who reads and those who hear the words of the prophecy and keep the things that are written in it, for the time is at hand.

4John, to the seven assemblies that are in Asia: Grace to you and peace, from God, who is and who was and who is to come; and from the seven Spirits who are before his throne; 5and from Jesus Christ, the faithful witness, the firstborn of the dead and the ruler of the kings of the earth. To him who loves us, and washed us from our sins by his blood; 6and he made us to be a Kingdom, priests to his God and Father; to him be the glory and the dominion forever and ever. Amen.*

7Behold, he is coming with the clouds and every eye will see him, including those who pierced him. All the tribes of the earth will mourn over him. Even so, Amen.

8 "I am the Alpha and the Omega," says the Lord God, "who is and who was and who is to come, the Almighty."*

*9John, your brother and partner with you in oppression, Kingdom and perseverance in Christ Jesus, was on the isle that is called Patmos because of God's Word and the testimony of Jesus Christ. 10I was in the Spirit on the Lord's day and I heard behind me a loud voice, like a trumpet 11saying, "*What you see,* *write in a book and send to the seven assemblies: to Ephesus, Smyrna, Pergamum, Thyatira, Sardis, Philadelphia and to Laodicea."*

[12]I turned to see the voice that spoke with me. Having turned, I saw seven golden lampstands [13]and among the lampstands was one like a son of man, clothed with a robe reaching down to his feet and with a golden sash around his chest. [14]His head and his hair were white as white wool, like snow. His eyes were like a flame of fire. [15]His feet were like burnished brass, as if it had been refined in a furnace. His voice was like the voice of many waters. [16]He had seven stars in his right hand. Out of his mouth proceeded a sharp two-edged sword. His face was like the sun shining at its brightest. [17]When I saw him, I fell at his feet like a dead man.

He laid his right hand on me, saying: "Don't be afraid. I am the first and the last [18]and the Living one. I was dead, and behold, I am alive forevermore. Amen. I have the keys of Death and of Hades. [19]Write therefore the things which you have seen and the things which are and the things which will happen hereafter; [20]the mystery of the seven stars which you saw in my right hand and the seven golden lampstands. The seven stars are the angels of the seven assemblies; the seven lampstands are seven assemblies.

Prophecy

As stated in the preface, John writes Revelation in the prophetic style of 1) Things that were, 2) Things that are, and 3) Things that will be. These first twenty verses introduce the topic, names the recipients of the message, and shares how John received the message and from whom.

John addressed his message to the seven major branches of the Christian church in Asia: Ephesus, Smyrna, Pergamos, Thyatira, Sardis, Philadelphia and Laodicea. Each church represents one of seven stages of the corruption of my word from the time of my death in 33 AD until the end of time. Each letter begins with a salutation followed by praise and a warning. Notice that I am portrayed as holding seven stars (Divine inspiration for church mentorship) and seven candles (Divine authority for earthly mentorship.)

This first chapter predicts the slow corruption of the Christian church and its eventual downfall as the church turns away from its original inspiration (me) and eventually loses all authority for providing earthly mentorship for those attempting to find the Light of God. As you will see, each church (candle) holds a seed of potential downfall and I will discuss each separately as they are revealed by John.

Pay attention to this:

1. John addresses seven different weaknesses, one for each church of his time, and

2.   These seven different weaknesses can also be viewed as sequential weaknesses that occur in the history of the Catholic Church and subsequent Christian Churches over a long period of time.

As I said above, the Book of Revelations is about how these weaknesses bring about the long range downfall of the Christian Church and the restoration of the true authority of Godhood of the universe in time to come.

Parody

Note the dramatic description of me for this was done in the rhetoric of the day. The vision of me with a golden girdle, white hair, eyes of fire, with a mouth that spat a two-edged sword and with feet of brass, all conveyed to the people of the time my kingship, wisdom, knowledge, judgment and enduring power.

Notice that he describes me as separating the spiritual wisdom from the earthly authority of the churches. In one hand I held the seven stars (ongoing divine guidance.) In the other hand I held the seven candles (earthly authority to teach.)

The consequence to mankind due to the deliberate deviation from divine guidance by the churches and politicians stands front and center in Revelations. It was one thing for mankind to live in bondage of fear/guilt prior to my revealing the Truth, but it is quite another for the Church *to deliberately twist my words* in order to lead mankind back into bondage for its own gain. Much of the Book of Revelation parodies the behavior of the so-called Christian Church.

As I said before, John loved drama. I shared with him the facts and he chose to use horrific persuasion (based on Egyptian/Babylonian mythology) to frighten people into submission. Unfortunately his prophecy played into the hands of the churches—which to this day use fear to control the masses.

In this dialogue, I intend to set the record straight so that anyone who has eyes *will* see, and those who have ears, *will* hear the Truth: "The Father is not a God of Hell and Brimstone." Hell was actually a garbage dump outside of Jerusalem where trash burned night and day. John took Egyptian mythology and used it to turn Hell into a place, (in the symbolism of Hell) of eternal punishment. The churches found it a persuasive mind control device to usurp and maintain power.

Let me restate: I never intended to establish a church or *any* power structure to frighten *anyone* into submission. I came to tell the truth about mankind's true identity and mission on earth. My intent two thousand years ago was to establish an existential school where each person could grow in wisdom and love.

The Book of Revelation is not about how I, the Christ, intend to punish mankind; rather it is a story about the chaos mankind has brought upon itself. Liberation from the tyranny and mind control of the churches and governments is not something in the future; it is available to you now as you understand the true message hidden in Revelation.

Process

On one level, Revelation addresses the process by which the Christian Church removed itself from God's light (understanding and fulfillment) prior to "The Grand Ascension." (I define "The Grand Ascension" as a future time when a general awakening will occur in mass consciousness and many souls will assume new bodies and arise and join me in the "New Jerusalem"—which I prefer to call "Eden."

On another level, Revelation addresses the struggle of each individual man and the process used by the Remnant (those who understood and adhered to my words) to overcome the obstacles—set by the churches and government—in order to participate in life more abundantly while here on earth and to join in the dance of eternal life both here and in the future.

Progression

The preface introduces the concept of the seven steps in the progression of the Christian church AWAY FROM my teachings and leading up to the ultimate church/state world government, along with the collapse of civilization as you know it. Each of the churches in Revelation represents a time period from the time of my death until the end of time.

My teachings come from a combined understanding of the Kabbalah, the Books of Zohar (the teachings of the Ten Serifot that lay behind the Ten Commandments) and the teachings of the religious sects of the East, which date back to the Kabbalah. I spoke a language, Aramaic, that automatically arose from the idea of unity; ripeness/un-ripeness in terms of understanding, and of abundant and everlasting life.

Progressively, the seven churches followed seven sequential roads that: 1) Took the Christian school out of the hands of the Jews and placed it in the hands of the Gentiles who came from a completely different cultural background and understanding. 2) Turned my school into a compulsory religion under the thumb of the State. 3) Mutated into a compulsory religion that ruled the State. 4) Broke up into multiple religious sects that maintained the gentile mythology. 5) Retrenched into multiple duchies without much forward movement. 6) Experienced a mini-rebirth based upon a doctrine of self-help, and 7) Re-entered politics in the march towards world government.

As Jesus, I came to you as a man born of the union between Mary and Joseph, i.e. a natural human being. I was the effect of their union, one created by the natural process established by God; under the control of God and my parents, and a recipient of their charity.

After much advance study I underwent the Essenes rite of passage where I separated from my parents' house. At that point I took over responsibility for being the cause of all the effects in my life. Time for me became the distance between my actions and their effects. I took the reins as co-creator with the Father, with the ability to create my own experiences and share them with the Father.

I made the deliberate decision to STOP what I was doing; to deliberately NOT REACT; and to THINK about what was going on, and to ACT in a positive manner. In other words, I went from being a child in the home of my parents to becoming a man responsible for finding his place as God.

In the Kabbalah, we come from God and we are literally a piece of God. God hides himself from us so that we have time to mature into our Godhood. In other words, God allows us to EARN our Godhood, the same as a child earns the right to be considered a man. In order for us to grow, God hides his light and it is up to us to find it until ultimately we understand what it means to share in the one universal soul known as God.

This is an individual journey and can not be relegated to church membership. Churches might act as institutions of learning, but nothing more; certainly NOT what the Christian church has grown into. "Saved by the blood of the lamb" wasn't even in my vocabulary. If anything the notion of being "saved" would be an oxymoron.

Revelation addresses each man's progression in coming to full spiritual awakening while still here on Earth, and yes, you are hearing me correctly. The ascension into Eden is an ongoing process, a progression in divine understanding. The Kingdom of Heaven exists all around you. You can live in "Heaven" right now, if you so choose, and with me in Eden later on.

Your personal mission in coming to earth is twofold: 1) To find out whom you really are (an intimate piece of God and co-creator of the Universe) and 2) To learn how to live simultaneously as God and Man in peace and collaboration with The All That Is.

In order to assist you in doing this I have given you: 1) My words in the Bible and the Gospel of Thomas to let you know who I am and who *we* are; 2) The Ten Commandments of Moses to guide your spirit; and 3) Seven energy centers, or "Chakras" of the body, to guide your physical experience.

Everyone is given an equal chance to come to full awakening during his lifetime(s.) Some will decide to answer the call—in one lifetime or through many— but those who do not answer the call will remain here (on what will be left of Earth) to try again.

Each man has agreed to come to earth to work towards developing a prototype for body/spirit that can function in Eden. You arrive here as a blank slate upon which society writes its imprint. It is the duty of *each* individual to question his existence and to fulfill his mission. At the personal level, the seven churches represent various stages in man's journey away from fear/ego towards love/Spirit.

The Book of Revelation is NOT about crime and punishment, rather it is about:

1. God in his role of **Cause, Creator, Controller and Giver,** creating you and the universe. Consequently, the book is also about you starting out as the **Effect, Created, Controlled, and Receiver.**

2. Since your purpose in coming to Earth is to experience God's creations from inside his creation, eventually you must reverse roles and grow into a spiritually mature man. That means taking *personal* responsibility as the **Cause, Creator, Controller, and Giver/Sharer** of your own experience.

Can you see how the metaphor of "Father" and "Son" arises? Do we not come into the world subservient to our natural parents and then learn how to grow into parents ourselves? This transformation from spiritual child to spiritual adult is what is meant by being "born again." Once you understand this concept of one universal soul separating into pieces and then the pieces finding each other, all my sayings become clear. In effect, you have broken the code. Unfortunately, the churches try to keep you spiritually immature and in darkness for in that way you remain under **their** control.

Chapter 2
Part 2:
Verses 1–7

The Church at Ephesus: Stage 1 in the Corruption of the Christian Church 33 AD–270AD[1]

"To the angel of the assembly in Ephesus write: "He who holds the seven stars in his right hand, he who walks among the seven golden lamp stands says these things: [2] *"I know your works, your toil and perseverance and that you can't tolerate evil men; have tested those who call themselves apostles and they are not, and found them false. You have perseverance and have* [3]*endured for my name's sake and have not grown weary.*

[4]*But I have this against you, that you left your first love.* [5]*Remember therefore from where you have fallen and repent and do the first works; or else I am coming to you swiftly and will move your lampstand out of its place unless you repent.* [6]*But this you have; that you hate the works of the Nicolaitanes which I also hate.*

[7]*He who has an ear let him hear what the Spirit says to the assemblies. To him who overcomes I will give to eat of the tree of life, which is in the Paradise of my God.*

<u>Prophecy</u>

Notice that I no longer hold the seven candlesticks (the seven stages of Christian Church development) instead I walk in their midst. My walking among the candlesticks symbolizes my standing in their midst and offering the possibility of coming back to me and my teachings.

The seven messages I am about to deliver concern the progressive corruption to take place during the seven stages of church development from the time of my death in 33 AD until the end of time.

Thanks to the zealous nature of the Apostle Paul, the new Jewish Mystery school became overrun by pagans who received little training or support from Paul. He was so busy building his empire and adding numbers that he failed to lay a sound foundation. Consequently the church he built was doomed to failure from the start in terms of following my teachings.

This letter foretells the beginning stages of corruption of my teachings. "You have lost your first love," I tell them, "Your train has jumped the tracks." You have gone from teaching man about who he is and how to go about accepting the reins for his own spiritual development—to Paul setting up a political/religious empire. Because of this, I will take away my guidance to the church and it's authority to teach in my name.

I warned that I would take away Ephesus' candlestick (power.) Did this not happen to the Catholic Church during the Reformation and is it not continuing to happen today? Despite the fact that the Catholic Church and its Protestant offspring kept my name before the public all these years, it did so at the cost of its own integrity. The so-called "Christian Church" began as Ephesus exchanged the Truth about who man is and how to become spiritually fulfilled for power, control, and greed.

Parody

⁵**Remember therefore from where you have fallen, repent and do the first works; or else I am coming to you swiftly and will move your lampstand of its place, unless you repent."**

The figure of speech about the lampstand presents a metaphor for removing my light from you and your authority over my people.

Process

I intended for man to love his brother and to work collaboratively in deep reverence of all that exists on the earth and in spirit. I expanded and elaborated upon the Kabbalah and expected the elders to act as mentors for all who desired to follow my teachings as the gateway to accepting individual responsibilities and privileges of their divine nature. Already, however, the bean-counters at Ephesus are acting to overthrow my authority and to change my school into a governing body which stands between man and God.

The shift from Jewish Mystery School to Pagan Church occurred much the same as water turns to salt water, then turns to salt. You start with water and add salt, and then at some point the water becomes more salt than water. The water evaporates and what's left but salt. That process began happening at the Church of Ephesus. The Apostle Paul, lawyer and obsessive compulsive leader that he was, set about to convert the whole world to the Jewish Mystic School of "The Christ."

Like any salesman he was good at seeing the big picture and making lots of sales. Unfortunately he had no concept of how to build a good foundation or how to provide sound maintenance. He pulled more and more pagans into the school without sticking around to make sure they had a good foundation. He moved from place to place building members, and then shot back letters and laws, that he developed by the seat of his pants, to try to keep the Paulean Church empire in line. His efforts were destined to fail from the start. In his defense, he believed the world was about to end at any moment so it wasn't necessary to build a foundation. The Church at Ephesus dramatizes the work of Paul and predicts its sad end. Paul built a mighty empire, but he built it on tainted ground.

Each man is born into forgetfulness; then society gives him his identity. As the pagan religions infiltrated the Christian groups, gradually the nature of the institution changed, but the name remained the same. The water had become salt, but no one stopped calling it water or started calling it salt because the change occurred gradually and future generations believed the new mythology they were taught. The Gentiles gave the "Christian" Church its new identity.

How can you undo this process in your life? Step back and look around you and determine what the current beliefs of your time are and then break free from them. Dare to think for yourself! Although this advice may sound easy, believe me, it is not; for you face many hurdles in finding the Truth.

Many of you have been taught that to even THINK something different from what the church tells you results in a sin punishable by Hell. Therefore you must first overcome your own fear of even seeking the truth.

Once you begin to seek a different truth, what happens? I was crucified by my own people because I dared say that we are all Gods, so do you think it will be different for you? Disagreeing with your family/tribe can leave you alone or dead—and disagreeing with contemporary political power is equally dangerous to your health.

Once you know the Truth about your Godhood, you will no longer be able to act from fear and hatred. You will draw closer to your individual man, but farther away from current mass consciousness. What will that do to your government's edict to wage war? Then what?

I never said you should worship me, Jesus, I said: "Do as I do, live as I live, pray as I pray." I have sent you the Holy Ghost as a sort of Divine Internet from which you may seek knowledge and understanding. If you seek to follow in my footsteps then you must first develop the desire—and then ask for help. Don't go to some outside person or institution, go directly to the Father with your prayer; then set aside one hour a day for meditation. Clear your mind and allow the Holy Ghost to provide answers. You can heed the warning to the Church at Ephesus and renew your life.

Progression

The Letter to the Church at Ephesus represents the period 33 AD–270 AD. This period covers the reign of 26 Popes from the Apostle Peter to Felix I. The new Christians zealously preached my word to all of the then known world. Starting with a loose coalition of Christian groups who knew me and knew the culture from which I spoke, the school spread to groups of pagans who had no cultural preparation for my word and interpreted it according to their own understanding and myths about the purpose of life.

As the original Apostles die off, those who heard my actual words are replaced by a mixture of sincere seekers, legalists, pagans and greedy Christian want-to-be's with political agendas. In this letter to Ephesus you see the progression of my Jewish-based mystery school into an early gentile Church scattered throughout Asia.

Verses 8–11

Stage 2 in the Corruption of the Christian Church

8 "To the angel of the assembly in Smyrna write: "The first and the last, which was dead and has come to life, say these things: 9 "I know your works, oppression and your poverty (but you are rich) and the blasphemy of those who say they are Jews and they are not but are a synagogue of Satan.

10Don't be afraid of the things which you are about to suffer. Behold, the devil is about to throw some of you into prison, that you may be tested and you will have oppression for ten days. Be faithful to death and I will give you the crown of life. 11He who has an ear let him hear what the Spirit says to the assemblies. He who overcomes won't be harmed by the second death.

Prophecy

This letter prophecies the take over of my mystery school by the Roman Emperor Constantine as he codifies church law to fit his own agenda of world domination. My school becomes a state-run church based largely upon gentile mythology.

Parody

What is the second death referred to in Revelations? The first death is the death of the ego as you go from apprentice God to Man/God and take full control of your creation guided by the Ten Commandments. The second is the death of the body. He who overcomes the teachings of society, and understands my teachings, will realize that all that happens when the body disintegrates is like in your present day when you exchange cars—the old one gives out and you get a new vehicle.

Process

You were created with great power, energy and glory with the commandment to grow from apprentice God (spiritual child) to Man/God (fully evolved spirit). However taking responsibility for the results of your actions, recognizing yourself as a creator with unlimited powers, evolving from reactive to proactive and learning to give and take, represents a maturity process.

The early Christians, who wanted a church instead of a mystery school, resembled the early Jews who asked God for a King. They were like children who wanted to forever reside in the household of their parents—protected, controlled, reactive—and the recipients of handouts. This childlike desire to be led played right into the hands of Constantine who wanted to solidify his rule over the Roman Empire.

The Constantine Church deceived many who simply replaced me with their idol of the day. Constantine called the Council of Nicea and essentially told the bishops: "Hey look, boys, you codify a new religion that meets my needs and I put a stop to the persecution of the Christians. But I only have just so much patience. The last thing in the world I want is a group of people experiencing and creating their own belief systems. Forget arguing among yourselves, instead come to a general agreement and get it over with; otherwise I take another route and Christians will get persecuted worse than before."

Naturally the bishops did as they were told and birthed the "Holy Roman Catholic Church" under the rule of Constantine. Meanwhile, in parts of Turkey not conquered by Rome, the Aramaic speaking Jews continued to follow my words and grew as a Remnant…right up until World War II. At that point the West divided up the Middle East to meet Western interests without allowing the people to have a say in the matter. Many Aramaic speaking people were annihilated at that point.

The process of following my word stopped dead in its tracks after the Council of Nicea and began moving 180 degrees back into paganism and state government, thus setting the stage for the future World Government and the end times. Instead of empowering my people, the growing Catholic Church snatched power for itself. It then used my name, accompanied by threats of damnation, to institute a semi-pagan superstitious organization that had nothing to do with the *real* me.

The Father said: "I am the Lord thy God, thou shalt not have strange Gods before Me." Once the Catholic Church created idols and taught men to worship the Father as a schizophrenic dictator, the church leadership became no better then tinkling bells—and their spiritual mentorship evaporated.

The very church that I praised in my letter to Ephesus for rejecting false apostles became the church that eventually spawned them. To this day the Catholic Church and its seed continue to make awakening next to impossible.

So what does the letter to Smyrna mean to *you* individually? Do you remember in the Old Testament when the Jews asked for a King and I told them to beware of what they asked for? You have the same exact situation now. My words, my journey, are not that of a King and his followers. My words tell about your shared Godhood and about the journey where you take responsibility for *yourself.*

You can not leave your spiritual consciousness at home, accept a tyrant to rule over your spiritual awakening, and still follow me.

For centuries the Constantine Church and its offshoots have ruled over much of the earth, *but that time is coming to a close.* What I said to Smyrna was: "beware of wolves in sheep's clothing waiting to devour your soul," and that message has not changed in two thousand years!

Wake up, mankind! Read my words for yourself. You ARE a piece of the ruling God and you ARE the co-creator of all that is. I am in your brother as he is in me and I am in you. No man who wages war against his brother is of me. You, not me, are the savior of mankind. However, those who understand, love, teach the truth and collaborate to create a place of peace—are of me.

Progression

The message to Smyrna represents the period from 270 AD to 530 AD. This period covers the reign of 28 Popes from Eutychian to Felix III. It also includes the rule of the Roman emperor, Constantine and his declaration of Christianity as the Church of the Roman Empire in the year 323 AD.

The church at Smyrna represents the second step in the progression of the corruption of my word. The warning to the Church at Smyrna is this: "Wherever a power structure exists, there also exists a despot to turn it to his own use."

First the groups teaching my word became infiltrated by gentiles, and then the gentiles took over the Christian movement and codified regulations that concretized the church as a political tool.

As mentioned above, the early church became infiltrated by pagan Roman beliefs as the original Jewish Apostles died out and were replaced by opportunists. The most influential opportunist of all, the Emperor Constantine, saw the political advantages of adopting Christianity and in 323 AD declared Christianity the true faith of the Roman Empire.

The original church, started by me, was taken over by gentiles who knew little of the historic foundations of my teachings—and cared less. Constantine codified the teachings of the church that exist to this day. Gospels, such as the Gospel of Thomas, were re-written or eliminated. Only those writings which supported Constantine's megalomania remained. Fortunately, Constantine did not understand most of what I said, so you can still hear some of my original words today. Unfortunately most of you read them through the filter of one of the Christian churches.

The Gnostics literally disappeared into history as everyone not agreeing with Constantine's view of Christianity suffered martyrdom at the hands of the new gentile "church." When I speak in the Book of Revelations of those who purport themselves to be Jews, but are not, I refer to Constantine and the Church he founded. Let us say that the Catholic Church and most of the Christian churches are offshoots of the pagan Church of Constantine and have nothing *what-so-ever* to do with me or my work.

When I speak of the martyrs who gave their lives for me in this period of church history, I do not speak of the early Christian martyrs, but those who had been martyred by the Church of Constantine; and I speak of the underground movement during and after the time of Constantine that held true to my teachings.

Rather then having my followers identifying themselves as Christians, I would have preferred that they would have just known and professed their own Godhood for they didn't need a name and they didn't need to belong to a church.

To some extent it was their own political maneuvering that got them into trouble; for they got caught up into their own ego. They were really caught up in: "we are this group of people who are special and better than all the rest of you." They professed love…but they mis-understood the meaning of the word. Were some of the Constantine Church members' good people? Of course, many were, but their ego really was what caused them to ultimately deny me.

What about the "Christian" underground mentioned in this segment of Revelation? Did I want them to start a breakaway church? *ABSOLUTLEY NOT!* I never wanted them to go like victims to the slaughter waiting for me to come and rescue them; rather I wanted them to pass on their knowledge behind the scenes until today, when the time has now come for everyone to know the truth about the inheritance of mankind.

Versus 12-17

Stage 3 in the Corruption of the Christian Church

12 "To the angel of the assembly in Pergamos write: "He who has the sharp two-edged sword says these things: 13 "I know your works and where you dwell, where Satan's throne is. You hold firmly to my name and didn't deny my faith in the days of Antipas my witness, my faithful one, who was killed among you, where Satan dwells.

14But I have a few things against you, because you have there some who hold the teaching of Balaam, who taught Balak to throw a stumbling block before the children of Israel, to eat things sacrificed to idols and to commit sexual immorality. 15So you also have some who hold to the teaching of the Nicolaitanes likewise.

16Repent therefore, or else I am coming to you quickly and I will make war against them with the sword of my mouth 17He who has an ear, let him hear what the Spirit says to the assemblies. To him who overcomes, to him I will

give of the hidden manna; I will give him a white stone and on the stone a new name written, which no one knows but he who receives it.

Prophecy

This letter tells the people of Pergamos that they dwell "where Satan's throne is" i.e. under the jurisdiction of Rome. It predicts the growing power of the church and its turning the tables on Rome as the church goes from a religious tool under the thumb of Rome to ruling Rome…and the rest of the then known world. It also predicts giving the keys of the kingdom to the faithful and the ultimate triumph of those who hold true to my word.

Parody

The two-edged sword coming from my mouth represents the truth about who God is and who you are in relationship to God. It also represents the truth about the so-called Christian Church. Satan's throne refers to the "Holy Roman Catholic Church" and its offspring. Manna refers to the key to understanding my sayings.

Here is the key:

1. God created you from his own universal soul.

2. No separation exists between you and God, God and the Universe, you and the universe. *"I and the Father are one"* (John 10, 30) *"On that day ye shall know that I am in my Father, and ye in me, and I in you."* (John 14, 2).

3. Don't believe anything anyone tells you, test my truths and find they stand on their own.

4. You are NOT involved in a battle of good versus evil. Rather you are undergoing the natural process of growing from spiritual child to spiritual adult. You come into this world a physical baby, created by your parents, living in their home, under their control, receiving from their beneficence. However the natural progression is for you to grow into a spiritually mature adult, capable of stopping and thinking things through before you act; responsible for the effects of your actions; in control of your actions; responsible for creating your own physical experience and willing to share what you have with others. When you hold the above key, nothing will remain hidden from you.

In my time "The White Stone" had many connotations:

1. A person taken to court and acquitted was given a white stone as a symbol of his innocence. In a voting situation, "The White Stone" meant acceptance, the Black Stone meant rejection.

2. Victors of athletic events were given "The White Stone."

The symbolism of the white stone in Revelation meant that he who obtained the key to my words, then went on to use it to obtain spiritual maturity would be innocent in the eyes of God, would be accepted among the remnant, and would be the victor who successfully ran the face of life and came to know himself. The secret name on the stone refers to the name of the person as determined in the bible code or Kabbalah.

Process

The dark ages of the church corresponds to the dark ages of the soul and represents the next step in spiritual awakening. You grow up in a church or you don't. Regardless, at some point you begin to break away from the beliefs of your parents and start searching for your own spiritual meaning. It's like the man who attends church on Sunday because that is the thing to do; it gives him status or political advantage—particularly in the Catholic and Mormon societies. One day the angst of separation from his soul grows so strong that he throws himself into Christianity in earnest. He becomes a fundamentalist Christian, a Catholic or a Mormon and turns himself over to their rule.

What started out as attending a religio/political organization turns into the organization taking complete rule over the man. The church makes the rules: disobey the church rules and you burn eternally in hell…much like the strangle hold of a cult.

During your own dark night (and everyone goes through it) you try to find meaning in your life by drawing closer and closer to church or spiritual doctrine. "If you could just be the perfect Catholic saint, the perfect fundamentalist Christian, the perfect "spiritual" person, all your cares would end." HA! The harder you try the worst the pain. Since the Christian doctrine is completely upside down, the more you buy into it, the farther you wander from your own divine nature as God and Man.

Non Christians, Agnostics and Atheists also go through their own dark night of the soul. But growing up in the pagan culture of Christianity, they find themselves affected by the separation between God and Man, and Man and Man: the same as their religious brothers. As long as you continue to view God as a being outside of yourself, and your brother as separate from you, the pain continues.

Have you ever played the game of Hot and Cold where someone hides a treasure then as you come near to it they tell you that you are hotter and hotter; as you move away they tell you that you are colder and colder?

Grace is like that. The more you believe you are a just a body or just a body with a soul, the colder and the more painful your journey becomes. The more you draw close to realizing that you are a spirit inhabiting a temporary vehicle and that your spirit is the same as the spirit inhabiting all the bodies around you, the warmer your journey becomes. Then one day you realize that everything you see about you is an illusion, a setup to allow God to experience himself in many bodies and many objects.

Picture this: are you over here daydreaming about the cat on the windowsill…or is the cat on the windowsill daydreaming about you? Both and neither! Your experience here *feels* real, but so do your dreams; so read my words since the Church didn't understand them enough to change them and you can still see them in the five gospels. The most faithful rendering of my words occurs in the Gospel of Thomas.

Where the church DID recognize that the threat of: "The kingdom of heaven is all about you and you do not see it," you will notice that the Catholic Church tried to eliminate that statement.

<u>Progression</u>

The Church at Pergamos represents the third stage in the corruption of the Christian Church which took place *530* AD–1530 AD. This encompassed the reign of 26 Popes, from Bonaface to Clement VII. During the period of the Church at Pergamos, the effects of the pagan religion of Rome continued to mutate and grow in strength. Notice this very important mutation:

1. During the rule of the Church at Smyrna, the Roman Empire ruled the church.

2. During the Period of Pergamos, the Church ruled the Roman Empire.

As the influence of Rome diminished, the political influence of the Church remained, grew, and spread to other empires, until it held a strangle-hold on much of Europe and Asia. Notice that I refer to the Catholic Church of this period as Satan himself and that I only reserve praise for those who resisted this ultimate marriage of religion and politics and held true to my Word.

Truly the lives of those who remained faithful to me hung in continuous danger from "The Seat of Satan:" the "Holy Roman Catholic Church," which hunted them down and martyred them for its own political ends.

The Church at Thyatira:
Versus 18-29

18 "To the angel of the assembly in Thyatira write: "The Son of God, who has his eyes like a flame of fire and his feet are like burnished brass, says these things: 19 "I know your works, your love, faith, service, patient endurance and that your last works are more than the first.

20But I have this against you, that you tolerate your woman, Jezebel, who calls herself a prophetess. She teaches and seduces my servants to commit sexual immorality and to eat things sacrificed to idols. 21I gave her time to repent, but she refuses to repent of her sexual immorality.

22Behold, I will throw her into a bed and those who commit adultery with her into great oppression unless they repent of her works. 23I will kill her children with Death and all the assemblies will know that I am he who searches the minds and hearts. I will give to each one of you according to your deeds.

24But to you I say, to the rest who are in Thyatira, as many as don't have this teaching, who don't know what some call 'the deep things of Satan,' to you I say, I am not putting any other burden on you. 25Nevertheless, hold that which you have firmly until I come.

26He who overcomes, and he who keeps my works to the end, to him I will give authority over the nations. 27He will rule them with a rod of iron, shattering them like clay pots;2 as I also have received of my Father: 28and I will give him the morning star. 29He who has an ear let him hear what the Spirit says to the assemblies.

<u>Prophecy</u>

This letter blatantly prophesizes the fall of the Catholic Church and the governments with which it has committed fornication. It also predicts the "children" of the Catholic Church (the Protestant Churches) which maintain the same pagan belief system of virgin birth, original sin, guilt and punishment and salvation through "The Blood of the Lamb." These too will come to a no good end.

Those however, who have not been subjugated to the rule of the Catholic Church and who have no knowledge of its corrupt teachings will find it easier to grow from spiritual children into spiritual adults. They will not be hindered by the mind control of the Catholic and Protestant religions. Those who see my teachings and abide by them will eventually survive, thrive and inherit the morning star.

By telling you that those who follow my word will inherit the morning star, I tell you that I will provide those who seek my message the enlightenment, information and tools to bring about a Spiritual Awakening in mass consciousness. Mankind has literally witnessed the rapid rise and slow fall of the major roadblock to awakening: the false, pagan church built in my name, the mother of all blasphemies.

---

2 2:27 Psalm 2:9

Parody

Jezebel is a parody on the Holy Roman Catholic Church which grew more and more corrupt as time went on—even to the point of selling indulgences and guarantees of going to heaven. It also serves as a parody of those political officials who "committed adultery" with her. The prophecy states that all that issues from this coming together of the political State and the Catholic Church will eventually perish.

The parody carries over to the Protestant Churches which maintained essentially the same belief system of separation and "Redemption by the Blood of the Lamb" as the Catholic Church. Their offspring also shall perish at the time of the final world government.

The Morning Star symbolizes the coming dawn (that is all ready in place but has not manifested as yet) of the great Spiritual Awakening about to occur at the fall of the World Government. At that time the Word of God (the Spiritual light) will be renewed world wide—and resurrected throughout the world.

The Morning Star also harkens back to: "Blessed are they who mourn for they shall be comforted." The Aramaic translation of this is, "Blessed are they who soften the hard places in their soul for they will become ripe to receive my word." It isn't until man lets go of his ego and experiences those events that will break his hard heart and make him ripe, empty of false pride and ready to fully let go of old ideas, that he will accept the miracles awaiting him.

Process

The process from here to the fall of world government will be the progressive breakdown of the Catholic Church, the initial rise of its Protestant children and the awakening consciousness that "something isn't correct" about the false pagan teachings of the so-called Christian Church.

The fall of the Christian guilt cult will give rise to the dark night of the soul in mass consciousness. During the dark night of the soul, many of you will go from church to church seeking me—or some other authority figure—to lead you. <u>Do not be misled</u>, for ANY church that attempts to lead you through fear and doctrine is but another version of the tyranny of the Catholic Church.

I used the metaphor, in the previous letter to Pergamos, of the Catholic Church being the seat of Satan; now let me warn you that Satan wears many faces. Because an organization claims to represent me, does not mean that it does. Beware of those religions that claim you are separate from God and separate from your Brother—for your soul *IS* God and you *ARE* connected to every other human being through your soul.

As long as your body and mind remain blinded to the illusion of separateness, your ego rules you through fear and becomes your own private Satan. So what can you do to get through your own third temptation—that of thinking that some organization out there can serve as the instant pill to salvation?

Explore various Christian churches if you must—but: keep an open mind. Give no person or organization your complete spiritual alliance, for in doing so you blind yourself to the meaning of "Love God above all things and your brother as yourself." Learn from each, but keep in mind my judgment against them. They are like blind men who think they can construct a rocket ship to God. Don't purchase a ticket.

Explore various churches outside of Christianity, for truly you will find more truth in many of the Eastern religions than in those religions seemingly dedicated to me; yet keep your own counsel, reserve always the right to think your own thoughts. Do not get caught up in *ritual* and cult-like attractions as a substitute for truth and do not get caught up in the "Woo Woo" of the New Age cult.

Use Love as your yardstick. Any organization that preaches separation between you and your brother; that leads you toward war; that rules you through fear of punishment and guilt—betrays its own face of Satan. Any organization that portrays you as sinful, with me as your savior and my crucifixion as your salvation, lies to you and is part of the seat of Satan.

You were **not** born in sin; you can **not** sin and I did **not** die to appease the Father. You are here to learn who you truly are and to learn sufficient spiritual balance to rule and co-create the universe with your brothers, **Period!** Your *own* fear creates Satan—which is but your own ego trying to trick you into thinking you can control others through power, guilt, and fear. Why do you think the Church mutated from a State organization to a spiritual cult—for what greater control could the Pope and his henchmen have than the human fear of eternal punishment?

Meditate daily. Let the love that comes from your heart guide you. Love is the absence of fear, so ask each day to make decisions based upon a complete lack of fear, knowing that I walk beside you. Be more concerned with establishing peace in your heart than in struggling to survive, for in truth no struggle is necessary. Your ego causes fear because it tries to think its way out of problems. However, the ego only knows what *it* has experienced. It does not know of the other possibilities—particularly those that lie in the hands of your brother. When you are afraid, come to me in meditation and let me connect you with your brother.

Progression

Letter to the Church at Thyatira: 1530 AD-1730 AD. This period covers the reign of 26 Popes from Paul III to Benedict XIII. The Church of Thyatira embodies the time span of the Reformation, the Renaissance and the Establishment of the Protestant Churches.

So far we have seen the Church start out teaching my words, but beginning to stray into paganism (Ephesus). Then the Church took on the cloak of Roman Government where it adopted rules and policies intended to control the masses with its new pagan beliefs (Smyrna). From there the Church expanded its power, mutated and assumed religious ruler ship over the political world (Pergamos).

Does this not resemble a virus mutating to accommodate changes in its host? In this next period, the Church of Thyatira, the church mutates again. This time it splits into two segments: Catholic and Protestant, yet the Protestant Churches maintained many of the same pagan beliefs as the mother church—same song, third verse.

I praised those who back then held out for their right to read and interpret my Word and live the life given to them in the Ten Commandments/Attitudes. I told them I would send a Morning Star to guide them. That Morning Star, my light, the Holy Ghost (or Holy Spirit, whatever you wish to call my messenger) comes to you in meditation as a deeper understanding of spiritual truth.

The Christian church has now past its heyday and the advent of mass awakening lies on the horizon.

Chapter 3
Part 2: The things that are continued.
Verses 1–6

"And to the angel of the assembly in Sardis write: "He who has the seven Spirits of God and the seven stars says these things: "I know your works that you have a reputation of being alive, but you are dead. [2]Wake up and keep the things that remain which you were about to throw away, for I have found no works of yours perfected before my God. [3]Remember therefore how you have received and heard. Keep it and repent. If therefore you don't watch, I will come as a thief and you won't know what hour I will come upon you.

[4]Nevertheless you have a few names in Sardis that did not defile their garments. They will walk with me in white for they are worthy. [5]He who overcomes will be arrayed in white garments and I will in no way blot his name out of the book of life, I will confess his name before my Father, and before his angels. [6]He who has an ear let him hear what the Spirit says to the assemblies.

Prophecy

This letter is a prophecy that in time, the Protestant sects and the remnant of the Catholic Church will eventually settle down into self-satisfied little kingdoms with very little spiritual growth. The church communities will be busy recruiting new members and carrying on social activities—but spiritually will be dead.

Parody

The parody here is that of a church community that has become self-satisfied; seeks no truth nor provides a service to the community. God reminds the community to: "Wake up and remember what you were taught in the beginning, at least keep what little you have!" Otherwise, the church is told, God will come like a thief in the night. The smug churches were being warned that their membership will fall off as believers cease to believe in the church and start seeking God on their own.

Process

The process of moving from my Aramaic teachings to Westernized Christianity has been slow and painful. In my language and thinking, separation simply did not exist. If you were an Assyrian looking outdoors at your garden you would see yesterday, today and tomorrow. In other words, all that had gone into preparing the garden, how the garden looks today and what it will look like this fall. Our concept of time flowed like a river, or like the time between cause and effect.

In Greek mythology the gods were timeless and perfect (in their own way.) Man was time-limited and imperfect, and most certainly separate from the gods. As my words were translated into Greek, Latin, etc. the meanings got lost in the cultural exchange. God became separate from man—and time became separated into intervals. Good and bad became absolutes instead of on a continuum between ripe and unripe. In other words, changing languages and customs corrupted the nature of my teachings.

Now in this 5th period of church history we see retrenchment and infighting. The spirit of my teachings cannot be found. The churches have a reputation of being alive, but they are dead and their teachings are dead.

So…how does this impact you? While going through your dark night of the soul, you had to struggle to find truth. Along the way you have had to reject a multitude of false teachings and resist social pressures to conform, but now those battles lie behind you. Now no one tells you what to think or how to act, for you have come to the place where you are ready to accept your own Godhood.

You are like a rubber band that has been stretched to the max and what happens when the tension releases? You got it—you go right back to your comfort zone; life intervenes and you neglect your meditation. Taking charge of your life requires constant vigilance, but without outside pressure you go back to sleep. New world crises erupt and mob mentality says: "Nuke 'um, turn those non-Christian terrorists to glass," and what do you do? You go along with it.

The lull before the storm is probably one of the most challenging spiritual events thus far. Right when you need to become a force for good, a pro-activist in living and proclaiming my word…you go to sleep and you become afraid to speak your truth. You relinquish your personal spiritual leadership—and to whom? The churches! So what can you do at this point?

Pray and Meditate: if ever you needed to go back to my original words, now is the time! Get out the Gospel of Thomas and meditate on one saying a day. For example: From the viewpoint of all my teachings about your godhood, what am I telling you? How can you apply it to your life **right now**? When does the thief come? He comes in the night when all is quiet.

There is no standing still, for the moment you cease to pray, act and move forward, you begin moving back into the world. Fear takes on a new life as you get caught up in trying to stay alive; the ego rises from the dead and you become an "enlightened" lunatic.

Detach: from judgment against your brother—and that is easier said than done for how can you detach and watch world events as if they are only an illusion—particularly when your government goes from yellow alert to orange alert to red alert—to attack this country or attack that country? Remember this: "Nothing matters anyway." Can you control what terrorists do, what your government or your boss does? Unlikely! Can you control your *own* thinking and actions? Absolutely!

Let your light shine: I told you: "ye shall know the truth and the truth shall set you free." How does a free man act? He speaks his own truth—at least to himself. He dares to act "as if" he *is* a piece of God and he returns good for evil. If you really believe in me, to what extent are you giving of yourself, your goods and your spirit to others?

Have you moved from judging others to accepting them just the way they are? Do you go out of your way to say a kind or encouraging word to everyone around you? Do you set standards based upon the Ten Commandments/Attitudes and hold yourself to them? When is the last time you complimented a competitor, and why do you see anyone as a competitor in the first place? What's there to compete for when you know who you are?

I tell you, instead of all the churches fighting among themselves to prove who has the best understanding of my word; they might far better look outside of their own organization and think about what they might do to encourage and help *all* people—with no thought of personal gain.

Progression:

This letter to the Church at Sardis covered the period 1730 AD to 1880 AD and the reign of 26 Popes from Clement XII to Pius IX. I, Jesus, mentioned earlier: wherever power and money reside, there too can corruption be found.

From the days of the Church at Ephesus, usurpers piggybacked on my name and reputation to seize control of the population for financial and ego gain. I tell you that trying to spread my message through the churches has been like trying to grasp a marshmallow. Squeezing one section simply causes a new bulge to pop out somewhere else.

Truth existed nowhere except in the few individuals who had separated themselves from the organizational struggle for power and had dedicated themselves to actually living the life mandated by my teachings.

At this point, the initial battle between the Catholic and Protestant churches had ended. Teachings become less important than retrenching. The Catholic Church will never again hold itself out as the only church dedicated to my teachings and the Protestant Churches are busy splintering off into various sects.

None of what the churches taught, after the splintering and retrenching, had anything to do with me or my message. Rather it had to do with the formation of little duchies—each with its own center of power. As I said before, the Christian church is a clever virus that mutates to sustain the lowest level of spiritual knowledge and the highest level of worldly power.

The Church at Philadelphia:
Versus 7-13

"To the angel of the assembly in Philadelphia write: "He who is holy, he who is true, he who has the key of David, he who opens and no one can shut and who shuts and no one opens, says these things: 8"I know your works (behold, I have set before you an open door, which no one can shut) that you have a little power and kept my word and didn't deny my name.

9Behold I give of the synagogue of Satan; of those who say they are Jews and they are not but lie. Behold, I will make them to come and worship before your feet and to know that I have loved you. 10Because you kept my command to endure, I also will keep you from the hour of testing which is to come on the whole world, to test those who dwell on the earth.

11I am coming quickly! Hold firmly that which you have, so that no one takes your crown. 12He who overcomes, I will make him a pillar in the temple of my God and he will go out from there no more. I will write on him the name of my God and the name of the city of my God, the new Jerusalem, which comes down out of heaven from my God and my own new name. 13He who has an ear let him hear what the Spirit says to the assemblies.

Prophecy

This prophecy differs from the others in that it is written to the Remnant that actively sought out and kept my teachings. As I said before, some of these remained in Eastern Turkey, Iraq and Iran until the West divided up the Middle East for Western advantage. I also had beloved people here and there who dared to think for themselves; broke from the churches and explored the original meaning of my words in Aramaic; who studied my culture and who successfully found the true meaning of my sayings. This prophecy is for them.

Many of you in this modern age find yourself part of the mass awakening—the return to God and to His teachings. Unlike other times, enough of you will go forth with the true Word that you will protect one another, and I tell you this one last time, hold true to what you know to be Truth.

Parody

Once again I parody that "Synagogue of Satan"—the Christian church, which calls itself a leader of my disciples—but lies.

Process

Once the Protestant Churches ceased fighting among themselves and with the Catholic Church, no one challenge remained to awaken them and they in effect fell asleep. Isn't that what happens in any situation when a person or a people cease to refresh themselves?

Yet, how far you have come, my brother, for by the time you reach this point in your own spiritual development you have endured much, and I am sending in a new breed of humans to help you along in your journey. You have already noticed the subtle change and refer to them as "the new children." They come as participants in my promise that the door you have opened will not be closed. They come to earth remembering their connection to the universal soul and with a different type of intelligence. Your society is like blind men who now have among them children who can see.

You diagnose them as ADHD (Attention Deficit Hyperactivity Disorder) because they quickly grow bored with your slowness and then you drug them and try to force them to fit into your system. Eventually, however, there will be more of them than you and they will know how to nurture their children; whereas you are too caught up in making money and maintaining power to know how to nurture them. Your mission, and that of the new children, is to awaken as many of your brothers as possible so that they may have time to spiritually mature before Earth renews itself.

Remain steadfast: in your pursuit of truth.

Remove completely all judgment: of your brother.

Live in peace: with yourself in your rightful role as God/Man.

Co-create your future: by living in collaboration with your brother and treating all things as if they were your brother—for they are.

Enjoy the ride.

Progression

This Letter to the Church at Philadelphia dates from 1880 AD to 1967 AD. This period covers the reign of six Popes from Leo XIII to Paul VI. The Christian Church, during the almost two centuries following my death, progressed from my original teachings to becoming paganized; to becoming a state-ruled organization; to becoming an organization that ruled states; to breaking apart into Catholic and Protestant factions; into wars and into complacency.

After the letter to the Church at Philadelphia, the word "church" is not mentioned again in Revelation until my "second coming;" the time when those who have awakened, and accepted co-responsibility as God/Man, will come with me to Eden.

The last prophecy of Revelation ended in 1967 with the six day war when the Jews reclaimed Jerusalem, and as predicted, the population has become complacent.

Thus far I, the Christ, have emphasized two points: 1) I never intended to start a church, rather I intended to start a school where each man would grow in wisdom and knowledge of my word until in adulthood he would assume his rightful role as God/Man on earth. In childhood he would be taught the words of Moses from his elders and in maturity develop them as Ten Attitudes for spiritual enlightenment.

My words are *not* about forming an institution that engages in judging others; developing mind-control or political control over nations. Rather about developing a spiritual maturity that results in mankind respecting each other and their environment. It is about Man becoming a divine co-creator of the universe as he lives in collaboration with his brother and the forces of nature. 2) I keep pointing out a Remnant that has understood and kept my word—this letter is about them.

Through the ages a small number of people have truly asked for enlightenment. Some gathered this knowledge from father to son. However, the vast majority—like you—came to enlightenment through your own efforts. You prayed, you read my words, some of you read the writings of other mystics before you—whatever it took, you broke away from mainstream Christianity and refused to be held captive by the ritual, false teachings, false judgments and social pressure of the political organizations that I refer to in this letter as the "Seat of Satan." Good news and Bad news. The "bad" news is that you are now in the final period of spiritual revival. The "good" news is that you will be protected and preserved as you spread the Truth.

Notice that for the first time in this letter, I begin talking about environmental catastrophes. Yes indeed, environmental upheavals have changed the face of the earth, both before the advent of modern man and since. Have you not in your present time found tropical animals preserved at both poles where no vegetation grows and no climate exists to allow for such large reptilian existence? Well, it's about to happen again—soon!

Once again an earthly life form—man—is about to bring about his own destruction. In this letter I am telling you those who hold true to my teachings, as I have told life forms before you—"do not be afraid." You yourselves, acting alone as well as collaboratively, have opened the door to the truth about Man's mission here on earth and I will not allow it to be shut. Yes, you will leave your body to be reborn, as you have so many times before. This time, however you will not return to this planet. This time you will come with me to Eden, for you have earned the right through your perseverance, patience and courage.

A Remnant of human life form will remain on the new earth to start over again on the eternal journey of self-discovery. These humanoids will receive breath from the universal soul and continue to refine life forms that can live in harmony in Eden.

Of course the soul *is* God and will never be discarded. However the body/mind combination that has evolved from fear and physical survival will not be used again. Like you, they (the new ones) will receive a body/mind capable of awakening to its connection to God, and thus, the process begins again.

The Church at Laodicea:
Versus 14-22

14"To the angel of the assembly in Laodicea write: "The Amen, the Faithful and True Witness, the Head of God's creation, says these things:15"I know your works, that you are neither cold nor hot. I wish you were cold or hot. 16So, because you are lukewarm and neither hot nor cold, I will vomit you out of my mouth.

17Because you say, 'I am rich and have gotten riches and have need of nothing; and don't know that you are the wretched one, miserable, poor, blind, and naked. 18I counsel you to buy from me gold refined by fire that you may become rich and white garments, that you may clothe yourself and that the shame of your nakedness may not be revealed; and eye salve to anoint your eyes, that you may see.

19As many as I love, I reprove and chasten. Be zealous therefore and repent. 20Behold, I stand at the door and knock. If anyone hears my voice and opens the door, then I will come in to him and will dine with him, and he with me. 21He who overcomes I will give to him to sit down with me on my throne, as I also overcame and sat down with my Father on his throne. 22He who has an ear, let him hear what the Spirit says to the assemblies."

Prophecy

The term "church" is no longer used because in modern times the Christian religion has become so watered down, corrupted and useless that it has no redeeming grace left in it. It has become like foul water presented to those who thirst. These *are* the end times! Abundant life and eternal life are not to be found anywhere in the Christian movement. Yet those who actively seek my words and thirst to understand the culture from which my words come will find me and I them.

Parody

This letter goes beyond parody to condemnation of the Christian movement which in modern times has come to rely on "touchy-feely" and feel good motivational speeches in place of the Divine. I tell them: You are neither hot nor cold and I vomit you out of my mouth, for you have no more idea of whom and what you are, or why you came to this earth, than that rock over there.

Process

The churches have come full round from paganism of Rome and Greece with their Gods of the upper realm, to the Paganism of the West with it's: "if it feels good, do it" doctrine and colonial actions.

Taking responsibility for your own shared Godhood has been no easy matter. It is like the woman who bakes a chocolate pie, drops the pie on the floor and sits weeping while waiting for someone to clean it up—until finally she realizes no one is coming. If the mess is to be set straight, she must do it herself. What a shock! And what a shock to your spiritual nature for I am *not* coming to clean up the mess! If the environment is to be renewed, poverty eliminated, the sick healed, and war to cease, then YOU must do it YOURSELF.

Going to church on Sunday will not "save" you. Saying prayers, giving alms, living rich, or living in poverty will not "save" you. Attending self-help seminars and engaging in political battles or peace rallies will not "save" you—since there is nothing to save. Wars, poverty and illness do not exist because of lack of abundance—or because man does not know right from wrong—rather they occur because man DOES know right from wrong, but believes *he* is right and his brother wrong.

Cease looking outside of yourself for the answers! I am in you and around you—*I AM you*—as you are me, and *I am* the universal soul. My words have been preserved for you to read—particularly in the Gospel of Thomas. You are not "saved by grace" you *are* grace. You are not "saved by the blood of the lamb," *You ARE* the lamb. There is nothing to "save" anyone from—except their own dream-state of complacency.

Instead of "doing," learn to "just be." Meditate daily upon my words. Find out who you are and *study* the Ten Commandments/Attitudes. Work on YOUR-SELF until you realize that the words of Moses are not about what "*Thou Shalt Not* Do;" they are about "What Thou Shalt remember to BECOME"

Take responsibility for who you truly are. It isn't up to your priest/minister, your president, or even some old man who sits on a cloud playing a harp, to take responsibility for your actions. Love isn't some romantic feeling towards unknown people. Love is recognizing the true identity of the guy next door who plays loud music or whose dog goes on your lawn. If you can not maintain peace with your next door neighbor who doesn't want to be friendly back, how can you maintain peace with Iraq? First become friends with yourself and with me; then you will know how to make peace with your neighbor.

Take responsibility for what you think. The world is not in chaos because chaos is the natural order of things; it is in chaos because the *mass consciousness* sets up chaos with mixed goals. Society has taught you to fear your brother and to seek wealth—I tell you to *first* seek my words. Humans possess the unique ability to work together to solve problems and create a new earth, so why hasn't it happened? Because someone(s) doesn't WANT it to happen, that's why. Satan is not outside of you; Satan is in your own thoughts, wishes, desires and fears.

Take responsibility for your own perceptions. Once you understand my words you will know that the only one or only thing that you have to control is yourself—and your own ego. Who gives meaning to the events about you? YOU do. Only you can develop perceptions or label events and things as "good" or "bad." Look around you and ask yourself who gave meaning to that tree, that car, or that desk. YOU, THAT'S WHO, for nothing has any meaning other than what *you* give it. You are like a child who, being given a paintbrush, paints on a canvass and begins to give meaning to the picture he paints. The child gets caught up in his own illusion—and so do you.

Take responsibility for what you say and do. Remember that this time of complacency is YOUR time to get YOUR act in order. Do I want you to sit and do nothing? Of course not, for doing and creating is the reason you came here with appendages and a brain, so have fun! You are a body and a brain enjoying life in the Universe that *we together*, created—and that is what I want you to do.

What I don't want you to do is come into conflict with your brother. It is much easier to give a buck to the homeless man on the corner whom you judge "poor" or a "scam artist," than it is to be loving towards your neighbor who is in your face day after day and whom *you* judge to be "disrespectful."

Rather than punching your neighbor in the nose, or finding a cutting remark to get even for his dog peeing on your lawn or his kids running through your garden, first ask yourself what you were meant to learn from this situation. Then handle the situation as love—your own God-self, would handle it. In other words, don't just romanticize about being God/Man, *BE* God in human form. Become who you truly are by acting the part.

Progression

This letter represents the time from 1996 to the present including the rein of Popes John Paul 1 and John Paul ll. Western Society in particular, has replaced my words with self-help seminars and self-righteous belief in "salvation" and "judgment" against their fellow man. The Bank of God has been replaced by the Bank of America, as those with wealth lounge in comfort rather than taking responsibility for their true God nature.

My teachings have been replaced by a historic and romantic memory of me doing all the work, including my crucifixion, so that you could follow a bunch of church rules while waiting for me to come and rescue you. Nothing could be farther from the truth for this *is the final opportunity* for you to take responsibility for your own spiritual awakening and "rescue" yourselves.

Chapter 4
Part III
Verses 1 through 11

After these things I looked and saw a door opened in heaven and the first voice that I heard, like a trumpet speaking with me, was one saying, "Come up here, and I will show you the things which must happen after this." [2]Immediately I was in the Spirit.

Behold, there was a throne set in heaven and one sitting on the throne [3]that looked like a jasper stone and a sardius. There was a rainbow around the throne, like an emerald to look at. [4]Around the throne were twenty-four thrones. On the thrones were twenty-four elders sitting, dressed in white garments with crowns of gold on their heads.

[5]Out of the throne proceed lightnings, sounds, and thunders, there were seven lamps of fire burning before his throne, which are the seven Spirits of God. [6]Before the throne was something like a sea of glass, similar to crystal.

In the midst of the throne and around the throne were four living creatures full of eyes before and behind. [7]The first creature was like a lion and the second creature like a calf, the third creature had a face like a man and the fourth like a flying eagle. [8]The four living creatures, each one of them having six wings, are full of eyes around and within. They have no rest day and night, saying, "Holy, holy, holy[3] is the Lord God, the Almighty, who was and who is and who is to come!"

[9]When the living creatures give glory, honor and thanks to him who sits on the throne, to him who lives forever and ever, [10]the twenty-four elders fall down before him who sits on the throne and worship him who lives forever and ever, and throw their crowns before the throne, saying, [11]"Worthy are you, our Lord and God, the Holy One,[4] to receive the glory, the honor, and the power, for you created all things and because of your desire they existed and were created!"

<u>Review of happenings to date</u>

Up to now I have shown you the weaknesses inherent in the early churches and how those weaknesses played out over the centuries as human beings twisted my teachings:

First: from a post-Essenes school into a gentile church dominated by a synthesis of pagan/gentile/Jewish theology (Ephesus) which mutated into:

Second: A political instrument of Rome (Smyrna) that mutated into:

Third: A much more powerful Papist instrument to rule over multiple political structures of the then known world (Pergamos) that mutated into:

---

3 4:8 Hodges/Farstad MT reads "holy" 9 times instead of 3.

4 4:11 TR omits "and God, the Holy One,"

Fourth: A Papist/Protestant split giving the illusion of returning to my word (Thyatira) which dissolved into:

Fifth: A time of stagnation where the various Protestant churches bickered over who would sit at the Captain's table on the Titanic (Sardis) which evolved into:

Sixth: A mini spiritual revolution where the remnant of those who truly followed my word began to find each other as travel and communication increased (Philadelphia.) The last prophecy is fulfilled as the Jews retake Jerusalem and promise to hold the door open for the Remnant and begin to discuss the environmental catastrophes to come.

This then evolved into a time when the Churches turned from my word to political discussions and self-help groups (Laodicea) and, with even further increases in communications and travel, my word becomes available to all men.

This is a waiting period where all human life is given the opportunity to get its act together.

Behind the scenes, heaven has been happening. I have told you that the kingdom of heaven is all around you, now I am telling you that *it* evolves as *you* create and evolve your human experience. Heaven is a place you can see with human eyes (Earth) and a place you see in meditation through the Seventh Chakra (the Doorway to the Divine.)

Even if you are familiar with them, you may want to stop here and read the section on the Seven Chakras for this interpretation is more enlightening and I believe should give you a deeper understanding. Otherwise picture them for the moment as the seven maturation steps the physical body takes in realizing its Godhood; starting from birth as a physically dependent and immature being through becoming a mature sage, fully cognizant of your Spirituality.

Prophecy

Up until now I have been concentrating on the spiritual/cultural influences on the Christian Church and the mutations that eventually lead to its death as a spiritual entity. In your time, it might just as well be called a Grange or a Health and Wellness Center, but certainly NOT anything to do with my teachings.

Now the book shifts its emphases. From here on out I will no longer try to call the church back to its spiritual foundations. Rather I will talk about the repercussions of spiritual duality and death. I start out by describing the 24 prophets of the old testament and the Seraphim, or healing Angels (living creatures) assigned to weed out the awakened from the un-awakened, i.e. those who have passed from spiritual infancy into spiritual maturity.

Parody

John tells the story of Heaven and Hell in the Greek tradition of his upbringing; where God, his Angels and Saints, sit on high while Man plows the earth down below. It's all a story, a parody of the meaning of life. Unfortunately the Christian Church concretized it as if it were real.

In reality there is no Heaven, no Hell, no physical Supreme Being, no saints, no Angels—in fact there is no time. In modern times you might see such a vision by watching a movie or by playing a holographic game where your senses "saw" happenings as if they were real. In the Divine, only the "Now" exists. The "Now" reflects the actions of the past, shows us the present creativity going on all around us and serves as a predictor of the effects of the creativity. Time is merely the space between an action and its effects.

What are Angels? Angels are archetypes of the Divine and *you* see them as "helpers." In actuality they are reflections of your own connection to the Universal Soul. What are Saints and Prophets? They are shadows of the humanizing of pieces of the Divine Soul that existed in the past and continue in the archetype of your soul—like shadows of yourself.

Process

John entered the space of the Universal soul through the process of passing through the door of his Seventh Chakra, the Gateway to Spiritual Unity with the Father. Behold, there he saw a throne (which represents the ruling element of the Universal Soul) and seated upon that throne was God Himself, the thinking and living creative source of the Universal Soul.

What did God look like? John didn't try to photograph God; instead he painted an impressionistic picture since in Aramaic no words existed to describe God and John was receiving his impressions from me, the Christ. John saw a translucent brightness sparkling with many colors (Jasper), and within that stone were set elements of red—the Sardine-stone. These represent the creative, all knowing aspects of the Universal Soul mitigated by balancing the ying/yang of love, wisdom and discernment.

Around the throne John saw a rainbow (the symbol of renewal) that glowed like an emerald, representing the ever changing and reviving nature of the Universal Soul. John was seeing a metaphor of what all things in the Universe look like before they come into physical form. Notice the brilliance, balance and joy of your true self.

Is it any wonder that you felt a sense of loss upon transcending from this place of joy to a physical body, the First Chakra? Yet, through growth in understanding of my word, you experience both the spiritual excitement and the physical manifestation of this glory: the Seventh Chakra. John wasn't just seeing a vision, he was *experiencing* God.

Sitting around the throne, John saw 24 elders dressed in white with crowns on their heads. I have told you that you agreed to enter into a body in order for the Universal Soul to be able to experience its creations on earth as well as many other places in the Universe. These 24 elders represent the 24 prophets of Israel, as well as the unification of the 12 tribes of Israel and also the manifestation of the Remnant that held true to the teachings of the 12 Apostles.

In other words, the unification of all humanity who diligently strive day and night to know who they truly are and who make the journey through the seven Chakras. The 24 elders are *you* who have heard my voice and heeded my message through the ages. Notice how the 24 elders sing, day and night: "Glory to the Father and to the Son and to the Holy Spirit." Have you not learned to do the same? The Father is the Universal Soul of which you are a part. The Son represents me, the Christ, and others who have come to earth to teach you the Truth and the Way back to your Godhead.

Out of the Throne came lightning, thunder and voices. Lightning and thunder represent Truth and Authority. The voices represent Truth interpreted and transmitted to the physical aspects of God and in this case, Truth is transmitted to you through my words—*as stated in the original Aramaic.* Moreover, the Universal soul inhabits many kingdoms, Earth representing but one. I tell you this so you will not think you are alone in the Universe.

The Seven lamps of fire in front of the throne represent The Holy Spirit/Holy Ghost, the communications system that enables you to stay in constant contact with your Universal Soul through meditation.

The Holy Spirit/Holy Ghost embodies seven mindsets:

1. THE SPIRIT OF CHRIST IN YOU

You have actively sought out my word for I've been with you more than once. I have been known by many names, all of which are the Christ and all of which spoke with the same message about your role as God/Man.

2. THE SPIRIT OF WISDOM (TRUTH)

Many messengers bang on your door; notice, for instance, the malignant mutations of the so-called Christian Church. For those of you who hunger and search for truth, I have given the spirit of discernment. In your journey through the seven stages (Chakras) of spiritual wisdom you may get trapped in one mis-statement of the truth or another, for short periods of time. That is why I tell you to meditate constantly, for maturing spiritually takes time. You must see the truth and experience its ramifications before passing to the next. I promise however, that whoever seeks unendingly will ultimately find the answer.

3. THE SPIRIT OF INTERCESSION

How do you know what to ask? You can only ask to the extent of your experience. If you think yourself poor, you will ask for a donkey cart to go to the store. If you think yourself a bit richer, you will ask for a Rolls Royce. But when you know you are God, you ask for the store to come to you. I refer to The Spirit of Intercession aspect of the Holy Spirit when I compare it to the Internet. Put in a word and use the search engine or just chant "God" and I come to you with information beyond your understanding.

4. THE SPIRIT OF JOY

How do I know my own? I know them through their joy. How can one be joyous in the face of war and persecution? They can't if trapped in ego and fear, for only those who know and follow my Word realize the truth: nothing on earth matters—OTHER THAN—that you do what it takes to release yourself from your own judgmental nature and that of your neighbor. When you can truly love your neighbor and find a way to collaborate with him in your joint awakening, joy rules.

5. THE SPIRIT OF COUNSEL

From birth, ego separates you from your brother and tells you what sneaky trick to pull next to gain power over him. How do you free yourself from the tyranny of the ego? By hearing and following my Words!

When you walk the path of the Seven Chakras, knowing that you have come here to learn to be God/Man experiencing your own creations in human form—all changes. Your perspective and actions become incomprehensible to the world at large for you send love, where they send hate; you create, where they seek security; you collaborate, where they compete.

How do you know what to do? Simple: meditate. Normally you will know what to do next by following your joy. There will be times however, when you will be called to give up security and everyone and everything known to you, to journey into the wilderness. Only those who have drawn close to me, however will be asked to do the "impossible."

You will know that the new action required from you comes from me when 1) It obeys the Ten Commandments/Attitudes and 2) When the call comes gently and persistently over a period of time. These will be the times when you will hear "Call so and so." Or "Quit your job and move here." These "leaps of faith" come only during the development of the Fifth, Sixth and Seventh Chakras, when you are strong enough in your faith to answer the call.

6. THE SPIRIT OF POWER

Again, this is a Fifth through Seventh Chakra stage of development in your spiritual growth in human form. As said earlier, your actions as God/Man appear insane to men in their First/Second Chakra stage of development. Yet I tell you, when you know and understand my words and when you act on them in a spirit of complete selflessness, I will take over when you can go no further. You by yourself can only change yourself, however from the realm of the Universal Soul, I can change anything. The Holy Spirit brings you the power to do, be and have more power to complete the ordinary every day missions and the supernatural missions assigned to you.

7. THE SPIRIT OF LIFE

The spirit of life is to collaborate with your neighbor and to create new experiences in which the Universal Soul can experience life. Those who do not know my word live in a world of shackles, slaves to the ego of the power mongers—and mostly they sleep. As one of mine however, you live a life of extraordinary creativity, joy and excitement. You will know you are mine when each day brings a new adventure; when you follow your bliss and your bliss stirs the creativity of others; when jobs are created for you, not the other way around.

The life of the awakened man reflects the results of passion and grace. See yourself as an artist before a canvas. On the left hand side you see charcoal outlines made by me for you to color in. In the middle you see directions for what colors go where. But at the end—behold—you see a blank canvass for you to create all the splendor of life. The Holy Spirit suggests the theme—*you* create the picture. Does that explain the Holy Spirit/Holy Ghost for you?

In the middle of the throne John sees a lamb with its throat cut, the symbol of Jewish sacrifice. To John, influenced by the "Blood of the Lamb" mythology, this lamb represents me. Notice I am not yet sitting on my throne as Lion and Ruler as that will come when *you* are ready to join me in Eden.

Before the throne John sees a sea of crystal glass. This represents the joint ability of the Universal Soul to see all things with crystal clarity; as well as your ability to tap into the divine consciousness through prayer and meditation. In the beginning stages (Chakras 1 thru 4) you see through the glass darkly, as if through smoke. This is where the Holy Spirit intervenes to provide power and insights not yet available to you. In the later stages (Chakras 5 thru 7) your vision clears allowing you to commune with God directly.

Sitting on the throne and encircling it are four living creatures: a Lion, an Ox, Man, and an Eagle. All contain six wings and multiple eyes embedded throughout. They sing praise to the Universal Spirit and to the Eden to come. These living creatures represent the Seraphim, the angels of healing. Why all these eyes, what are the wings and what are these living things?

- **The eyes:** Perfect vision. The eyes represent the ability to see clearly above and below, within and without on all sides. They see what has been and what needs to be done to fulfill the promise of Eden.

- **The wings:** These wings represent the healing power of the Seraphim, or "Healing Angels." The wings cleansing and purifying the soul in preparation for becoming ripe to accept one's Godhood. The first set brush the dust from your body, i.e. brush away negativity and ego. They clean up the first Six Chakras by:

    a. Removing the sense of being at the mercy of and under the control of something outside yourself—1st Chakra.

    b. Giving back the confidence that you can manage your own life—2nd Chakra.

    c. Bringing you back into contact with your true nature—3rd Chakra.

    d. Helping you accept both your bright and dark sides and marry them into a single unit—4th Chakra.

    e. Begin understanding the nature of your own ability to speak out (use the Divine Breath) to create miracles—5th Chakra.

    In terms of the Kabbalah, this would be like removing the earthly shrouds of the Serifot, the veils that enable Man to remain grounded until we mature enough to begin to accept our Godhood. By cleansing your physical energies, the Seraphim place man on the threshold of spiritual awakening and prepare him to move from Man to Man/God.

    f. The second set of angelic wings brush the dust from your souls, sort of like a divine internal feather duster. They open up the mystical "third eye," the internal vision of the Divine in order to reveal to you who you are, why you are here, and your Divine Mission—6th Chakra.

    In terms of the Kabbalah, this is like removing half the spiritual shrouds of the Serifot. By opening the eyes of your soul to your Divine oneness with God, the cleaning process prepares you to become God/Man.

    g. The third and last set of angel wings brushes your vision so your reflection becomes clear. Finally, you look in the mirror and see your Divine Nature reflected back to you—7th Chakra.

The last shroud of the Serifot fades. God breaths the divine breath of abundant and eternal life into your consciousness and you inhale your full spiritual maturity as God walking the earth.

- **The four living creatures. The four Seraphim, healing angels: steps in changing from Man to Man/God to God/Man.**

  (1) The Lion—The warrior king who obeys my word and peruses his true divine identity with his whole heart and soul; and who accepts his place as guardian over his physical realm.

  (2) The Ox—The servant Man/God who obeys the Ten Commandments/Attitudes and seeks God's direction in all things.

  (3) Man—Man as Man/God entering physical form in order to experience his divine creations.

  (4) Eagle—God/Man representing man's Divinity.

When the Four Living Creatures worshiped their source—the Universal Soul—the twenty four elders took off their crowns and fell down before the throne to worship God. This symbolizes absolute adherence to the First Commandment: "Love God Above All Things." The twenty four elders (all who awaken and arrive at their Seventh Chakra) take off their individual crowns in order to participate in the Universal Divine Soul.

You like to think yours is the only time of the habitation of your planet but it is not, for even before you have gone other civilizations. In the dawn of your civilization, you had the situation where it was dog eat dog, for animals neither planted nor sowed the fields—they lived off one another. In the representation, the "Lion" was the time before man's memory.

I've told you already that not only are you God, but that other things are also God: be it the earth, the dirt or the television you watch; all of these are the essence of God in one. Mankind has learned to harness some of that essence so your television set isn't just a box, it receives messages and signals just as *you* also receive messages and signals; but because of your lack of knowledge your reception is limited, thus the Lion represents the beginning stages of creation.

The "Ox" represents the time when man went from being the hunter gatherer to becoming more agricultural. Man was beginning to think he could make things easier by conquering the earth and growing his own food. The "Man" represents the time when man became more civilized, began to study and to learn; then tried to figure out in his head what it meant to be God. I gave Man the Ten Attitudes to guide the way. They were intended to uplift and encourage Man on his journey. However, man chose to be led rather than to lead and turned the Ten Attitudes into the Ten Commandments.

The "Man" represents the humanity of mankind, the time when the brain evolved to the point where it could think, feel and analyze. Man, among all beasts, has the ability to see the "dog-eat-dog" mentality and find ways to overcome it, to create a new world where peace and harmony reign.

The "Eagle," represents flying above the mind as a spiritual being capable of existing as both God and Man. So we see the progression of pre-man to hunter/gatherer, to agrarian, to scientist and then to a spiritual being. Those who awaken then go into the "Eagle" or "Spirit" realm.

The Four Living Beings have eyes all over them because at each stage they are trying to see clearly the will of God. Notice that as you go from the Lion to the Ox to Man, then to the Eagle, you start seeing not only earthly visions but spiritual visions as well.

Progression

Remember, I told you that time represented the space between an action and its consequences? Up until now I have told you about the seven stages of the churches and the actions taken by false priests and rulers to control your soul. From here on out I will be telling you about the consequences of those actions. So far, John has set the stage to tell you a metaphor about how those consequences arise and play out.

Chapter 5
Verses 1–14

I saw in the right hand of him who sat on the throne, a book written inside and outside, sealed shut with seven seals. 2I saw a mighty angel proclaiming with a loud voice, "Who is worthy to open the book, and to break its seals?"

3No one in heaven above or on the earth or under the earth, was able to open the book, or to look in it. 4And I wept much, because no one was found worthy to open the book, or to look in it. 5One of the elders said to me, "Don't weep. Behold, the Lion who is of the tribe of Judah, the Root of David, has overcome; he who opens the book and its seven seals."

6I saw in the midst of the throne and of the four living creatures and in the midst of the elders, a Lamb standing as though it had been slain, having seven horns and seven eyes, which are the seven Spirits of God sent out into all the earth. 7Then he came and he took it out of the right hand of him who sat on the throne.

8Now when he had taken the book, the four living creatures and the twenty-four elders fell down before the Lamb, each one having a harp and golden bowls full of incense, which are the prayers of the saints.

9They sang a new song, saying: "You are worthy to take the book *and to open its seals: for you were killed and bought us for God with your blood, out of every tribe, language, people and nation,*10 *made us kings and priests to our God and we will reign on earth."*

11*I saw and I heard something like a voice of many angels around the throne, the living creatures and the elders; and the number of them was ten thousands of ten thousands and thousands of thousands;* 12*saying with a loud voice, "Worthy is the Lamb who has been killed to receive the power, wealth, wisdom, strength, honor, glory and blessing!"*

13*I heard every created thing which is in heaven, on the earth, under the earth, on the sea and everything in them, saying, "To him who sits on the throne and to the Lamb be the blessing, the honor, the glory and the dominion forever and ever! Amen!"* 14*The four living creatures said, "Amen!" The* 5*elders fell down and worshiped.*

Prophecy:

This segment establishes the authority of the "Lamb" (me, the Christ) to open the seven-sealed book.

---

5 5:14 TR adds "twenty-four"

Parody

This lays a heavy parody on the churches. Notice that not one church, priest, religious or political leader, was worthy to open the book.

This passage has remained a mystery until now because of the guilt-cult spread by the Christian Churches; the few who ventured to try to understand this difficult book assumed that I, the lamb, was worthy because I had sacrificed my life for the sins of mankind. Consequently this book made it past Constantine and the Council of Nicea because it suited the Roman Empires' purpose and also because the Emperor didn't understand a word I was saying.

The Catholic Church tagged along and the offshoots of the Catholic Church—the Protestant Churches—tagged right along with it. Instead of teaching my words, the Protestants took the paradigm of their fathers and just went back to a purer understanding of the WRONG message: a message of "Saved by the Blood of the Lamb, Good versus Evil, Sin and Damnation." Not one of them dared to think outside the box. Consequently, no one but me was worthy to open the seals.

Up to now the prevailing Christian doctrine proclaimed that the Lamb of God died for the sins of man. I did *not* die for your sins; rather I died to show you how to live. I died because of the truth about you, and how to live an abundant life. I died in order to conquer my own ego and to show you by my example the necessity of allowing yourself to ripen and be ready for the true word of God. I died because the churches of the time could not compete with my word. I died because the Christian church could not survive my words, at least not as thrones of power and corruption.

The one thing I DID NOT DIE FOR is to make amends to a psychotic God for sins over which you have no control. "Original Sin" and the creation story *were not* about man sinning; it was about man maturing and taking responsibility for earning the right to be a physical manifestation of God.

Man's leaving "Paradise" was not a *bad* thing, it was a *good* thing. The same as your children leaving home to live a life of their own is a good thing. If anything, I died because that message was and is the last Truth in the Universe that a guilt-cult, fear ridden, corrupted, money-loving church wanted to hear.

Process.

You have lived many lives, yet I lived but once. I accomplished all that I needed to accomplish in my one lifetime, for I came to a complete awakening before I died. I overcame my fear of death and I surrendered to it; I went through it, I experienced it and I finally gave up my spirit. So the interpretations of the rest of the Book of Revelation are going to be much different than you think they are going to be.

Progression

Notice how your society has progressed from the "Breadbasket of Civilization" to instantaneous communication between continents not even known in my time. Why did I let the gentile guilt-cult of Christianity prevail all these years? Well, think about it. When in history has Earth had the communications systems you have now; the educated population or the freedom to read and understand for yourself the words written in the five gospels of Matthew, Mark, Luke, John and Thomas?

Look at the Remnant who maintained the Truth and at what happened to them and their writings before this time! See what I mean? Do you think even now that the good church-going people will accept the true message? Not likely. Yet the Book of Revelation is written specifically about them and for them so that as many as possible will awaken and accept responsibility for their own Godhood in the time that remains.

Throughout history, individual man has sought the Truth about who and what he is and why he came to Earth. Indeed, mass consciousness has sought the same Truth. The elders before the throne lived through numerous lifetimes trying to attain the sixth and seventh Chakra level of spiritual development, and even I, the Christ, have come to you in many forms. However as the individual named Jesus, I had only one birth and one death. I attained all seven Chakras—and more—in that one lifetime.

The teachers who came before me brought forth spiritual conscientiousness and left behind their writings and their teachings (of which I was quite familiar) that helped me to awaken much earlier than anyone else in history. Since I only had one lifetime, my awakening was greatly accelerated. Most men do not reach the level of the sixth Chakra until around age 50 or 60. I attained the sixth Chakra around the age of twelve and the seventh Chakra and beyond by age 20.

I spent my life up to age 20, focusing on learning to live as God in a human body; I then focused on teaching others to do the same. I didn't die to save you from your sins; I died for my own faith, my own beliefs. I died to *my* ego so that *you* could learn to die to yours.

Listen to me! You think you are tied to your body—but you are not. You are the Universal Spirit who has agreed to take on a body—just as I did, and you came to rule (Lion/King) just as I did. But your kingdom is not that of an earthly despot, your kingdom is the universe.

Your job is to rule in cooperation with every other human—and your entire environment. I sacrificed my body to show you what it means to be free from fear. You are here to live life to the fullest, to believe in the impossible (knowing that nothing is impossible to the Universal Spirit) to serve as guardian to your environment, and to create your own joy and bliss in cooperation with all men.

The Christian guilt-cult attracted spiritually blind men and power mongers who represented me as a narrow doorway, to which they had the only key, so *they* could use my authority to rule over you—and they certainly weren't going to give you the key to awaken to your Godhood.

Does the Father love me? Of course! Does he love you? Just as much, for *we* and the Father are one! The Christian church has conditioned you to think that you are hopelessly lost and in need of their intersession: **Utter Nonsense.**

Celebrate, for now I have opened the door and the staircase waits, so follow me! I have told you over and over again that I am the way; that no one comes to the Father except by me. I never said that you had to "worship" me, rather I told you to wake up and read my words! The message is right there in front of you; albeit misrepresented and hidden all these years by the "Church Fathers."

Take responsibility, for you are the savior, not the savee. Your generation, as a team, must accomplish what you came here to do: to prepare a place where God can assume form and enjoy his own creation.

The upcoming seven seals are not about the "wrath" of God. The seven seals are a "warning" about the destruction that the majority of mankind is bringing upon itself, because like the Israelites before you, you prefer to be lead by blind men rather than to take responsibility for your true inheritance.

Chapter 6
Verses 1–2
The First Seal

I saw that the Lamb opened one of the seven seals and I heard one of the four living creatures saying, as with a voice of thunder, "Come and see!" [2]And behold, a white horse and he who sat on it had a bow. A crown was given to him and he came forth conquering and to conquer.

Prophecy

This first seal prophesies that the Jesus teachings will be spread through the world prior to the "End Times."

Parody

The metaphor of the white horse: Truth, the Light of God, riding out with great power and speed, bringing the message of the seal to the world.

Process

I mentioned earlier that I, the Christ, have come to you both before and after the time of Jesus to help spread the truth to many cultures. The God-representation, Jesus, however only came to you once. We see me as Jesus, riding out on a white horse (white equates knowledge and truth; the horse equates power and stamina.) I come forth as Man/God with the crown (authority of the Father) carrying a bow and arrow. (The Bow equates my speaking the truth, and the Arrow equates the truth continuing on beyond my time.) I ride out to all the then known world to spread the Truth. It isn't until the present time, however, with the invention of unparalleled communication, that the Truth finally becomes available to all people in its original text, unsoiled by *religious* interpretation.

Progression

This first seal represents the first action taken in progression towards attaining divine consciousness. Notice that I ride out—I don't sit home and wait for the world to come to me. The First Seal represents the beginning of your redemption (remembrance of who you are) and the opening of the First Chakra level of spiritual awakening.

Who among you, from a small child, has not felt that you were born a stranger in a strange land (that you didn't quite "fit" on earth) and that you came here for a purpose? The seed planted manifests itself as the angst of separation from your real "mother and father," (the Universal Soul) to be transplanted to a new soil where you may or may not flourish.

Innately you *know* you are more than just Jimmy or Jane in an imperfect body, but you don't know what to do about it. Without angst, would you have looked for the truth? Doubtfully! Yet driven by the need to find your *soul* parents, you begin conducting a search. You hire a detective (the church) only to find yourself among the blind leading the blind. You hold my words (Mathew, Mark, Luke and John…and maybe the Gospel of Thomas, if you are lucky) in your hands, yet going from church to church you find yourself being ripped off by Christian Pharisees and money changers.

The pains of separation remain, but deep inside you know you are not evil and you feel guilt that I should have come and gone through the agony of the crucifixion to satisfy a lunatic "God." How could anyone love me or the Father? Little by little you separate yourself from the mythology of your childhood, and then you feel angst at the separation from your family and society.

The Chakra system acts as a gyroscope. As a child the Chakras drive you towards union with your tribe/family. As you grow in knowledge and spirit, the Base or First Chakra of seven, pulls you towards your soul family, yet holds you grounded to Earth by your need for an earthly family and friends.

Can you see that the first Chakra involves battling against the notion of separation: your separation from God; your introduction to your earthly family; your reunification with God; and finally (in the higher Chakras) your unification with the All That Is?

With the dawn of spiritual awakening, you too ride forth on your white horse (spiritual awakening) to search for Truth (the Holy Grail) and end separation. When you finally learn the truth that we are all one, the first Chakra balances itself and you become whole.

In the process of balancing your spiritual/physical energy do you not give up all you have, leave home and birth family to seek the truth? Are you not at that stage my Apostle? "Come follow me," resides in your genes. Why do you think I came to you as Moses, as the Buddha and other Elders, long before I came to you as Jesus? Even from birth are you not stirred to the very base of your being although you still do not know me? "ET, call home" represents the Universal Soul calling its own.

As we move into the plagues later on, I will discuss what happens when you open your first Chakra—the first chapter of the book of life; and how the Father installed within you a gyroscope to help you avoid false teachings in order to build your house (awakening) on a sound foundation.

Verses 3–4
The Second Seal

³When he opened the second seal I heard the second living creature saying, "Come!" ⁴Another came forth, a red horse. To him who sat on it was given power to take peace from the earth and that they should kill one another. There was given to him a great sword.

<u>Prophecy</u>

The second seal appears on the surface to represent God's wrath. In truth it represents a stage in your spiritual development when you first separate from the System and then learn to find your individual peace and cease to need the System's approval.

When you read the Seventh Beatitude, "Blessed are the peacemakers, for they shall be called children of God," I talk about "peace" as opening a place in the fertile soul where seeds of peace may be planted long before they sprout and bear fruit. In order for man's soul to become ripe and fertile however, man has to seek the Truth as spoken by me, Jesus, or by my other incarnations as one of "The Christ's."

The churches, however, made it practically impossible for their members to ever inquire that deeply into their souls. Instead, they taught the opposite to my words such that peace became just a word used for not going to battle with those who believe the same thing as the church taught. If you don't believe me, notice how lightly man goes to war—eagerly even. Notice how the US became incensed at the attack on its World Trade Tower and went to war with first Afghanistan and then Iraq. Did you never question any of this? NO!

Well, the red horseman has ridden fourth, nor was he sent by God; he was sent by the centuries of false teaching by the Christian, and other churches—and by government rulers. He first rode out during the persecutions of my true followers at the start up of the Christian church. Now he rides forth in the Middle East during this, the end times.

It is natural for you to separate from the system in order to obtain spiritual maturity. It is natural for the system to persecute you because you no longer fit in. Your challenge is to establish your own separate peace in the midst of chaos.

<u>Parody</u>

The second seal represents the parody of the Catholic Church, the Protestant Church and clandestine world government/church's riding out (in my name of course) to subdue all who disagree with the" System" and its ways.

The early gentiles wrestled control of the "Christian Church" out of the hands of the Gnostic remnant who held true to my teachings; and persecutions hallmark this era in Christianity. First Rome persecutes the Christians; then Constantine usurps Christianity for his own agenda; then Rome persecutes the Remnant and all non supporters of Roman rule—all in my name of course.

The rider on the red horse represents the powerful and passionate alliance between Church (the rider) and State (the horse). You see a mini-revival of the red horseman in the 2000th millennium as once again Western and Eastern politicians use their dog and pony show of political power while riding on the back of religious zeal and then persecuting areas rich in environmental resources for financial gain. Notice that the US attacked oil rich Iraq, not environmentally poor Haiti to "free" it from a despot.

The process

Let me start out by saying that anyone who truly understood and believed in my words would never go to war. That does not, however mean they would not be warred upon for breaking with "the system."

What happens when you come home one day and say: "Mom and Dad, I've decided to leave the Catholic (Mormon, Bible Baptist, Presbyterian…) Church? I've read Jesus' words for myself and realize that the so-called Christian churches have turned Jesus' words completely upside down. I no longer want religious zeal in my life; rather I seek a sound spiritual foundation built upon the life and teachings of Jesus."

Do they say, "At last son, you see the truth and the truth has set you free?" Highly unlikely! And, depending on which time in history you did this, you most likely would find yourself an outcast, burned at the stake, excommunicated from church and family—or simply excommunicated from your brother.

Why do your family and friends freak out? Think about it. First the Christian church teaches about the loss of your immortal soul…and what parent wants that for his sons and daughters? More deeply buried however lies fear of the unknown. Your proclamation of independence from the tribe threatens their house of sand. Pull out one pebble and soon other pebbles break away until their fortress of separation washes out to sea.

Tribal survival depends upon blind loyalty. Have you noticed that direct confrontation with the "guilt-cult" results in massive outreach to drag you back into the fold? Have you also noticed how much easier it becomes to say: "Mom and Dad, I've noticed a lot of non-believers out there, send me on my way and I'll go bring the truth to those outside the fold?" You gain the same results: your freedom. One approach threatens prominent beliefs, but the other gains support. Say your tribe "liberates" you. Then what? Then you must find peace within yourself independent of the good will of others.

This second period of Christianity bears the scars of bloody persecution. I told you that I did not come to wreak the peace, but to wreak battle against members of the same family. I also told you that as my follower you could expect society to treat you exactly the same way society treated me. Do you think if I appeared today that the world would welcome me? Who do you think would be the anti-Christ? Me, that's who! Can you imagine me flying a bomber over Iraq? Think about that one.

My point: The second seal represents a time of war between you and your brother. Separation and reunification on a higher level comes encoded in the genes of all social beings. The fledglings leave the nest to later reunite in migration. So too, do you separate for a space of time—and then reunite.

You come into this world with a spiritual sense that there is more to the world than can be seen and that you have a special mission. Without that longing, you would never ride out on your quest for the Holy Grail.

You also come with a gene recognizing the tie between you, your brother and the environment. However society writes on the blank slate of your childhood memory by teaching you that you belong to this tribe—and not that one. In the worst of scenarios it also teaches you to separate from yourself and your sexuality. Can you see the roots of separation? As you begin to awaken, the gyroscope in the second Chakra begins to move you in the direction of separation from the System, reunification with your soul and then coming to a separate peace with the System—independent of the good will of others.

The first seal taught you about your dual membership in the Universal soul and humanity. What does that make your brother? Is he not also God/Man? In spite of, or maybe even because of your own persecution by your brother, little by little you cease to "see Christ in your brother," rather you see your brother *is* Christ, *is* your savior.

Savior from what? The Savior from the illusion of separation, that's what! Can your thumb bludgeon your little finger into submission? No, neither can you use force nor fear to successfully "control" your brother, for brothers can not live side by side with brothers in an atmosphere of fear. Your communion (First vial) with your brother can not last for the long term built solely upon charisma or sexual attraction. What happens when your brother steals from you or bombs your buildings? Society sticks him in prison or nukes him into glass—and how well has that worked?

The second seal is all about the process of separating from the System and the war like process the System uses to bring you back into line or destroy you. It's also about establishing your own inner peace so that you remain united with your soul truths, no matter what.

Progression

You came to earth to learn how to build a community of humans who could live and create cooperatively. The second seal (second stage of spiritual "ripeness" to receive my word) involves the process of: 1) Separating from your mother and father, sister and brother in order to begin the process of spiritual maturation. 2) Experiencing the exponential pain of separation. 3) Realizing that you and your brother are one. 4) Sublimating your desire to hold on to your body and your fear of death into overwhelming love and unity with the Universal soul, and 5) Reuniting with your brother on the soul level that allows no separation.

How do you know when you have progressed through these five steps of the second seal?

- You see no fault in your brother. The actions of his ego may seem Satanic, but you are one and the same soul. He is learning and teaching, and your job is to teach and learn from him.

- Retribution no longer exists in your vocabulary.

- Separation and criticism (judgment) no longer is your business! *You* can not balance *his* spiritual energy through fear, force, or rejection since fear increases his separation, yet love reduces it. The only way you can help is by showing him loving kindness, no matter what. That is what I meant by turning the other cheek.

- Your existence is not about you teaching your brother's ego a lesson; it is about helping him to reunite his soul with yours. How much harder is it to be patient and loving with your spouse, child or even your next door neighbor, than with the missions in Africa? Your obnoxious brother remains right in your face forcing you to balance and rebalance your second seal until you cease professing phony love and instead *become* love.

- Kindness towards friends/aggressors becomes second nature. What did you think I was talking about when I said: "love your brother as yourself?" Did you think I meant feed the hungry when politically/financially convenient, but bomb the hell out of them when they get in your face? Sorry, you got the wrong Jesus. Why did I allow Constantine to ride out on his red horse? Because nothing happens until one soul rubs against another. Got it?

Verses 5–11
The Third Seal

⁵*When he opened the third seal, I heard the third living creature saying, "Come and see!" And behold a black horse and he who sat on it had a balance in*

his hand. ⁶I heard a voice in the midst of the four living creatures saying: "A choenix⁶ of wheat for a denarius and three choenix of barley for a denarius! Don't damage the oil and the wine!"

Prophecy

The third seal prophesizes how the Church/State System will attempt to establish power by controlling mankind's ability to obtain the essentials of life.

The black rider represents the pernicious nature of the Christian Church, and the black horse represents the powerful spread of the malignant virus of so-called Christian teachings throughout the then-known world. Rather like viruses spread from computer to computer in the present age. First the virus infects the host and then it mutates, reproduces, and sends itself to every name in the host's computer.

Who held the ability to give or withhold life substance from the people in the 4th period of the church? The Catholic Church that's who! The Catholic Church certainly ran rampant and rode roughshod over the majority of the ancient world at that time. Like the Pharisees and money changers, the church pillaged my temple for their own ends—with a sale of an indulgence here, a duchy there.

In the End Times the ability of man to obtain sustenance will be regulated by the "Mark of the Beast" (codes that allow mankind to access finances needed for sustenance—and what do you call your present day credit cards?)

Parody

What happens when a virus makes you ill? First the body ingests the virus and then the virus ingests the body. The Third Seal represents a parody on first the Catholic Church of the sixth through eighteenth century; then it represents the church/state alliance of the twenty first century. In the early years of the Catholic Church, the most powerful political body in the ancient world (Rome) first ingested the church, and then the mutated Catholic Church ingested Rome— followed by every other political body within reach.

The Catholic Church became very inventive at filling its coffers by offering salvation to the rich and poor alike. So yes, it does in a way pertain to a time in prophecy. However, I told you that Revelation is only partially prophecy since it also contains elements of an overlying allegory. Notice that the symbolism of the infectious worm (Red rider) precedes the spread of infection (Black rider) to all Christianity not protected by a virus program (the Remnant) and this occurs over a long period of time.

---

6 6:6 A choenix is a dry volume measure that is a little more than a litre (a little more than a quart).

Since this seal talks about groceries, let's say the Catholic church of that time—and even now—sold the world "a bill of goods." In fact, in the Third Seal we will talk about the quality of the goods being sold, for wheat and barley are only as good as the life left in them.

Notice the black horseman holds the scales of "justice;" also notice the mention of not fouling the oil and the wine. During the Dark Ages the Catholic Church forbad individuals from reading the bible. In effect they withheld the ingredients necessary to make flour into bread—and the wine to wash it down. For a time the Catholic Church held complete control of the bodies and souls of men and, as Priests of the Inquisition, became judge, jury, torturer and executioner, thus the scales.

Tell me something. During the American crusade on Iraq, who held the keys to awarding huge contracts for repairing the oil fields, subverting the locals and supplying goods to the troops? How were those contracts let out? "A measure of wheat for a penny"…get it? The church/state alliance in your present age is another viral mutation and "those who fail to learn from history…."

Process

What happens now when you go against the teachings of Christianity—fundamentalist Christianity in particular? Can you see the slow invasion of religio-politics into your political System? Can you see the fear and the hatred in the actions of the far right Christian government of the US? Has not religious warfare consumed modern consciousness?

Let's take a look at what I said about all this in the Eighth and Ninth Beatitudes:

"Blessed are they which are persecuted for righteousness' sake: for theirs is the kingdom of heaven."

"Blessed are ye, when men shall revile you and persecute you, and shall say all manner of evil against you falsely for my sake. Rejoice and be exceeding glad for great is your reward in the heavens."

I predict here that once you go against the System, the System shall go against you. I told you to let your light shine. I also told you to be careful of spreading pearls before swine. During this tender first step towards becoming Man/God, tread lightly. Be careful with whom you share your truth for this is not the time to "spread the word"—that will come later in your growth.

Take time now—in meditation—to grow your truth and test it by your actions; keep your silence and lead through example. You do not need to tell your brother you love him; you need to learn to love and respect yourself through a thorough understanding of my words. THEN, ***show by your demeanor,*** the calm centeredness that exists inside of you and the unrelenting love and acceptance you feel towards him. Loving someone is much more difficult than words.

As the Remnant waited through the ages, keeping their counsel, sharing their light; so too must you learn to walk in faith while you wait. Will you be tested? Just try speaking about peace, prayer and forgiveness when a terrorist bombs your capital.

In truth, the System does you a favor by forcing you out of your comfort level and causing you to examine your values as you learn who you truly are and become confident in your abilities to provide for yourself.

Progression

I came so that everyone after me would have access to the Truth about whom and what they are and their mission on earth. Through a slow progression, my word was usurped by the Gentiles, the Roman Government, and the Catholic/Protestant Churches, leading up to the upcoming unveiling of World Government.

Have you ever seen a string of lead pendulums hung by string on a rod? When you pull back the first ball it strikes each succeeding ball until all the balls swing in harmony. Click. Click. Click. Click. Eventually a more powerful force, gravity, causes all the balls to be still. Gravity neither screams nor strikes back; it merely "is." When all about you react with force, let your centeredness be the unseen force that centers your brothers.

So too, World government will take over and try to eliminate my Word one last time; but shall be overcome by the power of Universal Truth, the God Force that pervades the universe.

Verses 7–8
The fourth seal

[7]When he opened the fourth seal, I heard the fourth living creature saying, "Come and see!" [8]And behold, a pale horse and he who sat on it, his name was Death. Hades[7] followed with him. Authority over one fourth of the earth, to kill with the sword, with famine, with death and by the wild animals of the earth was given to him.

---

7 6:8 or, Hell

Prophecy

This seal predicts first the death and demise of the Catholic Church, followed by a brief resurrection of the Christian Church alliance with World Government, followed by the downfall of the latter.

Parody

The pale (spiritually lifeless) Catholic Church rides out with its own death in the saddle. Close behind comes replica Protestant religions preaching the same pale beliefs until they evangelize half the world. "Here," they say: "Come into our tent. It's made of the same fabric (basic beliefs) as the dead one over there; same canvass, better structure." Now the churches martyr each other—all in my name of course.

I'll bet you thought the Pale Horseman represented victory of the mainstream Christian Church over all other religions. That's one of the reasons the Book of Revelation has remained a mystery. Do you believe the Christian Church would admit its mistake or predict its own demise? Protestants might predict the demise of Catholics or other Protestant sects, but their own false teaching? Never!

Yet the fourth seal parodies the death of the "Prominent Man" or Christian Church. *Yeshúa says: The Sovereignty of the Father is like someone who wishes to slay a prominent person. He drew forth his sword in his house,[1] he thrust it into the wall in order to ascertain whether his hand would prevail. Then he slew the prominent person.* (See the Gospel of Thomas.)

Process

Have you noticed your journey gets more difficult and less defined as you move towards higher spiritual awakening? So too for the Remnant during the two thousand years since my death. The hardest lesson thus far for you, my followers, has been learning to keep your head when all around are losing theirs and attacking you.

What happens to anyone who disobeys orders from the powers that be? Can you imagine a whole nation of people who truly kept my word? What a political nightmare. How do you rule a whole nation of people who work cooperatively together to create bounty, who find ways to invent new resources, who refuse to invade other countries, who refuse to fight and who come together in meditation seeking my help when attacked? What would become of the approval rating of a "War President" under those circumstances? Can you see why the Christian church rides a pale horse with Hell following?

Wisdom asks: "How would Love handle this?" Why does God need you to pick up a sword to defend yourself—or Him? You will know you have truly attained mastery over the fourth Chakra when you can release your own agenda and act in a manner that turns the other cheek, giving the thief your cloak when he tries to steal your shirt, and return good for evil. You can not change other people, you can change only yourself. When you learn to hold all you have—even your very life—in an open hand, then I, the Christ, will change other people for you.

How do you expect peace to reign in the Middle East—or any where else—when the Church's that claim to spread the "Word of God" in my name remain centered in the same fear, greed and ego as the people it tries to convert? Where do you see a historic portrayal of me with the Old Testament in one hand and a sword in the other? Want to take over a hostile land? First, Christianize the population: same song, second verse.

Progression

In the beginning, my followers understood their role in the universe and put their faith in God. In modern times, bombs, wealth and power have become your nations' God. Too bad your governments hold my power in such low esteem. Quite a test for individual wisdom, is it not?

As a people, you have progressed from standing on the verge of spiritual enlightenment to worshiping at the altar of a mob-led, spiritually un-awakened world government.

I never told you to lie down and become a doormat for ego-driven political structures and I certainly never told you to make yourself slaves to false teachings. Instead I tell you this: when religious fervor sweeps over the land, realize who and what *you* truly are: God inhabiting a limited human body in order to have a human experience. Be like Gandhi and maintain your center in the face of conflict; neither give in, nor fight back: just be (God.)

Verses 9–11
The Fifth Seal

⁹When he opened the fifth seal, I saw underneath the altar the souls of those who had been killed for the Word of God and for the testimony of the Lamb which they had. ¹⁰They cried with a loud voice, saying, "How long, Master, the holy and true, until you judge and avenge our blood on those who dwell on the earth?"

¹¹A long white robe was given to each of them. They were told that they should rest yet for a while, until their fellow servants and their brothers, who would also be killed even as they were, should complete their course.

Prophecy

This seal predicts a short period during which those who have awakened and those who are awakening will be protected in order to help as many as who desire to know the Truth to be able to find it. The works of the modern day Remnant build upon the works and understanding of all the en-fleshed beings who went before and who actively sought the truth.

If you are reading this work, most likely you are among those who seek the Truth and are included under this seal regardless of how much progress you have made to date on moving from spiritual infancy, to adolescence, to apprentice God, and to knowing and acting upon your true identity.

Parody

This vial parodies the notion of "the living and the dead." The dead lie underneath the altar while the living go about the work of completing their ripening—like tomatoes on a vine. In my language and culture, the living and the dead were one. You were considered a soul who started out in the Eternal Breath of God (Universal Soul), en-fleshed, experienced physical life, and then returned to the Eternal Breath of God.

Process

During this extended period, the church went from ruling the world to splitting up, to bickering among itself and then to essentially dropping dead. Meanwhile, the remnant continued to persevere. These, the Elders, held the light for you through all those difficult and dangerous times. Some passed on their knowledge through secret writings, but far more simply meditated and prepared a place in the mass consciousness for you.

You see, the Universe balances its energies the same as you balance your Chakras. In order to hold a place for you in these end times, beings from all over the Universe have meditated and opened the Mass Wisdom of all previous ages for you.

Progression

Many, who held the Truth wrote about it, taught it to their descendents and yet never lived to see the outcome of the human experiment. Could man learn to live a centered life where he could share his Godhood with his brother and environment? Could God walk the earth in human form for ever and ever? Been tried before! Failed before!

My mistakes lie at the bottom of your oceans hidden by earth changes. Will I be able to use this earth or will I need to remove the workable models of man to another place, Eden, where they can enjoy life as God/Man while I return the earth to "Go" and start over with a new model?

It's not about vengeance, it's about practicality. What do you think the chances are of Israel and the Palestinians living in harmony? What are the chances of Asia, Europe and the United States ceasing to rape the less developed countries? Do you really believe the U.S. builds high tech snooping devices, tracks your records, censors your reading material and cuts down on your human rights to "rescue" you—from what?

Who really holds weapons of mass destruction? Who just bred more terrorists than the world has ever known? Read the history of the Barbarians, understand the forces that formed their power structure, and then ask yourself if the world is headed towards love. I think not!

It is one thing to know the Truth about your beingness and quite another to act upon it. During the complacent, dead days of the Christian church, more souls found liberty to awaken and begin to give voice to their beliefs. During this period, truthful teaching about my Word rose exponentially from off the bottom of the charts to moving up towards the top ten, and Mankind received its last chance…The Sixth Seal.

Verses 12-17
The Sixth Seal

12I saw when he opened the sixth seal, and there was a great earthquake. The sun became black as sackcloth made of hair and the whole moon became as blood. 13The stars of the sky fell to the earth, like a fig tree dropping its unripe figs when it is shaken by a great wind. 14The sky was removed like a scroll when it is rolled up. Every mountain and island was moved out of their places.

15The kings of the earth, the princes, the commanding officers, the rich, the strong and every slave and free person, hid themselves in the caves and in the rocks of the mountains. 16They told the mountains and the rocks, "Fall on us and hide us from the face of him who sits on the throne and from the wrath of the Lamb, 17for the great day of his wrath has come and who is able to stand?"

Prophecy

Beginning in the 1880's and lasting up until the Jews regained Jerusalem in 1967, a general spiritual revival took place. The Christian Church attempted to return to the truth; however, not knowing the meaning of my words, the best they could come up with was self-help seminars and political rallies. Meanwhile the Remnant grew in Wisdom and began reading my words in a larger and larger wave.

It became a race between the sluggish mass consciousness of the self-satisfied and needy, and the mass consciousness of spiritual renewal. Not everyone needed to attain knowledge and respect for his heritage, not even 50%, but simply a smaller critical mass. Had that happened in time, the earth could have populated itself with beings capable of taking responsibility for their own power. Didn't happen though. Oops.

Now begins the period of earth changes and chaos. The prophecy changes from wars to earth-changes as the earth is reinventing itself. It starts with the usual earthquakes, storms, and melting of the poles, leading step by step to the shift of the earth on its axis.

Often interpreted as gloom, doom and wrath, the real message of the Sixth Chakra proclaims that the Remnant must hold a spiritual balance while the Remnant, along with the new children, help many to awaken while there is still time.

Parody

The Sixth Seal definitely serves as a metaphor for the world falling apart. For many—particularly the rich and politically influential—their worlds will indeed fall apart since they built the foundations for the meaning of their lives on the sand of wealth and power.

Process

At the sixth seal, members of the Remnant become the first vice president in charge of the universe as they fully recognize their place as aspects of God walking the earth as Man. They know they can't rule alone, just as every finger on the hand is needed for the hand to act as a hand. They know their own Truth. They speak their own Truth and they follow the lead of the Universal Soul through prayer, meditation and adherence to the Ten Commandments/Attitudes. They take their place among the Elders…and they wait.

Meanwhile, the leaders of the Church/World government federation continue to do more of the only thing they know how to do: destroy, rampage and hate, all in the name of God.

Progression

Those of you reading this work most likely ARE the Remnant. Some of you are writers; some teachers; some health care professionals, etc. Each of you knows who and what you are and your job in the *short* space of years to come. You stand on a mountain top and as a storm approaches, all black, blue and threatening below you on the rolling green hills, you see many shepherds with their flocks. These are the Fifth Chakra workers I have placed among the Remnant, each charged with awakening the flock in his care. You who have reached the Sixth Chakra hear my voice: "Go tell the shepherds to bring their flock's home."

The earth itself begins to undergo strong physical changes as the moon recedes from the earth, gravitational changes occur, changes in the earth's crust cause volcano's to erupt and earthquakes to reshape the face of the planet.

Chapter 7
Versus 1-17:

After this, I saw four angels standing at the four corners of the earth, holding the four winds of the earth, so that no wind would blow on the earth or on the sea, or on any tree. ²I saw another angel ascend from the sunrise, having the seal of the living God.

He cried with a loud voice to the four angels to whom it was given to harm the earth and the sea, ³saying, "Don't harm the earth, neither the sea, nor the trees until we have sealed the bondservants of our God on their foreheads!"

⁴I heard the number of those who were sealed, one hundred forty-four thousand, sealed out of every tribe of the children of Israel:

⁵of the tribe of Judah were sealed twelve thousand,

of the tribe of Reuben twelve thousand,

of the tribe of Gad twelve thousand,

⁶*of the tribe of Asher twelve thousand,*

of the tribe of Naphtali twelve thousand,

of the tribe of Manasseh twelve thousand,

⁷*of the tribe of Simeon twelve thousand,*

of the tribe of Levi twelve thousand,

of the tribe of Issachar twelve thousand,

⁸*of the tribe of Zebulun twelve thousand,*

of the tribe of Joseph twelve thousand,

of the tribe of Benjamin were sealed twelve thousand.

⁹*After these things I looked, and beheld a great multitude, which no man could number, out of every nation and of all tribes, peoples, and languages, standing before the throne and before the Lamb, dressed in white robes, with palm branches in their hands.* ¹⁰*They cried with a loud voice, saying, "Salvation be to our God, who sits on the throne and to the Lamb!"*

¹¹*All the angels were standing around the throne, the elders, and the four living creatures and they fell on their faces before his throne and worshiped God,* ¹²*saying, "Amen! Blessing, glory, wisdom, thanksgiving, honor, power, and might, be to our God forever and ever! Amen."*

¹³*One of the elders answered, saying to me, "These who are arrayed in white robes, who are they and from where did they come?"*¹⁴*I told him, "My lord, you know." He said to me, "These are those who came out of the great tribulation.*

They washed their robes and made them white in the Lamb's blood. [15]Therefore they are before the throne of God, they serve him day and night in his temple.

He who sits on the throne will spread his tabernacle over them. [16]They will never be hungry, neither thirsty any more; neither will the sun beat on them, nor any heat; [17]for the Lamb who is in the midst of the throne shepherds them and leads them to springs of waters of life. And God will wipe away every tear from their eyes."

<u>Prophecy</u>

This prophecy talks about separating the wheat from the chaff, i.e. those life forms who have actively sought spiritual awakening, from those life forms not willing/able to achieve enlightenment.

I've told you already that a Remnant preserved and maintained my teachings through the ages. Some passed the word from father to son, while others, through their own diligence, actively sought out my word and, through prayer and meditation began their solitary trip through the seven Chakras of spiritual understanding.

As the world now stands on the brink of great civil upheavals, leading to separating the chaff from the wheat, those capable of becoming God in human form, identify themselves. They come from the 12 tribes of Israel and from all humanity for everyone is eligible to come with me to Eden. After all, that is why the Universal Soul came into all human forms in the first place…to identify prototypes, who by their own free will, chose to rise above the illusion of separation and live cooperatively, free from fear and ego.

But not everyone chose the spiritual path. Many chose "What you see is what you get" and therefore have lived their whole life without ever clearing even the First Chakra. Nonetheless, the Father, the Universal Soul, has been patient and has awaited the time when communications allowed my words to reach the entire earth. (Understand that many of those who came before me and those who never had access to my words worked it out for themselves through industrious searching, prayer and meditation; they now stand as the elders before the throne awaiting the coming of Eden.)

Some of the Elders, those of you who "awakened" in the 1980–90's, have returned to help awaken (seal) the remainder of humanity. Those of you who are Elders already know who you are. Also walking among you are the "New Children," additional Elders who have come back to assist the last awakening. Because of time restrictions, the new ones came into human form completely awakened and ready to serve.

Process

I told you earlier that many of you are Elders who, in previous lifetimes, achieved the spiritual level of the Fifth through the Seventh Chakra. Your job now is to identify each other and work collaboratively to spread the Truth to all who seek to know who they are.

"I DO NOT MEAN TO GO ABOUT EVANGALIZING!"

The earth has seen quite enough of that—thank you anyway, for earth does NOT need more churches or egotists. Rather it needs gentle individuals who love God above all things and their neighbor as themselves. Speak among yourselves. Help one another to re-member. Write what you know—and teach those who seek you out.

Those who seek truth will identify you by your demeanor and your works. Keep your ego out of it; point them to the Holy Spirit and let the Seven Attributes of God do the work. Simply make my words available to them and answer their questions. If they don't ask, don't volunteer, as they will ask to the extent that they see me in you. Rather work relentlessly on your own spiritual growth, lest your ego sneak in like a thief in the night.

Progression

These verses describe the time when spiritual progression comes to a close. Those who could pass through the stages from spiritual infancy to spiritual maturity have done so. Those who could not are now separated out.

Up to now, "Sealing the Saints" has been interpreted by "good" Christians as setting them aside because they attend church and do everything the Christian Churches demand. Not so! Your time on earth is NOT about belonging to the proper church or doing ritualistic acts, passively waiting to be rescued or actively condemning those who disagree with your doctrine. It's about overcoming the angst of separation, recognizing the mass soul and actively participating in Divine Creation. Those who come with me to Eden will be recognized by their attitude and their actions; not by their religious zeal or sentimental membership in any organization.

Will Church members be among those sealed? As I said: Those who come with me to Eden will be recognized by their attitude and actions, *not* by religious zeal. From groups within the same church one will be taken, while the one standing next to him not taken. For the self-righteous, the war mongers, the judgmental, the discouragers, the spoilers and all who chose not to live in harmony with others—*their pride will be its own reward.* The last shall be first and among the church leaders it will come as a surprise to many as to who comes and who stays.

Are those sealed only Christians? Don't be absurd, I have come in many forms! My truth exists in MANY religions—some of which have brought it forward in time with much more purity than the "Christian" Churches. The Book of Revelation was written by John to the early churches professing to teach in my name. That is why emphasis is placed upon them since I dictated the book to him addressing my followers, just as I dictated this one. As I said, I and the Father know you by your attitude and actions and anyone who truly seeks will indeed find the truth inside himself.

During the great upheavals to come, some of the awakened will die natural deaths and return to the Universal Soul to await the advent of Eden. Others will remain in safe places on the earth to help with enlightening the Remnant, which are still awakening. Of those who are not yet fully awakened, many will be caught in the midst of the tribulation but will come out upon finishing their spiritual journey.

A Short Digression Concerning The Origins of Earth

Before proceeding with the Seventh Seal, I need to set the record straight about the origins and meaning of life, for with the opening of the Seventh Seal— here comes Armageddon. Sounds like I am coming to get you, doesn't it? Well, I am, but not quite in the way you think.

The Father is not a peevish lunatic God who finds it necessary to take revenge, for that is nonsense. I am *you* and *you* are me. Who creates the illusion of earth…*YOU do*, that's who!

I told you that the Book of Revelation is an allegory; now let's talk about Satan for a minute. According to your mythology, I am the Universal Soul sitting up here in the dark getting bored so I created these disembodied beings, Angels, that are separate from me, even though they are a piece of me. One of them becomes crabby and decides to unite a bunch of other disembodied spirits to get rid of me and become the Universal Soul. Then this naughty son decides to depose his daddy king, and…well, who could account for kids in those days!

Apparently I didn't just create angels, I split my personality in half to make things more interesting, for how could I create "evil" unless evil were inside of me in the first place? Anyway, the "good" me acts out of complete love, the "insubordinate" me, Satan, acts out of complete fear (ego.) Father against Son and God against God—Good vs. Evil: the Chaos theory. I must have REALLY been bored…and *I* get piqued with you for acting the same way?

Well, apparently the angel experiment didn't work out, so now I create a limited edition: Man. At least man is earthbound and controllable. I give him free will, but if he doesn't do what I want him to do, I squish him like a bug and once he dies and gets back home, I torture him forever—I'm just that kind of guy, a really loving God. Satan then whispers in Man's ear to make him afraid and evil. In other words, "The Devil made you do it." Meantime: there stands man, a pawn in the spiritual battle between good and evil.

Then I get so mad that I turn my back on man and pout, however I'm still bored, so being a raving lunatic, I pick sides. I separate out one group, the Jews, and play them against Satan's side—everybody else. But what's in it for the Jews? I tell them I'll send them a savior if they play on my team, and they think they are going to get a warrior king. Instead, I take a piece of me, embody him as God/Man and send him to earth in order for the bad guys to torture and kill him.

That makes me happy since man is redeemed by killing off my family and I open the door to heaven once again. Only this time I appoint an out-of-control church to guide the way. Satan takes over the church and it's my entire fault for creating Satan and the church in the first place; therefore Man's unhappy and God's unhappy. Boink! I hit myself on the side of the head for when will I ever learn—bring on the "End Times"—thus Armageddon.

Man fights man and man fights his environment, then the environment fights man and man fights God. Finally I get sick of the whole thing; dump the project, dump Satan, take the good guys with me, torture the opposing team forever, build a new city…and we all live happily ever after. Suuuuure….!

I created Man in my image and likeness; then Man created me in his. "Is there another God up here somewhere?" Ever know how to tell a really good lie?…put just enough elements of truth into it to make the lie believable.

Let me tell you something. Millions upon millions of life-bearing planets exist in the Universe—each in various stages of evolution; and each planet creates its own mythology of creation depending upon the stability of its surface and its ability to maintain life forms long enough for them to evolve into supporting full knowledge of the Universal God-spirit in all things.

Of all the planets, Earth remains the most unstable, tilting on its axis every few billion years to begin life anew. Man's vision therefore remains askew because of your short evolutionary history, plus your short lifespan. Imagine a termite trying to explain how the tree it was living in turned into a house…well, that's Man trying to explain the Universe.

Neither enough time nor space exists in this book for me to fully explain myself to you. Know this however:

- I, God, evolve endlessly.

- Man gets bored. I do not.

- I do not need to be worshiped, loved, or feared, for you and I are one.

- Other planets exist that currently support eternal life.

- My ultimate plan is for earth to support eternal life.

- As part of my creative nature I seeded Earth with fragments from some of the faster evolving planets.

- Your understanding of your spirit nature evolves *with* the life forms, not separate from them. In other words, I/you planted earth the same as you plant tomatoes and cucumbers, then wait for the garden to evolve into higher consciousness.

- From those fragments you evolved as part of—*not separate from*—but part of the original mutating seeds.

- You are not separate from anything in the universe. Separation is an illusion *you* created.

- Man is not more highly evolved than anything else in the universe, *you* simply created/limited yourself in order to experience different functions; in fact some plants hold higher spiritual consciousness than most humans.

- The angel, Satan, ***does not* exist**. However *fear does* exist and your ego has created the equivalent of Satan by convincing you that you are separate from God and your brother. This belief inhibits trust in me and in your brother and your ability to move past the First and Second Chakra.

Here are some additional facts:

- Earth can support eternal life, but not until its guardians (you) evolve fast enough to be able to control the motion of the planets and stars in your lifetime.

- There exist other planets where evolving spirits wait in highly evolved "bodies" to rest and reincarnate in order to help populate the universe with spiritually awakened guardians.

- You originate from them. In other words, you originate from Me, take on life form then either return to Me when you leave your body or accept another intermediate life form on other planets. You have been here before and are now receiving help from higher evolved beings who are still arriving—another evolutionary step for man.

- <u>**Your planet is about to tilt on its axis—speeded up by your own foolishness.**</u>

- Some of you spiritually evolve slower than others.

- Those who have attained the Fifth through the Seventh Chakra will go with me, God/Jesus, to Eden to rest and decide whether to come back to Earth and try again or do something else.

- Those who did not grow spiritually will be turned under to become the loam from which the new seeds grow, sort of like alfalfa.

- Armageddon is not about punishment, it is about "renewal," but you foresee change and re-creation as punishment because of your ego's attachment to the body.

- The story of Armageddon is the story of man and the church's mistakes through the ages.

- Armageddon is also the story of present day happenings and of things to come—a box within a box.

- Armageddon is simply change and renewal. Stop fussing and help your brother awaken.

I tell you about these things not so you will be afraid, but rather that you will center in your spiritual consciousness and recognize the signs, but not to become emotionally attached to the outcome.

Herein resides the big question: "After all the planets become inhabited with spiritually aware beings, which recognize and cooperate with each other to produce harmonies, what will we (together) create next?"

Now let's get on with the changes about to result from natural forces and/or from man's carelessness with his environment.

Chapter 8
Versus 1-6

When he opened the seventh seal, there was silence in heaven for about half an hour. [2]I saw the seven angels who stand before God and seven trumpets were given to them. [3]Another angel came and stood over the altar, having a golden censer. Much incense was given to him, that he should add it to the prayers of all the saints on the golden altar which was before the throne.

[4]The smoke of the incense, with the prayers of the saints, went up before God out of the angel's hand. [5]The angel took the censer and he filled it with the fire of the altar and threw it on the earth. There followed thunders, sounds, lightnings and an earthquake. [6]The seven angels who had the seven trumpets prepared themselves to sound.

<u>Prophecy</u>

The Seventh Seal literally prophesizes earth changes that will occur in end times. Heavenly bodies will impact both the moon and the earth causing the moon to move back and the earth to tilt upon its axis. Gravitational pulls will change, thus greatly causing changes in the tides, in the movement of the tectonic plates and in the volcanic activity that continuously rejuvenates the earth.

Changes will occur in the atmosphere protecting the earth and in the sub atomic particles bombarding earth and sea. All these things have happened before in Earth's history and will happen again. An enlightened mankind could have developed ways to avert the problem; however Man has been far too busy proving himself right and everyone else wrong to put his energies into the required spiritual growth.

<u>Parody</u>

This whole segment of Revelation is told in powerful metaphor.

The seven trumpets occur both simultaneously with the seven seals, and independently as real events in modern time—another example of how the Book of Revelation resembles a box within a box.

My dictation to John for this Chapter starts with the Seven Angels and with the Seven Trumpets standing by to sound their warning for man to awaken and take his place as God/Man and guardian of the earth. However all heaven pauses as one angel comes forth with incense, fills the pots of the elders and lights the censer (a swinging incense holder such as used by the Catholic Church over the years) and the pots before the throne.

The incense represents my intercession with the Father on the behalf of man to allow more time for awakening of the Mass Consciousness. In the hands of the Elders, it also represents the intercession by all who have awakened and who will share with you the experience of living in physical form as God/Man in the Garden of Eden.

Overall Progression of the 7 Trumpets

Now, who I am, for the time has come to talk about that.

I have already hinted that Jesus is not the only Christ, since the term "Christ" refers to an overall title given to my many manifestations. You have known me as the prophet Moses, as Buddha, Jesus, Mohammed…and the list goes on, for together we all serve as The Christ.

The man, Jesus, stood out from all the rest because Jesus lived but one lifetime and attained all seven Chakras in that lifetime. The aspect of God writing this book for you is Jesus, represented in Revelations as the "Lamb" and "King of Kings." That portion of the Spirit of God that existed in the vehicle Jesus is the one who will be with you in Eden. Don't expect me to come in riding on a cloud however, because that "ain't the way it's gonna happen."

I, first as God and then later as God/Man, have held high hopes for Mankind ever since the Universal Soul thought up the idea of existing in a physical form on this limited life support system you know as Earth.

We will talk about how you and I have planned to hook up before going to Eden later in Revelation; but for now, I want you to let go of your romantic illusions of me as a blond haired, blue eyed Nordic prince who walked around with a light separating me from everyone else—with music playing in the background.

My nails were often dirty from helping with the family business. I had scars on my fingers from woodwork—particularly on my right thumb which I nearly sliced off when I turned 13 and was given my first set of tools. I had head lice quite often and therefore frequently wore my hair short until I got rid of the infestation. On some days, after hard work in the hot sun, even I could not stand my smell. So even though this book describes riches and grandeur, I want you to get those giddy pictures out of your head. I may be represented as the "Lamb" of God, but do you know what sheep smell like?

Now back to the incense. In John's vision, the angel lights the censer and casts it to earth causing all sorts of commotion.

Verse 7
The First Trumpet

7 The first sounded and there followed hail and fire, mixed with blood and they were thrown to the earth. One third of the earth was burnt up, one third of the trees were burnt up and all green grass was burnt up.

Prophecy

This prophesizes wars and environmental upheavals.

Parody

Fire and brimstone did symbolically fall from the skies as the Roman Empire spread, took over the Church, and then declined. The trees represent members of the Remnant who held true to my words, but who fell before the advancing armies or were martyred as Constantine took over the church. Do fire and brimstone literally fall from the heavens in your time? Well how about the atomic bomb; how about the Gulf War and what about "Ethnic Cleansings?" How about your present terrorist and anti-terrorists attacks? Can you see the parallel?

"Destruction of the Earth" happens every few billion years as the earth tilts on its axis—and it's on the verge of that happening soon. Only this time, Man is bringing earthly changes on even sooner than scheduled by his own misuse of weapons of war. World War III will not resemble the two preceding wars. This time the lines will not be nearly so clear, nor will the Western Empire's "Weapons of Mass Destruction" prevail against the seeds of mass hatred the West has sown throughout the world in the name of "Peace, God, Survival"...and of course..."global business."

Like the Roman Empire before you, modern day "Good Christian Men" send bullets, missiles, napalm and bombs to kill off the infidels in my name—and in the name of commerce. How many regiments and how much artillery did I commission when the Jews and Romans came for me? I tell you this, better for your country had your leaders' waged war in their own name and in the name of power and greed, than to have once again used my name in vain. Indeed, "The First Trumpet" *has* blown for the first and last time in the modern age—and you have not recognized it.

Process

To a large extent, this segment of Revelation discusses the process of letting go of judgment. Why do bad things happen to good people? Actually they happen to everybody, the good just think they should be exempt. First of all, what makes you judge events as "good or bad?" How can anything be good or bad unless it threatens your comfort in some way? And what is comfort? Does a comatose patient experience comfort or the lack of it? By definition, no; so fear accompanies concerns about bodily health and emotional safety. The point being that it will last as long as you persevere in thinking that security really exists, and that you belong to your body, not your soul.

Fear of death and loss; isn't that why the West attacked Afghanistan and Iraq? Why did I die on the cross? Not to rescue you, but to convince you to let go of your fear of death in order to lead a full life of spiritual peace. The first trumpet sounds for you the moment you feel your survival threatened. It keeps on sounding as you watch your favorite illusions about security—like trees—crash and burn.

The more you hold onto security as your God, the louder the trumpet blows: "It's time to get up, it's time to get up, it's time to get up in the morning." Disaster blows the awakening call at the dawn of your spiritual journey. Either you worship survival and move through life like a scared rabbit, or you worship God above all things and move through life with serenity and peace, taking each obstacle as a new opportunity to recreate your experience.

Verses 8–9

The Second trumpet: ⁸*The second angel sounded and something like a great burning mountain was thrown into the sea. One third of the sea became blood* ⁹*and one third of the living creatures which were in the sea died. One third of the ships were destroyed.*

Prophecy

First Constantine sees his window of opportunity and takes over the early Christian Church, molding it to his image and likings. Then, Rome (the great mountain) declines and loses its grip on the political power of the Church. The Second Trumpet has sounded.

What do we see happening early in *this* Millennium but politicians (with strong support from the Christian Right) waging war; trying to change laws and the U. S. Constitution to bring it into alignment with "Rightist" beliefs? In other words, we see politicians again riding on the tails of "Christianity" to gain and hold power—same song, second verse!

The recent joint venture between Church and State heralds the second and final call to awakening prior to the events about to take place in the remainder of the Book of Revelation—as church and state reveal *themselves* as the "Beast."

Process

To what extent is your world view affected by your religious views? If your President wants to wage war against Iraq because Sadam is a bad man with "Weapons of Mass Destruction," do you automatically fall into line because he represents himself as a Christian and member of your belief system? And just what is that belief system? Is it retribution and putting the killing of others above your belief and trust in God's ability to change hearts?

What happens if/when the West *goes bankrupt* and loses the "War on Terrorism" with a whimper instead of a bang—like the Soviet Union before it died? Do you think "the bad guys won?" If the first trumpet is about causing you to question security and your love of life over your love of God, then the second clarion calls for you to question the motives of people who try to lead you to break the Ten Commandments/Attitudes in the name of Jesus—and holy global money lenders.

Verses 10-11
The Third Trumpet

10The third angel sounded and a great star fell from the sky burning like a torch. It fell on one third of the rivers and on the springs of the waters. 11The name of the star is called "Wormwood." One third of the waters became wormwood. Many people died from the waters because they were made bitter.

<u>Prophecy</u>

As Rome declined, the Catholic Church grew like an Octopus, poisoning the mass consciousness (rivers and waters) with lies and misrepresentations of my words. The decline of the Catholic Church and its replacement by various other spiritually infected "want-to-be's," marks the Third Trumpet. Proclaiming that they had returned to my teachings, the Protestant sects essentially carried on the same message as their forbearers. Instead of cleansing their teachings and returning to my words and actions, the new religions cleansed some of the money laundering and sales of salvation, but continued to poison the mind of man.

In modern times, the Protestant sects enjoy mini-resurgence as the State rides the coattails of the Far Right on a rocket returning to earth, Dr. Strangelove style.

<u>Process</u>

Once you take the time to sit and read my words for yourself, chances are you will make the rounds of the churches seeking one where you can join in brotherhood with fellow members of the remnant. Remember that because someone claims to come in my name does not mean he has your best interest at heart. *Let the Ten Commandments/Attitudes be your guide.*

Verses 12-13
The Fourth Trumpet

12The fourth angel sounded and one third of the sun was struck and one third of the moon, and one third of the stars; so that one third of them would be darkened and the day wouldn't shine for one third of it and the night in the same way. 13I saw and I heard an eagle flying in mid heaven, saying with a loud voice,

"Woe! Woe! Woe for those who dwell on the earth because of the other voices of the trumpets of the three angels, who are yet to sound!"

<u>Prophecy</u>

On one hand, the darkening of the sun, moon and stars refers to a brief return to the dark ages of mind control. The picture, however, is not *entirely* a metaphor, for the sun, moon and stars will *indeed* darken for a brief time as a large mass moves between earth and the sun.

<u>Process</u>

From the time the first tribe emerged and set up camp, opposing mass consciousness became a dangerous act. Again and again governments have burned books, taken away civil liberties and intimidated humanity into falling in line. Do not think the future holds any different fate for you now.

In order to enter into World War III, it will become necessary for all sides in the battle for mind control, power and riches, to limit access to knowledge. Can a nation exist where the masses want to go to war but the Remnant will not? It depends upon how great a threat you pose to the religious/political coalition and the benefits to them of having you around.

This much I tell you: a nation that builds its existence upon my words has nothing to fear. Why do you think history now pauses to seal the remnant? It is not so *I* will know who you are; rather it is to empower **you** to remember who **you** are in the turbulent times to come.

Chapter 9
The First Woe
The Fifth Trumpet
Versus 1-12

The fifth angel sounded and I saw a star from the sky which had fallen to the earth. The key to the pit of the abyss was given to him. [2]He opened the pit of the abyss and smoke went up out of the pit, like the smoke from a[8] burning furnace. The sun and the air were darkened because of the smoke from the pit. [3]Then out of the smoke came forth locusts on the earth and power was given to them, as the scorpions of the earth have power.

[4]They were told that they should not hurt the grass of the earth, neither any green thing, neither any tree but only those people who don't have God's seal on their foreheads. [5]They were given power not to kill them, but to torment them for five months. Their torment was like the torment of a scorpion, when it strikes a person. [6]In those days people will seek death and will in no way find it. They will desire to die and death will flee from them.

[7]The shapes of the locusts were like horses prepared for war. On their heads were something like golden crowns and their faces were like people's faces. [8]They had hair like women's hair and their teeth were like those of lions. [9]They had breastplates like breastplates of iron. The sound of their wings was like the sound of chariots or of many horses rushing to war.

[10]They have tails like those of scorpions and stings. In their tails they have power to harm men for five months. [11]They have over them as king, the angel of the abyss. His name in Hebrew is "Abaddon" but in Greek, he has the name "Apollyon." [12]The first woe is past. Behold, there are still two woes coming after this.

Prophecy

Notice that no living thing is touched except the un-awakened man. This prophecy pertains to the first woe, the rite of passage from child to man, from aspirant mystic to mystic. What appears to be bad news, is in actuality predicting a period of "trial by fire" preceding a mass awakening by those who are ripe to receive my Word and walk the mystical path that I walked.

Parody

Notice also the fiery pit of hell and the master of the pit: Abaddon. This whole section parodies the term Abaddon, which prior to corruption by Christianity, referred to the rite of passage used by mystery sects.

---

8 9:2 TR adds "great"

A young man (star falling from heaven) would undergo an ordeal which put the aspirant into an altered state (darkness, visions of unnatural beings, thunder of war horses, and pain of scorpions). Obviously, this could be described as a "hellish" experience, but considered as absolutely necessary in the transformation from novice to fully awakened spiritual being worthy to be in a god-like state.

Process

Can you see where being sent to "Hell" can be compared to entering a rite of passage? You pass from childhood into a state of ripeness for manhood. Then one day the elders come to get you and from that day forth, you can never again reside in the house of your parents. You enter a hellish period of mind changing drugs, danger and terror—and the only way "out" is to "pass through."

Passing from apprentice God to God is like experiencing Abaddon. In normal times, man comes to earth and either enters and passes through his initiation or he comes back and tries again. In the end times, however, there is no coming back. The elders (spiritual forces) descend upon you, take you from your comfortable home and you no longer go where you wish to go, but rather where you are taken.

Christians normally translate this passage as all non Christians being tortured with fear of hell for five months. It's seen as a sort of sadistic punishment for not being "holy," but it is quite the opposite, for this passage predicts a time when all un-awakened men will be given the opportunity to become "whole" and pass into full spiritual maturity. It may not be pleasant, in truth it will be a very dark night of the soul indeed; yet by this period of testing—and only by this period of testing—do you earn your right to stand in the shoes of God.

Progression

Up to now man has been trained, prepared and allowed to wander over to the opening of Abaddon and jump in by his own free will. At the approach of the end times, those who are ready, those whose souls are ripe for maturity, will be thrown into Abaddon for their last opportunity to awaken. The initiates become initiated and the first woe has passed.

The Sixth Trumpet
Verses 13-21

13 The sixth angel sounded. I heard a voice from the horns of the golden altar which is before God, 14 saying to the sixth angel who had one trumpet: "Free the four angels who are bound at the great river Euphrates!"

15 The four angels were freed who had been prepared for that hour and day and month and year, so that they might kill one third of mankind. 16 The number of the armies of the horsemen was two hundred million. I heard the number of them. [17]Thus I saw the horses in the vision and those who sat on them, having breastplates of fiery red, hyacinth blue, and sulfur yellow; and the heads of lions. Out of their mouths proceed fire, smoke, and sulfur.

[18]By these three plagues were one third of mankind killed: by the fire, the smoke, and the sulfur which proceeded out of their mouths, [19]For the power of the horses is in their mouths, and in their tails; for their tails are like serpents, and have heads, and with them they harm.

[20]The rest of mankind, who were not killed with these plagues, didn't repent of the works of their hands, that they wouldn't worship demons, and the idols of gold, and of silver, and of brass, and of stone, and of wood; which can neither see, nor hear, nor walk. [21]They didn't repent of their murders nor of their sorceries,[9] or of their sexual immorality, nor of their thefts.

Prophecy

The sixth trumpet heralds the beginning of World War III—<u>a war which has already begun.</u> This war will not be won by weapons of mass destruction for the *enemy* lies within the hearts of men.

Parody

With the events of 9/11 and the over-reaction by the United States, mankind released the four angels holding back the great river Euphrates (Middle East.) You can imagine John trying to describe tanks, jet fighters, bombers and rockets, yet in his imagery you see the blue afterburners; the sulfur and the sting of their tails, and the devastation of present day.

The churches would like to think that the last part of this passage refers to "the other guy." The US government would like you to think it refers to the terrorists and Sons of Islam. Remember: the Book of Revelation is not about the Moslems, it foretells the rise and fall of the "*Christian*" Church.

The verses: *"[20]The rest of mankind, who were not killed with these plagues, didn't repent of the works of their hands, that they wouldn't worship demons, and the idols of gold, and of silver, and of brass, and of stone, and of wood; which can neither see, nor hear, nor walk. [21]They didn't repent of their murders, nor of their sorceries: of their sexual immorality, nor of their thefts"*—*predict* the hardened heart of the Christian Church/State federation.

---

9   9:21 The word for "sorceries" (pharmakeia) also implies the use of potions, poisons, and drugs

Process

The four winds have been released:

- The Wind from the "East"…launched a "holy war" on 9/11.

- The opportunistic and greedy Wind from the "West"…fell for the bait, birthing new nests of scorpions: scorpions of hatred throughout the world and scorpions of greed and power within its own borders.

- The money lenders from the "North"…fuel the fire of national debt.

- The third world of the "South"…bides its time.

When terrorists or government leaders send you to war, I want you to try picturing me as a suicide bomber or as a fighter pilot—or standing in the turret of a tank leading a war. Had I come to teach war, do you not think I would have led the Jews against the Romans?

Beware of the Beast that comes cloaked in the coalition of the false church of Christ and world power. Also: Beware of the Beast that comes cloaked in the coalition of a holy war and politics—for they are one and the same.

Progression

Up to now man has seen wars, earthquakes and famine. But communications were not such then that my word would spread to the whole world. Now however, all the prophecies have been met with the retaking of Jerusalem by the Jews in 1967. The first woe is in progress and many men are awakening. At the same time, World War III has begun and events are moving irreversibly towards the massive earth changes yet to come, for the chaff is now being separated from the wheat.

Chapter 10
Versus 1-11

I saw a mighty angel coming down out of the sky, clothed with a cloud. A rainbow was on his head. His face was like the sun, and his feet like pillars of fire. ²He had in his hand a little open book. He set his right foot on the sea, and his left on the land. ³He cried with a loud voice, as a lion roars. When he cried, the seven thunders uttered their voices. ⁴When the seven thunders sounded, I was about to write; but I heard a voice from the sky saying, "Seal up the things which the seven thunders said, and don't write them."

⁵The angel who I saw standing on the sea and on the land lifted up his right hand to the sky, ⁶and swore by him who lives forever and ever, who created heaven and the things that are in it, the earth and the things that are in it, and the sea and the things that are in it, that there will no longer be delay, ⁷but in the days of the voice of the seventh angel, when he is about to sound, then the mystery of God is finished, as he declared to his servants, the prophets.

⁸The voice which I heard from heaven, again speaking with me, said, "Go take the book which is open in the hand of the angel who stands on the sea and on the land." ⁹I went to the angel, telling him to give me the little book. He said to me, "Take it, and eat it up. It will make your stomach bitter, but in your mouth it will be as sweet as honey." ¹⁰I took the little book out of the angel's hand, and ate it up. It was as sweet as honey in my mouth. When I had eaten it, my stomach was made bitter. ¹¹They told me, "You must prophesy again over many peoples, nations, languages, and kings."

The mighty angel and the little book

Prophecy

This section of prophecy indicates that John will receive good news and bad news. The good news about the future would please him, but, like the story of Jonah, the fact that he would have to preach unwelcome news about the present lifestyle of the world scared him.

Parody

Notice the rainbow surrounding the head of the Seven Thunders, for here once again I hold forth the promise of calm at the end of the storm. My purpose is not now, nor ever was to destroy mankind out of spite. My purpose was/is to select as many of my fingers (you) as possible to come with my hand to the Garden of Eden, also this section represents the key to deciphering the Book of Revelation.

In John's mouth, the knowledge of my true message sounded as sweet as honey. However, realizing the possible reactions to the words left butterflies in his stomach…the same as with Jonah. After all, how many "Christians" would follow me if they realized what I actually preached? How would the world power structure react to John teaching them that Christianity teaches the complete opposite to my words? Not with open arms I dare say!

On the other hand, how did John feel about finding out there was no punishment for antisocial acts. (The story of hell did not even EXIST in my culture and language.) Or, even at the last moment, many could still read my words and awaken without being spanked for their bad behavior, for God still welcomes the prodigal son…Dang!

No wonder Jonah went outside of Nineveh sat in the sun and prayed to die. He went through all that Whale stuff and ridicule only to have Nineveh repent so that I didn't destroy it after all…what's a prophet to do? Well, what are YOU to do? I provided an escape hatch even at the eleventh hour; that's why John did not dictate this part of the message.

Like Jonah, by this point in the book, John began to look forward to mass destruction, hellfire and brimstone—and the bad guys getting their just comeuppance. Like Jonah he had to sit in the sun and go through his gourd exercise (see the book of Jonah, 4:6) until the bitterness left his stomach.

I, your Universal Soul, am *not* a God of wrath, retribution and exclusion. I am **not** a *God of* love—*I AM LOVE*—and I call my own to me. It is *you* who separates yourself and lives in delusion. This book is not about *my* "Divine Judgment," rather it is a book calling upon *you* to exercise *your* "Divine Judgment." Cease fighting among each other and unite to create a stable planet where you can "play nice" and continue participating in our divine creation.

Process

The process for obtaining peace, abundant life and eternal life involves turning away from the false message of the Christian Churches and actually reforming your own thinking in order to take responsibility for your own spiritual growth.

Progress

John has progressed, passed the warnings and is about to enter into information pertinent to the end times. The Christian church is not going to welcome this message, nor is he going to want to be the one to bring it to them. The message about the true meaning of my words however remains sweet in his mouth.

Chapter 11
Versus 1-2

A reed like a rod was given to me. Someone said, "Rise, and measure God's temple, and the altar, and those who worship in it. ²Leave out the court which is outside of the temple and don't measure it, for it has been given to the nations. They will tread the holy city under foot for forty-two months.

Prophecy

This chapter serves as a grand overview of the rise and fall of the church/state federation. As World government grows on the back of religion and slowly tyrannizes the earth in the guise of the "War on Terrorism," a simultaneous rebirth occurs in man's awakening to the true nature of my teachings. For a while, the federation appears to prevail, however the truth comes out and a spiritual renewal occurs resulting in civil wars and the final overthrow of the federation.

Progression

This chapter serves as a bridge, a progression from prophecy about the downfall of the seven churches, and the beginning of natural earth changes, into the rise and fall of the church/state federation.

Process

This segment restates the process of how the church became corrupt and answers the question: "Why was this false Christianity allowed into the outer court?"

Recap

1. At the dawn of creation, God-consciousness descended upon the earth. I, Jesus, came not to establish a new order, but rather to define the nature of God so that man might come to understand and put into words the purpose of his existence.

2. Remember, I told you that the "Gentiles," (i.e. the Romans) took my teachings and turned them to their own use and understanding, for is it not human nature for one culture to spread its mythology to another? Therefore, the new culture assimilates both new and old, thus giving birth to a new hybrid mythology.

3. The same thing happened with my teachings. Sayings that meant one thing to my Jewish/Essenes Apostles meant something completely different to the new Gentile church. Then under Constantine, an upside down Gentile Christianity prevailed in "the outer courtyard." God as separate from Man and Man as separate from Nature—thus Nature separate from God.

Why was Christianity allowed into the outer courtyard? For three good reasons:

1. Even though the Gentile church twisted the meaning of my words, the Catholic and Protestant sects, copied and printed them pretty much intact and distributed them world-wide; thus bringing them forward to modern times.

2. Even the writings exorcized by Constantine managed to be re-discovered and processed into modern day. As my name and teachings were brought forward in time, each generation had an opportunity to question, awaken and help his brother awaken.

3. Some brotherly love persisted within (in spite of the churches) and provided comfort to those seeking enlightenment. Mostly this love consisted of: "come into my tent and I will love you, otherwise be damned." Fortunately, enough soul level intuition remained to allow some individuals to love freely, regardless of the teachings of the church.

Verses 3–4

Two Witnesses prophesy for a thousand two hundred and threescore days.
3I will give power to my two witnesses, and they will prophesy one thousand two hundred sixty days, clothed in sackcloth." 4These are the two olive trees and the two lamp stands standing before the Lord of the earth.

Notice in the Book of Revelations that throughout the time of the apostate church (1,260 days = 42 months) I also provided two witnesses to keep the Truth alive and vital; neither did I allow the gates of hell (false teachings) prevail against them. Who are these two witnesses? Are they actually two human prophets? No, rather:

1. The first prophet represents a world-wide awakening consciousness that spontaneously arises in the first part of the 21st century. This movement has no particular leader, but many teachers. Instead of being called to follow a dogma and worship at the feet of this church, mankind is encouraged to research and seek out the answers to: "Who am I? Why am I here? What is my relationship with the Universe?" The spread of worldwide communications allows mankind to short circuit the control of the church in order to search the literature and his own heart for the Truth.

2. The second prophet represents a rediscovery/rebirth of my words as written in the original Aramaic and my teachings as represented in the mystic schools of the East.

As the Universal soul becomes more aware of itself, Man becomes more aware of his place in the Universe. Because you are a soul inhabiting a physical body, no amount of pressure from the pagan "guilt-cult" of Roman Christianity could erase my imprint on mass consciousness. And, because the true meaning of my words lay hidden from the Roman church and its' offspring, my words have survived intact.

With the opening of the Sixth Seal, the "beast" comes to destroy both God-consciousness and my words. I'll talk about the meaning of the beast presently. For now, I want you to look about at the increased use of mind-numbing drugs and the increased twisting of my words to support World War III. Look how both East and West revel in war and pat each other on their backs for terrorism and antiterrorism: thus history repeats itself <u>one</u> <u>last</u> <u>time</u>.

In the beginning, the oxymoron "War against terrorism" will be hailed glorious as the beast (government riding upon the false holy image of the Church) grows in prestige and power. Many of the population will be deceived as great miscarriages of justices are carried out by world political leaders who "proclaim" themselves as religious followers of Christ. *This will be particularly true in the United States.* However it will also be true in other regions of the world as puppets of world government proclaim themselves to be followers of the true god.

Beware. Not everyone who professes to come in the name of God can be trusted. It won't be until much later, when the true deeds of the government leaders become exposed, that a general uprising will occur. In the meantime, much of mankind will be lulled to sleep by the promise of "security" while the government removes their civil rights and replaces them with tyranny. Many parallels will occur between Western Government and the rise of Nazi Germany—but the *churches* will help its members to turn a blind eye.

The second woe
Verses 5–14

⁵If anyone desires to harm them, fire proceeds out of their mouth and devours their enemies. If anyone desires to harm them, he must be killed in this way. ⁶These have the power to shut up the sky that it may not rain during the days of their prophecy. They have power over the waters, to turn them into blood, and to strike the earth with every plague, as often as they desire.

⁷When they have finished their testimony, the beast that comes up out of the abyss will make war with them, and overcome them, and kill them. ⁸Their dead bodies will be in the street of the great city, which spiritually is called Sodom, and Egypt, where also their Lord was crucified.

⁹From among the peoples, tribes, languages and nations people will look at their dead bodies for three and a half days, and will not allow their dead bodies to be laid in a tomb. ¹⁰Those who dwell on the earth rejoice over them, and they will be glad. They will give gifts to one another, because these two prophets tormented those who dwell on the earth.

¹¹After the three and a half days, the breath of life from God entered into them, and they stood on their feet. Great fear fell on those who saw them. ¹²I heard a loud voice from heaven saying to them, "Come up here!" They went up into heaven in the cloud, and their enemies saw them. ¹³In that day there was a great earthquake and a tenth of the city fell. Seven thousand people were killed in the earthquake, and the rest were terrified, and gave glory to the God of heaven. ¹⁴The second woe is past. Behold, the third woe comes quickly.

Process

The second woe predicted the small skirmishes (9/11 and the Western invasion causing increased unrest in the Middle East) heralding WW III. Simultaneously, a groundswell of spiritual awakening has begun (the resurrection of the two prophets.) This awakening will not come from the churches, but rather from a grass-roots awakening of various populations throughout the world who, through meditation and my words, come to understand the truth. This opportunity for mankind to research and learn the truth for itself will continue until knowledge becomes available to everyone on the earth to awaken. During this time much dissension will occur in the ranks concerning the tyranny of world government and the churches that support it.

For a time, the church/state federation will prevail. Many righteous Christians will rejoice that "their side" has won the war and vanquished the troublemakers who questioned the ethics of yet more atrocities wreaked in the name of God. But when God calls forth the two prophets (a world wide media investigation of events leading up to and following the "War on Terrorism," and the truth comes out about the motives and actions taken by the church/state federation (the earthquake) governments will topple. Civil wars will claim the lives of many. Once again, the woe is not a punishment, but rather another step in awakening.

The seventh trumpet
Versus 15–19

¹⁵The seventh angel sounded and great voices in heaven followed, saying, "The kingdom of the world has become the Kingdom of our Lord and of his Christ. He will reign forever and ever!"

16 The twenty-four elders, who sit on their thrones before God's throne, fell on their faces and worshiped God, 17 saying: "We give you thanks, Lord God Almighty, the one who is and who was[10]; because you have taken your great power, and reigned.

18 The nations were angry, and your wrath came, as did the time for the dead to be judged and to give your bondservants the prophets, their reward, as well as to the saints and those who fear your name, to the small and the great; and to destroy those who destroy the earth." 19 God's temple that is in heaven was opened and the ark of the Lord's covenant was seen in his temple. Lightnings, sounds, thunders, an earthquake and great hail followed.

Process

The seventh trumpet sounds and I prepare to ride in on a cloud to reward the good guys and punish the bad guys, right? No, **not** right! In fact, two very different events are occurring at the same time as you enter the period of the seventh trumpet.

A portion of Mankind has evolved enough spiritually to finally see through the pseudo-religious coalition of church and state. Masses of the population reject the old world order and begin to prepare a place where the Universal Soul can experience itself in physical form as intended. Unfortunately great earth changes will make it impossible to do that on this planet at this time and the awakened will come with me to the place I have prepared for you: Eden.

As stated, <u>great earth changes are about to occur</u>. Through your own carelessness, man has caused changes in the ice fields at both poles. In addition to that, a large body will pass between the sun and earth causing a wrenching of the gravitational field, thus causing the earth to tilt on its axis.

Let me repeat. All these things are not about Divine judgment and retribution; rather they are about a giant step forward in Divine Consciousness as The All That Is becomes more aware of itself. No souls will be "lost" and no souls will "burn in hell!" Most souls will simply return to the Universal Soul, from which they were never separate in the first place. Other pieces of the Universal Soul will be transplanted into improved physical forms capable of sustaining life in Eden, which you refer to as "Heaven."

---

10 11:17 TR adds "and who is coming"

Chapter 12
A Woman Gives Birth
Verses 1–2

A great sign was seen in heaven: a woman clothed with the sun and the moon under her feet; and on her head a crown of twelve stars. ²She was with child. She cried out in pain, laboring to give birth.

Prophecy

As with the preceding chapter, Chapter 12 serves as an introduction to the process mankind will experience during the final days of spiritual renewal preceding the end times.

Parody

This entire chapter uses metaphor as a technique for explaining the birth of spiritual renewal during the end times.

Process

The process of rebirth involves letting go of childish notions and accepting responsibility for yourself.

Before we start on today's lesson, please turn off the heavenly music, get rid of the halos and let's talk facts. This verse is not about Mother Mary giving birth to the one and only Son of God and having to fight off the Devil. You will never understand Revelation as long as you hold romantic religiosity in your head. I've already told you that YOU are the son of God, the same as *I* am. In fact you and I are one at the level of the Universal Soul. I didn't come to rescue you, I came to provide information to help you wake up and take responsibility for your own destiny.

Parody

The symbolism of the woman travailing in birth clothed with the sun; with the moon under her feet and a crown with twelve stars, has been interpreted as the Mother Mary and the virgin birth of the Messiah to Israel. ***Wrong!***

The woman actually represents the feminine archetype of the creator-god. She comes clothed in the sun (Perfect vision, Perfect light and Perfect truth) with the moon under her feet—which is God-consciousness—God coming to know itself; and of Man coming of age and coming to know his *own* Godhood. Her crown represents authority as the creator of all things.

The twelve stars represent the remnant of mankind who share the feminine aspect of God: creator, caretaker and empowered. The stars also represent

God/Man: the twelve tribes of Israel, the twelve apostles, the twelve Chakras of spiritual growth and the twelve planets that participated in seeding earth.

The nativity of the man-child represents balancing the feminine and the masculine in the painful epiphany of sanity in human mass consciousness.

Versus 3-4

3Another sign was seen in heaven. Behold, a great red dragon, having seven heads and ten horns, and on his heads seven crowns. 4His tail drew one third of the stars of the sky, and threw them to the earth. The dragon stood before the woman who was about to give birth, so that when she gave birth he might devour her child.

Parody

These verses describe a great red dragon having seven heads with ten horns and seven crowns upon his heads. His tail drew the third part of the stars of heaven and did cast them to the earth, and the dragon stood before the woman which was ready to be delivered, as if to devour her child as soon as it was born. Sounds ominous, doesn't it?

However, this is representing "Good" (Mother Mary and Child) versus "Evil" (Satan)—the separation of a "good" God and a naughty tempter. "Just turn all your troubles over to the baby Jesus and he will save you from the boogey man." Rubbish! You ask who Satan is: *"Satan is man's ego-driven mass consciousness."*

Remember you evolved from primitive stuff: lizard eat lizard, dog eat dog. Back then, a good dose of ego went a long way. It helped you to run away from the dinosaurs, to realize you were smarter and to find a way of controlling them. Unfortunately, evolution has gone as far as it can go in terms of human survival.

There was a time, after you developed a brain capable of stepping outside of the "dog eat dog" paradigm, when you could have developed the "feminine" creative side of yourself and switched from competition to collaboration. It just didn't work out in the present human model. The reason? Peace and collaboration require a leap of faith—a trust in your awareness of your relationship to the Universal Soul and each other. Some people (the Remnant) "got it," but most did not.

So who is this dragon with seven heads, ten horns and seven crowns? The dragon is you—mankind—lost in fear, ego, control and separation. The seven heads represent the seven opportunities the church had to cleanse itself, but didn't. (Did I mention the dragon stank?) The seven crowns represent the repressive authority the seven churches have exerted over the minds of men from the time of my coming until the present.

The ten horns represent ten wrong attitudes complacently accepted by the Church in place of the Ten Commandments:

1. You are the Lord thy God—remain separate.

2. Idolize money, power and control above all things.

3. Pretend what you are doing is being done in the name of God. Defile the earth and its inhabitants in God's name. Attend a mainline church, throw around some platitudes and no one will question your authority to break the Ten Commandments of Moses as you order the murder, plunder and rape of whole nations.

4. Compartmentalize church and life. Spend a couple of hours giving lip service to God in Church one day a week. Then, spend no time reading my actual words or spending time with me in prayer and meditation.

5. Neither honor thy father nor thy mother, thy sister or brother. Be absent during the rearing of your children and neglect teaching them the Ten Commandments.

6. Let the TV bring up your offspring. Refuse to fund schools for the young or health programs for the elderly and, above all, get *yours* while the getting is good.

7. Murder anyone who gets in your way. Wage retribution against everyone who hurts you (and everyone within 1,000 miles of them.) It's OK to invade any country at any time provided you can come up with the right excuse. Collateral damage makes genocide work even better and faster, for the sooner you kill off everyone else—and their hopes and dreams—the faster you will become rich, powerful and famous.

8. Have sex with anyone you please as often as you please. Pay not attention to loyalty or partnerships. Shoot down other people's right to form partnerships different from the traditional man/woman, husband/wife, for love and loyalty mean nothing. Only the laws of the church and current culture matter— and even they don't matter much as long as you have a good time. Betrayal just means you weren't smart enough not to get caught.

9. Steal anything you want—just don't get caught. It's OK to take over other countries, use their resources and establish shady contracts that cheat the public: whatever, for it's OK to steal other people's dreams and their lives. He who gets the brass ring…wins. If you can fool other people into thinking you have created grand theft "in the name of God," even better yet!

10. Do anything it takes to put other people down and raise yourself above them. Spying on other people and misinterpreting truth are the ways of the world and is the smart way to get ahead. If you can't find real evidence to take another man down, heck, just make up new "facts." The biggest prize goes to the person who can lie about the biggest number of other people, attack them—and win.

11. Of course you should covet your neighbor's goods! How are you going to develop a plan to steal their wives and goods if you don't covet them beforehand?

Sounds like the seven churches? Sounds like governments throughout history—today included? Who needs Satan when man is quite clever at rationalizing on his own?

Conveniently man has interpreted the dragon as the Church, as Rome and as various wayward rulers. Nope. Know what I call that? A copout! First it is a refusal to take responsibility for yourself, and second, it is arrogance in thinking you are separate from God and your fellow man; that you know better than the Universal Soul how to rule the earth.

Do you really think the West invaded Afghanistan and Iraq because "God" told them to do so? I, the Christ, have told you the exact opposite, but who is it that thought they knew better? See what I mean about God-consciousness being a painful birth?

Verses 5–6

⁵She gave birth to a son, a male child, who is to rule all the nations with a rod of iron; her child was caught up to God and to his throne. ⁶The woman fled into the wilderness where she has a place prepared by God; that there they may nourish her one thousand two hundred sixty days.

Parody

We see here a little double entendre:

1. I, the Christ, was born to teach you the truth, yet the Remnant (woman, the underground church) had to flee into the desert in order to survive. Indeed, Divine Consciousness has had to protect man against the churches built in my name.

2. Balancing the masculine/feminine creative nature of God takes time, faith, trust and practice. Those who wished to live as I lived have had to separate themselves from the world as part of an underground movement of prayer and meditation for over 2,000 years.

I tell you, as long as you walk about singing Christmas Carols and blindly following your church and government leaders (the beast) as you blithely wait for rescue, yours is not the kingdom of sanity, much less the Kingdom of God.

Versus 7–12

7There was war in the sky. Michael and his angels made war on the dragon. The dragon and his angels made war. 8They didn't prevail neither was a place found for him any more in heaven.

9The great dragon was thrown down, the old serpent, he who is called the devil and Satan, the deceiver of the whole world. He was thrown down to the earth, and his angels were thrown down with him.

10I heard a loud voice in heaven, saying, "Now is come the salvation, the power, and the Kingdom of our God, and the authority of his Christ; for the accuser of our brothers has been thrown down, who accuses them before our God day and night. 11They overcame him because of the Lamb's blood, and because of the word of their testimony. They didn't love their life, even to death.

12Therefore rejoice heavens and you who dwell in them. Woe to the earth and to the sea, because the devil has gone down to you, having great wrath knowing that he has but a short time."

<u>Parody</u>

I told you that the Book of Revelation is both prophecy and allegory. Unfortunately, your leaders took the allegory, concretized it and passed it off as being only a prophecy.

Who is Archangel Michael in this section of Revelation? Was there really a war in heaven? Did some guy named Archangel Michael really vanquish a dragon and send him to earth to terrorize you? If you believe that, there is a bridge in Brooklyn that I have for sale…

Who is full of fear? Who invents stories to explain the necessity of "good" fighting "evil?" Not I. Why doesn't anyone ask the core question: "If God invented everything—including the devil—why couldn't He just take care of the mess Himself?" Why would I tell you to turn the other cheek, if in a past life with my Father/God, I had to raise an army and do battle with Satan?

When you are a child, you think like a child, and Man, caught up in his own fear and ego—still thinks like a child. But now you are being called to awaken and follow me. Put away these childish notions of good versus evil, of separation between you, God and your brother—of some source outside yourself being the bogey man.

God did not break into two pieces, one good and one bad! God did not fight against himself! No battle ever took place in heaven! The Archangel Michael in this story does not exist, nor has he ever existed, for the Archangel Michael represents a metaphor. Do you know who cast you out of heaven? The same person who looks at you in the mirror every morning, that's who!

Who is Satan but your own fear and ego! Who is Michael? Your own divine consciousness which calls you home even as we speak.

Versus 13–17

[13]*When the dragon saw that he was thrown down to the earth, he persecuted the woman who gave birth to the male child.* [14]*Two wings of the great eagle were given to the woman, that she might fly into the wilderness to her place, so that she might be nourished for a time, and times and half a time, from the face of the serpent.*

[15]*The serpent spewed water out of his mouth after the woman like a river that he might cause her to be carried away by the stream.* [16]*The earth helped the woman and the earth opened its mouth and swallowed up the river which the dragon spewed out of his mouth.* [17]*The dragon grew angry with the woman, and went away to make war with the rest of her seed, who keep God's commandments and hold Jesus' testimony.*

Parody

In this part of the story, Satan pursues the woman (Remnant) into the desert and sends forth a flood to drown her. Have you ever noticed that people act differently when in a crowd than alone? If you think man is capable of pulling some dirty tricks on his own, just look at what he does as a church or as a nation. And…why do you think man forms into organizations such as churches and nations in the first place—the "Us" and "Them?"

It is the same old tribal thinking, just as the cavemen or a pack of wolves. When seen through the eyes of mass consciousness, look at what churches and nations have done to the rest of mankind in order to maintain an illusion of control and security. You bet "Satan" (the mass fear consciousness) pursued the Remnant!

Without Satan man must take responsibility for his own actions. What happens to you if you refuse to play games with gangsters—"Them?" What happens to you if you refuse to join those who pursue and punish gangsters—"Us?" When you ignore the illusion of what is going on outside; when you return love for hate and when you work on what is going on inside—who looks insane to the rest of the world?

Without Satan do you need God? Who/what is God without the existence of an opposite? What is the benefit to you of seeing existence as a struggle between good and evil? Answer the last question and you answer the first two.

Progression

This chapter maps out a metaphor for the progression from spiritual childhood to spiritual maturity. When you were a child you thought as a child and boogey men hid in your closet (another metaphor) but now you are an adult and must think as one.

I, the Christ, am the *ultimate* pacifist and, "He who tries to save his life will lose it." Why? Because I know that no separation exists between man and man, or man and God. What frightens you, are you afraid you might lose something, someone or even your own body? The physical objects around you are just an illusion, an opportunity for God to experience his own consciousness through the appearance of separation. If you lose your body you lose nothing. However, if you lose contact with your soul, then you lose everything in life and your life becomes meaningless.

Chapter 13
Versus 1–10

Then I stood on the sand of the sea. I saw a beast coming up out of the sea having ten horns and seven heads. On his horns were ten crowns and on his heads, blasphemous names.

2The beast which I saw was like a leopard, his feet were like those of a bear and his mouth like the mouth of a lion. The dragon gave him his power, his throne and great authority. 3One of his heads looked like it had been wounded fatally. His fatal wound was healed and the whole earth marveled at the beast. 4They worshiped the dragon because he gave his authority to the beast and they worshiped the beast saying, "Who is like the beast, which is able to make war with him?"

5A mouth speaking great things and blasphemy was given to him. Authority to make war for forty-two months was given to him. 6He opened his mouth for blasphemy against God; to blaspheme his name, his dwelling and those who dwell in heaven.

7It was given to him to make war with the saints and to overcome them. Authority over every tribe, people, language and nation was given to him. 8All who dwell on the earth will worship him, everyone whose name has not been written from the foundation of the world in the book of life of the Lamb who has been killed. 9If anyone has an ear let him hear. 10If anyone has captivity, he will go into captivity. If anyone is with the sword, he must be killed. Here is the endurance and the faith of the saints.

<u>Prophecy</u>

Here begins the prophecy about the nature of the upcoming manifestation of the church/world government federation. The first "Beast" represents the Romanized Christian Church.

<u>Parody</u>

The two beasts have long been misunderstood, yet the answer lies right in front of your nose. Let's talk about the Beast of the Sea. Notice how he resembles Satan: seven heads and ten horns. Only this beast wears ten crowns on his ten horns (as opposed to wearing them on his heads) and his seven heads bear the name "blasphemy." He is like a leopard, with the feet of a bear, the mouth of a lion, and Satan gave him his power.

I already explained Satan as man's own fear-driven ego, that part of man that proclaims: I AM THE LORD MY GOD, I SHALT NOT HAVE OTHER GODS BEFORE ME. Satan arises from man's mistaken identity with the body and rejection of his heritage as the son of God (the Prodigal Son.) In his fear and blindness, man isolates himself from both God and mankind. Worse yet, he adopts the ten attitudes of Satan and tries to rule both God and his brother.

Yet man is God having a human experience and something strange happens when he denies his connection to the Universal Soul: he experiences the unbearable angst of separation, guilt and fear of retribution. What to do…for Man can live neither with himself nor without himself.

The metaphor at the opening of this Chapter:

1. **John sees himself standing on the sands (unstable ground) of the sea—the human mass consciousness of his spiritual origins.**

Although man may hate and fear both God and his brother, he fears the unknown even more. "Better the devil you know than the one you don't know" drives an unrelenting search for identity and the meaning of life. Man develops myths to explain these things: God against Nature; Nature against God; God against Man; and thus many belief systems spring up.

2. **Out of this untenable angst and paranoia comes a monster. (The Christian Church.)**

Ancient tribal wisdom dictates: "Strength lies in numbers," so uneasy coalitions develop among men of similar beliefs.

I come to bring the Truth: that you ARE God having a human experience and that you and your brother ARE one. Let the Ten Commandments/Attitudes given to Moses be your touchstone. Let go of fear, cooperate/collaborate with one another and war no more.

As the apostles bring my word, some seeds fall on fertile soil (those who, like me, understood the symbolism of Judaism and the Essenes.) However most of the seed falls on sand. (The ears of men steeped in mythology of good versus evil.) The Gentiles (mainly Roman) can not accept letting go of fear.

Addicted to and drunk with the Ten Commandments of Satan's making, mankind seizes upon the mythology of my death on the cross to build an extremely powerful guilt cult of Christianity. Instead of a teacher and bringer of the light, the leaders represent me as the sacrificial lamb that saves men from their sins. How convenient for now man can sing "Oh Little Town of Bethlehem" and await Santa Jesus to bring the gift of salvation.

3. **This monster bears seven heads. (The seven ages of the Christian Church.)**

Early on John warned the Churches about the perversion of my word by the Gentiles and of the consequences; yet his warnings fell on deaf ears. Fortunately, John's horrific writing style fit right into the Roman mythology. The upstarts had no clue about the true meaning of neither my words nor of the Book of Revelation. Consequently the book remained unchanged down through the ages

IN SPITE OF the Christian Church. The historical fulfillment of the prophetic nature of Revelation unfolded before their very eyes and they did not see it.

4. **On these heads is written the word "Blasphemy." (Man's attempt to build an earthly organization created in his own image and likeness.)**

Since the early Christian Church reinvented me as they went along, the word "Blasphemy" referred to any teachings counter to the *Church's* teachings. The same held true through the Protestant Reformation since those protesting remained steeped in the paradigm of: "Saved by the Blood of the Lamb."

The church fathers realized early on that the way to control the masses was to keep them away from reading my words for themselves and to indoctrinate the children in church teachings. Throw in fear of hellfire and damnation and Christianity had a headlock on the belief system of the day.

5. **One head (The Catholic Church) bears a mortal wound (The Protestant Reformation) which later heals.**

The Catholic Church received a fatal shot in the head during the Protestant Reformation. Fortunately, the Protestants held on to enough of the Catholic mythology to not raise much of a threat. The Catholic Church turned up the burners of physical and spiritual fear among its remaining followers and managed to make a comeback as an essentially dead religion enlivened in recent years by modern language, charismatic songs and livelier rituals. Like a rotting apple, its corpse rots from the inside out. The main difference, between modern times and the times before the fatal wound, is that now the rot hits the headlines.

6. **The beast also wears ten horns. (The Ten Attitudes of Satan described earlier.)**

Since the Christian Church arose, not from my words but from the ego of man, naturally it bore with it the mark of its author: ego.

By portraying man as naturally sinful, the Church opened the door for the continual rise and fall of man as he struggles against his own fear-based nature. It also created a loophole for itself by depicting me as the sacrificial lamb that died to intercede for them with a Zeus-like revenging god.

Instead of teaching that "Thou shalt use the Ten Commandments of Moses as the way to live in harmony with God, Earth, and your brother," it taught the Ten Commandments of Moses as laws which man continually breaks because of his sinful nature. By teaching "Thou Shalt Not" and then conveniently leaving forgiveness in the hands of the church fathers, the Catholic Church automatically opened the door to the ten horns. If anything, the ten horns added to the Church's death grip on its followers. Cross the church and expect eternal damnation…unless of course you came up with enough money to purchase indulgences and salvation.

The Protestant Churches continued the sin-based belief system, minus the indulgences. However, they still took responsibility off the shoulders of mankind to awaken and take responsibility for its own God/Man heritage. "Saved by the blood of the Lamb" still means: "Come into my tent and find salvation."

The separation between man and God and man and his brother remains. Children are still taught to see me in their brother rather than to know that we are one—and the consequence results in birth of situational ethics: You can do anything you want as long as you can justify your actions as preserving/spreading the "Word of God." Since the churches are not teaching my words, naturally the "Word of God" amounts to the sum of man's mass consciousness, for how else can you explain wars carried out in my name?

7.   **On each of these horns rests a crown. (The authority of Man over God.)**

The Catholic Church took the misrepresentation of my name to new heights during the Crusades when anything and everything was permitted—including murder of dissidents within its own ranks—in my name.

From the beginning, the Christian Church was the Church of Man, not the Church of God. You could break any of the Ten Commandments—as long as you found a way to rephrase what you were doing to justify the survival of the church. Be it the Crusades or the tacit approval of the War on Iraq, each of the ten horns wears the authority of Man *over* God—but in God's name of course.

8.   **He was like a Leopard. (Beast of Prey.)**

The leopard represents a beast of prey—fast, flexible, ruthless; consuming all flesh before it and unable to change its spots. Notice how quickly the Christian church spread, "able" to mutate into a new structure to suit its needs; ruthlessly, consuming governments and nations before it…yet unable to change its basic nature as a beast of prey.

9.   **With the feet of a bear. (Ponderous, Steadfast, Territorial.)**

The feet of a bear represent the Christian Church's ability to steadily conquer and retain control of large areas of the earth.

10. **The mouth of a lion. (Loud, Strong, Commanding.)**

Represents the Christian Church's ability to spread its doctrine and maintain fear in the hearts of all who would go against its teachings.

11. **And Satan gave him Satan's power. (Fear consciousness, ego and the need to control.)**

Christianity began with my Apostles spreading my word. In short order the Gentiles (Rome and other pagan cultures) mingled their fear-based mythologies with my teachings until nothing of me was left. First man attempted to rule God, and then man used the mythology of a vengeful God to rule man.

12. Yet one who leads into captivity shall go into captivity. (First man forms the church in order to control man; then man falls captive to the church.)

Man, acting through ego, tries to join with other men to develop a humanistic mythology of creation and salvation—one that lets him do whatever he wants as long as he can come up with a good enough excuse or can repent his mistakes. In the long run, his creation grows into a monster that in turn holds man captive. Instead of alleviating fear, man creates a guilt cult and a fear machine that rules him.

13. He who kills with the sword will be killed by the sword. Here is the patience and the faith of the saints. (Hints at my true message: "let yourself not be ruled by fear.")

The patience of the Remnant lies in their ability to discern the truth from my words: that only one soul exists, everyone and everything comes from it and shares in its' Godhead. You came to earth to experience God in physical form. No separation exists between God and Man. Man must learn to live in collaboration and cooperation with his brother, develop the *attitudes* of the Ten Commandments of Moses and live by them. He who tries to preserve his human life (ego) shall lose understanding of his soul. He, who tries to preserve contact with his soul, although he may lose his life, will maintain spiritual existence and come with me to Eden. He who lives by the sword (kill or be killed) shall die by the sword.

Verses 11–18

11I saw another beast coming up out of the earth. He had two horns like a lamb and he spoke like a dragon. 12He exercises all the authority of the first beast in his presence. He makes the earth and those who dwell in it to worship the first beast, whose fatal wound was healed. 13He performs great signs, even making fire come down out of the sky to the earth in the sight of people.

14He deceives my own people who dwell on the earth because of the signs he was granted to do in front of the beast; saying to those who dwell on the earth that they should make an image to the beast who had the sword wound and lived. 15It was given to him to give breath to it, to the image of the beast, that the image of the beast should both speak and cause as many as wouldn't worship the image of the beast to be killed.

16He causes all, the small and the great, the rich and the poor, and the free and the slave, to be given marks on their right hands or on their foreheads; 17and that no one would be able to buy or to sell, unless he has that mark, the name of the beast or the number of his name. 18Here is wisdom: He who has understanding let him calculate the number of the beast, for it is the number of a man. His number is six hundred sixty-six.

<u>Prophecy</u>

This segment prophesizes the rise of World Government and its federation with the Christian church.

<u>Parody</u>

To assuage his fear, man first built the church of man riding on the romanticism of my coattails, thus provided man with control over God and soul. The next logical step was for man to form a semi-stable (but easily changed) coalition with other men to gain control over the earth, i.e. street gangs grown up.

The Philosopher Rousseau said: "If there were a people of Gods, they would govern themselves democratically; so perfect a Government is not suited to men.[11]" That is true. If man recognized his Godhood and acted in Christ consciousness, democracy would be perfect. However, man rejected my teachings and installed his "ego" as God in my place, consequently most governments are little more than street gangs grown sophisticated.

In this second half of the chapter:

1. **John sees the second beast coming up out of the earth (the mind of man assuming political control.)**

Living in ignorance, fear and greed, man constantly runs amok of his fellow man. And, to maintain some jot of "safety," he forms governments: the second beast represents world government. Why do you think the Jews asked for a King? Same thing! The weak seek refuge in numbers and look for leadership from those who wish to use them; neighborhoods for street gangs. Nations form more sophisticated organizations called governments. Since these organizations represent the mass consciousness of a fear-driven society, they represent the same characteristics as the Churches with which they lay in bed.

2. **The second beast had two horns (political and economic control.)**

While Churches pretend to be sanctimonious, governments take the gloves off and go for the throat. In more primitive days governments gained control

---

11 Rousseau, Jean Jacques, <u>The Social Contract and other later political writings</u>. Cambridge, 2001 (Book 3. Chapter 4. Paragraph 8)

through weapons of mass destruction and some still go that route. Real power however lies in economic control. As nations evolved from an agrarian economy to an industrial economy to a technological economy, man became more dependent upon the ability to purchase the necessities of life.

War still allows larger nations to prey upon smaller ones. In modern times, however, war is a diversion. As long as man watches war on television, he does not watch the increasing debt of nations or the growing international structure that allows banks to accomplish a bloodless coup. World government exists; man simply does not see it…yet!

3. **…and Spoke like a dragon. (Fear-based power; power derived from Satan, power that transcends nations.)**

What do dragons do? They deceive, they frighten and they consume. In the early days of the Seventh trumpet, the hidden government (banking industry) will deceive men into thinking they should bankrupt their nations in order to wage a holy war against terrorism. Meanwhile, these large financial interests bankroll terrorists, gain financial control over large and small nations alike, and prepare to call in their debt.

4. **…and caused nations to worship the first beast. (Marriage of Church and State.)**

Dragons lie and act through deceit, for what better way to fool the masses than to "Come in the Name of Jesus!" Historically, Rome took over the church; then the church devoured Rome. In the time of the Seventh Trumpet, the banks and the Christian Church will fuse to form a one-world government. After all, the interests of the banks and the interests of the church are quite similar: Power, Greed and Ruthless Control.

5. **The second beast worked wonders and caused fire to come down from heaven. (Possessed of highly evolved technology—particularly weapons of war and invasion of privacy.)**

How can the banks gain financial control over nations? By bankrupting them! First the financial institutions place their own men in power in the industrial countries, men capable of bankrupting their own countries. Then they use the arrogance of the industrial countries to stir hatred and resentment, terrorism and holy wars in the countries with valuable natural resources. (Sound like the war in Iraq?) War weakens and demoralizes the poor and pours gasoline on coals of the arrogance of growing empires.

Empires grow suspicious of terrorists and then of the growing opposition of their own populations and produce "snooping" technology to track down both.

War and technology, working together, increases the grip of empires—and the men who own them.

6. **The second beast deceived mankind and built an image to the first beast. (Used religiosity to deceive the population.)**

Under cover of the religious right, governments begin to change laws, eliminate civil rights and build the impression of carrying on a holy war against terrorism as a distraction; meanwhile eliminating pockets of resistance, (Political prisoners held without redress) and cutting off legal and social channels for grass roots rebellion. Being equal opportunity employers, the financial magnets stir up the religious right of both Christian and non-Christian religions and fan the flames of holy war.

7. **Gave life to the first beast and caused those who failed to worship to be killed. (Revival of right wing Christianity.)**

Using religion as a guise to destroy whole nations—sound familiar? First strike fear into the hearts of man by using a holy war, apparently launched by an opposing belief system; then use the populations own fear-based religion to strike back. On the days after 9/11, who is going to criticize a bible thumping president who wants to turn "the enemy" to glass? At this point the highly emotional, but spiritually dead church becomes a front for waging war, unjust imprisonment, retaliation and loss of jobs for those who publicly disagree. In other words, physical and political death for those who oppose the rising power of world government.

8. **Placed a mark on the right hand (sword hand: political power, ability to self-sustain) or forehead (spirit of independence) of all men. No man can purchase life-sustaining goods without the mark.**

How would you survive today if denied all source of income and/or credit? Without money, paper or plastic, how would you obtain food, clothing and shelter? With your countries destroyed by war or driven into bankruptcy; with your ability to earn a living in the hands of a ruling party or in the hands of a government capable of tracking your every move; what controls your ability to survive? Currency!

Will you recognize world government when it comes? Not necessarily. You will recognize the carrot (the Christian Church and promise of salvation for its followers) and you will recognize the whip (the complete control of government over the people.) The Whip will make itself seen both in terms of political control (snooping devises, political prisoners) and in the correlation between being a "good" citizen and your ability to earn a living income. True political power rests better behind the scenes where it can grow rich, rather than in the limelight where it can be shot.

I tell you these things so you can see for yourself where you stand at this time in prophecy.

Here is wisdom. Let him that has understanding count the number of the beast; for it is the number of a man; and his number is Six hundred and sixty six.

So what is the meaning of 666? Let me tell you this: the reason that no one has cracked the code of Revelations prior to now is simple—no one asked!

Man, caught up in his arrogance and the churches caught up in theirs, kept trying to co-relate prophecy with specific events. Man believes that by just thinking hard enough he can figure everything out—and that is why Truth is given to the simple and uneducated for they let go of their paradigms and…ask.

The number 666 was an easy code for the ancients: 6+6+6 = 18; 1+8 = 9, the symbol of completion or harvest.

Man soon will reach the pinnacle of his evolutionary development, when he will, through the coalition of church and state, attain absolute power over the world. At that point he will put a halt to any new learning that might enable further spiritual development. He will not, however, have attained the ability to control his environment. If anything, he will continue to hasten changes at the poles and at the earths' core that will make earth even more vulnerable when the large body passes between the earth and sun. Atlantis all over again and not much progress this time around.

Those of you who have heeded my words and attained spiritual awakening however, will come with me to Eden—while the earth experiment begins all over again….

Process

The process of forming a world government piggy backed on religion is occurring right before your eyes, but you do not see it. Beware when your government spouts religious concepts in order to invade and wreak havoc on other nations! The war on Iraq is so thinly disguised it would seem that anyone who looks would see. But even more is to come. It will not be until the church/state federation comes back to bite its own population that the fullness of this prophecy will become clear.

Progression

The progression from inane religion and state government to imperialism to dictatorship follows the same old path as in centuries before. The only difference in modern day is technology. In retrospect you will look back and see a remarkable resemblance between the growth of world government and the growth of Nazi Germany. Right now you do not see it because it comes in the guise of self-righteous Christian religion warring agents of self-righteous Eastern Religion. Yet all this has happened so many times before…the peasants become pawns for the greedy kings who seek to become richer.

In modern times, the populations of the world continue to think small and remain parochial in their view of world dominance. Power does not lie in the Eastern religions battling the Western Religions; rather power lays in world chess players knowing how to maneuver the followers of each side into warring with each other.

In your vernacular, "world power isn't rocket science," and the World Bank has been around for quite some time. While the world is distracted by fear, wars and religious rhetoric, nations bankrupt themselves and remove civil rights in the name of defense. Remember: not war but *"finances"* brought down the Berlin wall. In the end times, war and fear will remove your civil rights, but national bankruptcy will bring about the world federation.

Chapter 14
Verses 1–5

I saw, and behold the Lamb standing on Mount Zion and with him a number, one hundred forty-four thousand, having his name and the name of his Father written on their foreheads.

²I heard a sound from heaven like the sound of many waters and like the sound of a great thunder. The sound which I heard was like that of harpists playing on their harps.

³They sing a new song before the throne, and before the four living creatures and the elders. No one could learn the song except the one hundred forty-four thousand: those who had been redeemed out of the earth.

⁴These are those who were not defiled with women for they are virgins. These are those who follow the Lamb wherever he goes. These were redeemed by Jesus from among men, the first fruits to God and to the Lamb.

⁵In their mouth was found no lie, for they are blameless.

<u>Prophecy</u>

As you have noticed by now, Revelations digresses every so often to summarize the lessons thus far. This is another of those digressions, a wrap of things past and a preview of events on the near horizon. Reminiscent of movie previews, Chapter 14 contains "Scenes from Next Week's show."

<u>Parody</u>

Thus far Revelation has set the stage for "The Last Judgment" by warning the Seven Churches; predicting the seals and the trumpets, and the joint venture between the two beasts to control all mankind through the mark of the beast (identifiers such as social security numbers that keep track of people and their earnings.) Mankind at this point, has reached the epitome of its evolution and has been found wanting.

The first vision of this digression shows me (The Lamb) and the 144,000, (all who have awakened to the truth of who they are.) They sing and rejoice that "they were not defiled with women for they are virgins," and have not prostituted themselves to man-made churches. In other words, they have come out from the masses, (as virgins) adhered to their new path of understanding and progressed up through the fifth to seventh Chakras in understanding.

Verses 6–7

⁶I saw an angel flying in mid heaven having eternal "Good News" to proclaim to those who dwell on the earth and to every nation, tribe, language and people.

⁷He said with a loud voice, "Fear the Lord and give him glory; for the hour of his judgment has come. Worship him who made the heaven, the earth, the sea and the springs of waters!"

The first angel announces the imminence of the hour of judgment. The earth stands on the brink of physical renewal as "Time" has run out and those who have awakened are about to be separated from those who have not.

Verse 8

⁸Another, a second angel, followed saying, "Babylon the great has fallen, which has made all the nations to drink of the wine of the wrath of her sexual immorality."

Babylon, the coalition of the two beasts (Church and State) has fallen. This does not mean that the final worldwide church state will be overcome by men. Rather it means that with the earth changes about to happen, man-made government will no longer control the earth. Like civilizations before it, this civilization is about to quicken its own destruction by mistreatment of the environment preceding the tilting of the earth on its axis.

Verses 9–12

⁹Another angel, a third, followed them saying with a great voice, "If anyone worships the beast and his image and receives a mark on his forehead or on his hand, ¹⁰he also will drink of the wine of the wrath of God which is prepared unmixed in the cup of his anger.

He will be tormented with fire and sulfur in the presence of the holy angels and in the presence of the Lamb. ¹¹The smoke of their torment goes up forever and ever. They have no rest day and night, those who worship the beast and his image and whoever receives the mark of his name. ¹²Here is the patience of the saints, those who keep the commandments of God and the faith of Jesus."

This section previews the doom of the Beast Worshipers. Now what are the Beast Worshipers exactly and what is the meaning of their doom?

The Beast Worshipers refers to those humans who remain caught up in the paradigm of separation and who have come to worship money and power. Instead of following the teachings of me, the Christ, they follow the teachings of the man-made church and the corrupt world government that uses the church as a pawn.

The hell fire and damnation of the Beast Worshipers refers to their soulless bodies being left behind as their souls return to the Universal soul and the earth changes consume their bodies.

Remember that John uses this horrific form of prophecy intended to scare mankind into submission. I repeat: I am not some petty despot consumed with revenge; I am *you* at your highest, most loving state, for I *am* the All That Is.

Verse 13

13I heard the voice from heaven saying, "Write: Blessed are the dead who die in the Lord from now on."

Some of you, through your own desire, intention and effort, have come to know who you are and have assumed personal responsibility for living the Ten Attitudes. Your souls and your soul consciousness will come with me to Eden to live as God in physical form. (No, you will not be bringing your present bodies with you. However your consciousness will renew itself in permanent physical form from which you may shift from full spirit to full physical existence at will.)

When I tell you that you will rest from your labors, I do not mean you will sit on a cloud and play a harp. Rather, I tell you that through the God consciousness that you have earned and achieved, you will set correct priorities and realize there was never anything to strive for in the first place.

Verses 14–20

"Yes," says the Spirit, "that they may rest from their labors; for their works follow with them." 14I looked and behold, a white cloud; and on the cloud one sitting like a son of man,12 having on his head a golden crown and in his hand a sharp sickle. 15Another angel came out from the temple, crying with a loud voice to him who sat on the cloud, "Send forth your sickle, and reap; the hour to reap has come for the harvest of the earth is ripe!" 16He who sat on the cloud thrust his sickle on the earth and the earth was reaped.

17Another angel came out from the temple which is in heaven. He also had a sharp sickle. 18Another angel came out from the altar, he who has power over fire, and he called with a great voice to him who had the sharp sickle, saying, "Send forth your sharp sickle and gather the clusters of the vine of the earth, for the earth's grapes are fully ripe!"

19The angel thrust his sickle into the earth; gathered the vintage of the earth and threw it into the great winepress of the wrath of God. 20The winepress was

---

12 14:14 Daniel 7:13

trodden outside of the city and blood came out from the winepress, even to the bridles of the horses, as far as one thousand six hundred stadia.

Process

All this time you have waited for me to come riding in on a White Cloud (God consciousness) to call you home. Well here I come! (Chuckle) How human. Listen, you don't need me to come rescue you. Throughout the ages, you have rescued yourselves through your own diligence and focus on your own Godhood. You are already with me, for you and I are one!

Progression

The description of Armageddon differs from human history to date in that previous ascensions of the soul have occurred at a slow but steady pace; however the renewal of the earth happens in a flash. When the earth tilts, primitive life will remain on the earth and even some human life will remain for a time: thus the meaning of the experience of hell and brimstone.

However, most human souls will ascend simultaneously to be reunited with The All That Is. Those of you, who have learned to live as God and Man on this planet, will then have the option of continuing your spiritual/physical evolution on Eden where there will be no wars or hardship. Those of you, who return to the All That Is, will be free to continue to create and to participate in the evolution of other physical forms on earth or in other places.

Ultimately Earth will evolve into full consciousness of itself. Remember: everything on earth continues to spiritually awaken all the time and Man does not have a lock on holiness (wholeness.) You may be surprised about who and what comes to Eden with you for "We" (you and I) are an equal opportunity employer.

Chapter 15
Visions of the angels of the seven last plagues,
and the bowls of the wrath of God.
Versus 1-8

I saw another great and marvelous sign in the sky: seven angels having the seven last plagues, for in them God's wrath is finished. ²I saw something like a sea of glass mixed with fire and those who overcame the beast, his image and the number of his name, standing on the sea of glass, having harps of God.

³They sang the song of Moses, the servant of God, and the song of the Lamb, saying, "Great and marvelous are your works, Lord God, the Almighty! Righteous and true are your ways you King of nations.⁴Who wouldn't fear you, Lord and glorify your name for you only are holy. All the nations will come and worship before you for your righteous acts have been revealed."

⁵After these things I looked and the temple of the tabernacle of the testimony in heaven was opened. ⁶The seven angels who had the seven plagues came out, clothed with pure bright linen and wearing golden sashes around their breasts.

⁷One of the four living creatures gave to the seven angels seven golden bowls full of the wrath of God, who lives forever and ever. ⁸The temple was filled with smoke from the glory of God and from his power. No one was able to enter into the temple until the seven plagues of the seven angels would be finished.

<u>Prophecy</u>

This very elegant and poetic prophecy predicts the final testing and cleansing of mankind. This is where the chaff is separated from the wheat.

<u>Parody</u>

The sea of glass represents mass unconsciousness, fire represents light and truth. Notice that those who waged victory over the beast, his image, mark and number, were standing **ON** the sea, hearing the harps of God…this represents the Remnant who, having come to full recognition of who and what they were (standing on the sea of glass) has reached full enlightenment. They had not done <u>battle</u> with the church, rather they had:

- Seen through the Church's charade and mockery of God.

- Been able to overcome their fear of the image of the Church power.

- Overcome their fear of the power of the State.

- Recognized the fulfillment of the scriptures and that the time of the Church State is now over.

Process

This segment reflects to progress by which the Remnant remained faithful to my teachings. These are those who have recognized the Ten Commandments of Moses ("…sing the song of Moses,") not as laws, but rather as *"Attitudes"* to guide their pathway to enlightenment; they have read my words in scripture and studied Aramaic traditions in order to understand the times and traditions in which I lived and taught. They have recognized and rejected fear and ego in favor of the greater Wisdom required by living in harmony.

Progression

"Then, one of the living beings that worshiped before the throne of God (the Lion) gave each angel one of the seven vials of plagues to be poured upon the earth." Sounds pretty awesome, doesn't it…NOW we'll all get the hellfire and brimstone and wrath of God too, right? Wrong, for now you will learn how man, through his own ego and foolishness, has brought these plagues upon himself. The progression from spiritual childhood to spiritual maturity is not one of hell and brimstone. Those words/concepts did not even exist in my language/culture.

When you are a babe (spiritual childhood) you need rules and security as well as outside love to protect and nurture your human form. As you mature, all these things (security, rules, outside assurance) are removed so that YOU can learn how to create, control, give love, and rule as God. The plagues are not about punishment; they are about growing up and assuming your rightful place in the ongoing creation story.

Chapter 16
The Seven plagues

Prophecy

Chapter 16 graphically portrays the final events that occur during the end times.

Parody

This entire chapter is one long parody of the growth of the banking industry and it's assumption of world political power in collusion with the false Christian Church. It also parodies man's willingness to defile his own nest—something that even the lower animals know better than to do.

Process

Bowl by bowl and plague by plague; Chapter 16 leads us through the rise and fall of church/state government in the end times. Largely the process follows misdirection of the attention of the populous through staged wars and religious zeal as the money interests and the far right church's limit civil rights and set the stage for a dictatorship. The chapter also outlines the process by which misuse of natural resources by big business and the inability of man to pull together to control cosmic influences, leads to mass earth changes.

Progression

This chapter outlines the ultimate progression away from my words and views, towards fear-based dictatorship.

Verse 1

I heard a loud voice out of the temple, saying to the seven angels, "Go and pour out the seven bowls of the wrath of God on the earth!"

The seven vials/bowls pertain to two phases of plagues brought about by the man made church/state federation of world government (which is already in place but not yet evident.)

Phase 1: As the money brokers seek to expand their power world wide, they both deliberately and inadvertently initiate spiritually and environmentally disastrous "holy wars" between the false churches of the East and West.

Phase 2: The actions of men speed up naturally occurring earth changes leading to a sudden tilting of the earth on its axis.

Verse 2

²The first went and poured out his bowl into the earth and it became a harmful and evil sore on the people who had the mark of the beast and who worshiped his image.

Having gained control over much of the Western World, the money brokers behind the hidden world government turn their attention to the wealth and natural resources of the East; instigating and encouraging flair ups of "holy wars" and localized acts of terrorism. Simultaneously, they increase their "spiritual" influence on the West, putting into place regimes capable of carrying out their agenda of world government.

When the situation ripens, the war brokers encourage and aggravate the extension of localized terrorism into world terrorism. Thus the symbols of the followers of the Beast breaking out in boils (reminiscent of the plagues of Egypt in the time of Moses: the *first* warning and the *first* visible sign of fulfillment of the prophecy of Daniel, Jesus and Revelation—that the end is upon us.)

Verses 3–7

³The second angel poured out his bowl into the sea and it became blood as of a dead man. Every living thing in the sea died.

⁴The third poured out his bowl into the rivers and springs of water and they became blood. ⁵I heard the angel of the waters saying, "You are righteous who are and who were you Holy One, because you have judged these things. ⁶For they poured out the blood of the saints and the prophets and you have given them blood to drink. They deserve this." ⁷I heard the altar saying, "Yes, Lord God the Almighty, true and righteous are your judgments."

Water, as always, represents the mass unconsciousness. Notice that the unconscious assault upon the minds of men occurs in two phases:

1. By awakening world-wide fear and stirring harbingers of World War III (Poisoning of the sea—the 9/11 attack of East on West—and subsequent overreaction) resembled running the flag up the pole to see who would salute. This relatively small, but brutal attack served its purpose for it has bankrupted the United States, fueled mass fear and retribution consciousness and—flushed the semi-hidden Western Alliances into the open. It also commences the takeover of the Eastern wealth and natural resources.

2. Individual fear contributing to the growth of WW III (Poisoning the streams and fountains that pour into the sea.) Remember that I, Jesus, came to tell you the Truth about who and what you are. However, church and state leaders corrupted my teachings to suit their own ego needs. Up until modern

times the church state coalition maintained limited mind and physical control over various regions of the earth. In modern times however, absolute power became attainable. Now absolute power (media control, invasion of civil rights, development of snooping technology) is setting the stage for <u>absolute</u> corruption of the West.

First you will see an open coalition of Western Governments seeking to overthrow Eastern Leaders. This movement will piggyback on the growth of the far right man-made Catholic Church and its daughter, the Protestant churches. This modern day Crusade will serve to distract the Western population from the erosion of their freedom as it instigates new pockets of hatred and resistance in the East.

You would expect the East to retaliate against the visible church/state federation; this would happen IF the *political* West attacked the *political* East. However, the "holy war" nature of WW III instead aligns the non-Christian East against the Christian West. Thus terrorism spreads to its easiest targets, the seemingly "uninvolved" Western nations.

This outbreak of terrorist attacks on seemingly "innocent" nations (fueled by the secret world government) causes intensification of the "Us" and "Them" mentality needed for world takeover of the church/state federation, i.e. "The Beast."

Notice that the takeover begins as self-righteous indignation and counterattack by the West on the East; however, the true players in the overthrow of all Western Governments, along with the takeover of the East, have not as yet made themselves evident.

Verses 8–9

8The fourth poured out his bowl on the sun and it was given to him to scorch men with fire. 9People were scorched with great heat and people blasphemed the name of God who has the power over these plagues. They didn't repent and give him glory.

With the fourth vial, man commits the ultimate insult upon his own planet. Up to this point, the money brokers cared little about pollution and destruction of the ozone layer so long as it did not negatively impact their own nests. To some extent, the secret world government could publicly deny global warming, pollution and the impacts of nuclear weapons. Terrorism however, once initiated in the name of God, is not so controllable.

I told you earlier in this writing that man's carelessness with the environment would set in motion the premature tilting of the earth on its axis. Two major juggernauts have already activated.

1. Erosion of the ozone layer from pollution resulting in global warming, melting at the poles and changes in the mass of the earth.

2. Changes in the heat and polarity of the earth's core from underground nuclear testing resulting in pending changes in the magnetic poles.

As terrorism increases, expect regional attacks on the environment from rogue groups. Some of the terrorism will be sponsored and controlled by the hidden world government; some of it will result from mass fear—and—will be completely out of control. As these things come about, the general population of both the East and West will continue to sleep, steeped in the belief that I am the God of vengeance and that I am on "their" side.

The Remnant of my people, who have agreed to remain on the planet during this period, will observe and recognize the signs but will not partake in the politics, as they work to awaken as many as are ready to receive my word.

Verses 10–11

10The fifth poured out his bowl on the throne of the beast and his kingdom was darkened. They gnawed their tongues because of the pain 11and they blasphemed the God of heaven because of their pains and their sores. They didn't repent of their works.

Again, Revelation remains a book within a book. The symbolism of darkness pertains to the blind adherence of the Christian right to the doctrine of fear, guilt and self-righteous retribution as manipulated by the money brokers. The symbolism also foretells the coming of the asteroid that is about to pass between the earth and sun resulting in the tilting of the earth on its axis.

Verses 12–16

12The sixth poured out his bowl on the great river, the Euphrates. Its water was dried up that the way might be made ready for the kings that come from the sunrise. 13I saw coming out of the mouth of the dragon and out of the mouth of the beast, and out of the mouth of the false prophet, three unclean spirits something like frogs; 14for they are spirits of demons, performing signs; which go forth to the kings of the whole inhabited earth to gather them together for the war of that great day of God, the Almighty.

15"Behold, I come like a thief. Blessed is he who watches and keeps his clothes so that he doesn't walk naked and they see his shame." 16He gathered them together into the place which is called in Hebrew, Megiddo.

Ignoring the earth changes, the growing world government continues its takeover of the East. Armageddon, a real place in the Mid East, represents the site of the last battle for World Control. Notice this is NOT a battle of good verses evil or of Satan versus the Angels of God. It is a battle between the mass fear and ego of the East and the mass fear and ego of the West—Man battling man for World control.

Verses 17–21

17The seventh poured out his bowl into the air. A loud voice came forth out of the temple of heaven from the throne saying, "It is done!"

18There were lightnings, sounds and thunders; and there was a great earthquake, such as was not since there were men on the earth, so great an earthquake, so mighty. 19The great city was divided into three parts and the cities of the nations fell.

Babylon the great was remembered in the sight of God, to give to her the cup of the wine of the fierceness of his wrath. 20Every Island fled away and the mountains were not found. 21Great hailstones, about the weight of a talent, came down out of the sky on people. People blasphemed God because of the plague of the hail for this plague is exceedingly severe.

Soon after the passing of the asteroid, the earth will tilt on its axis, ending this civilization just as it has eliminated advanced civilizations of the past. Accompanying this event expect great upheavals in the earth and a shower of meteorites from the heavens.

The third woe has passed—it is finished.

Chapter 17
Verses 1–18

One of the seven angels who had the seven bowls came and spoke with me, saying, "Come here, I will show you the judgment of the great prostitute who sits on many waters ^{2}with whom the kings of the earth committed sexual immorality; and those who dwell in the earth were made drunken with the wine of her sexual immorality."

^{3}He carried me away in the Spirit into a wilderness. I saw a woman sitting on a scarlet-colored animal full of blasphemous names, having seven heads and ten horns. ^{4}The woman was dressed in purple and scarlet, and decked with gold, precious stones and pearls; having in her hand a golden cup full of abominations and the impurities of the sexual immorality of the earth.

^{5}And on her forehead a name was written, "MYSTERY, BABYLON THE GREAT, THE MOTHER OF THE PROSTITUTES AND OF THE ABOMINATIONS OF THE EARTH." ^{6}I saw the woman drunken with the blood of the saints and with the blood of the martyrs of Jesus. When I saw her, I wondered with great amazement. ^{7}The angel said to me, "Why do you wonder? I will tell you the mystery of the woman and of the beast that carries her, which has the seven heads and the ten horns.

^{8}The beast that you saw was and is not; and is about to come up out of the abyss and to go into destruction. Those who dwell on the earth and whose names have not been written in the book of life from the foundation of the world will marvel when they see that the beast was, and is not, and shall be present.

^{9}Here is the mind that has wisdom: The seven heads are seven mountains, on which the woman sits. ^{10}They are seven kings. Five have fallen, the one is and the other has not yet come. When he comes, he must continue a little while. ^{11}The beast that was, and is not, is himself also an eighth and is of the seven; and he goes to destruction.

^{12}The ten horns that you saw are ten kings who have received no kingdom as yet, but they receive authority as kings with the beast—for one hour. ^{13}These have one mind and they give their power and authority to the beast. ^{14}These will war against the Lamb and the Lamb will overcome them, for he is Lord of lords and King of kings. They also will overcome who are with him, called and chosen and faithful."

^{15}He said to me, "The waters which you saw, where the prostitute sits, are peoples, multitudes, nations, and languages. ^{16}The ten horns which you saw and the beast, these will hate the prostitute and will make her desolate; will make her naked, will eat her flesh and will burn her utterly with fire. ^{17}For God has put in their hearts to do what he has in mind and to be of one mind; and to give their

kingdom to the beast until the words of God should be accomplished. [18]The woman whom you saw is the great city, which reigns over the kings of the earth."

Prophecy

This entire chapter describes the ultimate fall of the false Christian Church as mankind wises up to the church/state federation.

Parody

Although the ultimate downfall of the false Christian Church is told in metaphor, the keys to the metaphor are easy to identify and follow.

Process

And, although John and many of the bible-thumping right-wing Christian sects like to think of the Father coming in wrath to destroy all non-Christian fundamentalists, quite the opposite occurs. The church and state have been in bed with each other for so long that they forget about the power of public opinion. As world government unravels, so too does the power of the church. The Christian Church ultimately becomes responsible for its own undoing.

Progression

Again, this Chapter lays out the progressive undoing of the false Christian Church in vivid detail. The church/state federation has operated in the dark for so long that its own arrogance becomes its ultimate undoing. Having come this far, can any mysteries exist concerning the identity of Babylon, the Great: Mother of Harlots?

Here are the main characteristics of Babylon:

1. Great whore sitting upon many waters.

2. Committed fornication with kings of earth.

3. Made inhabitants of earth drunk with wine of her fornication.

4. Arrayed in purple, decked with gold and precious stones.

5. Golden cup in hand full of abominations and filthiness of her fornication. Name written: MYSTERY, BABYLON THE GREAT, THE MOTHER OF HARLOTS AND ABOMINATIONS OF THE EARTH.

6. Drunken with blood of saints and martyrs of Jesus.

7. Riding upon the scarlet beast who was, and is not; that shall ascend out of the bottomless pit and go into perdition.

From what I have told you thus far, the above should be self-evident. The great whore sitting upon many waters stands for the man-made "Holy Roman

Catholic Church" and its Protestant offspring's that maintain a strangle hold on the deep seated beliefs of the inhabitants of many nations. Throughout the seven stages of Christian Church development, this abomination formed church/state alliances with many rulers, selling its power to the highest bidder; in doing so this so-called Christian church led astray vast populations, many of whom were forbidden the opportunity to read my actual words. In modern times, you may read my actual words, but are too drunk with the promises of ready-made salvation to dare to think for yourself.

The Christian Church sits upon the scarlet beast full of names of blasphemy, with seven heads and ten horns. The seven heads represent the seven ages of the Christian Church during which, wearing the purple cloak of authority and wealthy beyond measure, the Christian Church allied itself with political leaders. These politicians, following the ten anti-commandments, twisted every commandment to the federation's agenda (names of blasphemy.)

The golden cup represents the Christian Church's grip on the Holy Grail—the symbol of man's search for meaning. Instead of offering man the opportunity to study my words and complete his existential reason for existence, the Christian church so twisted my words for its own agenda that its followers came to believe the exact opposite from my original sayings.

The Christian church has indeed earned its name: MYSTERY, BABYLON THE GREAT, and MOTHER OF HARLOTS AND ABOMINATIONS OF THE EARTH. The only way the church could support its mis-interpretation of my words was to proclaim them a "Mystery" and open its own mystery-school.

Like Babylon of old, "Babylon the Great"—the man-made Christian Church—seeks to usurp the power of God. As "Mother of Harlots," the Christian Church has sold itself throughout the ages to the highest bidder. As "Mother of Abominations on the Earth," the church has led—and continues to lead—hellacious crusades against anyone who gets in its way.

Now, as a co-conspirator with major governments, it still supports war, unlawful imprisonment and mass murder of all who oppose the church/state federation. And, who has murdered or supported the murder of more of the Remnant—than this so called *"Christian Church?"* Yes indeed, look upon this present day Christian Church: This Holy Roman Catholic Church and its' Protestant Daughters, and behold them riding upon the scarlet beast of world governments.

Here are the characteristics of the scarlet beast:

1. It was:

2. And is not:

3.   That shall ascend out of the bottomless pit:

4.   And go into perdition.

During the early days of the church, the scarlet beast of Rome ruled most of the then known world. At present, the world government exists only in the background for the time has not quite arrived for the banking interests to show their true face. However, the hidden government is beginning to place its puppets into positions of power: these will appear to be "Good God Fearing Men" in the beginning, but not until the last hour will the puppets' true sponsors become evident.

Through man's own ego-driven fear and drive for control, he hastens the effects of natural elements about to cause the oceans to cover the existing earth masses. Had man accepted my words and worked collaboratively with his brother and with the "All That Is," he could have made peace with the forces of nature. Instead, with the help of the Christian Church, he chose the road to perdition— annihilation!

<u>Let me repeat, everything that I predicted as of this writing, has now occurred with the exception of the world government coming into the open.</u>

None of this was the work of the Eternal Soul; rather it resulted from the ego-needs of man to become his own self-limited human god.

Oh Christianity! You are no better than the other man-made churches you seek to replace. You have prostituted yourself to the politicians and the money-lenders and have formed the perfect symbiotic parasitic marriage. Each preys on and benefits from the other. The State needs the Church for mind-control over the masses and the Church uses the State to enforce its man-made rules—the ten anti-commandments. And, because the Christian church has built itself upon lies and fear, and because it relies on government to enforce its power, it remains barren.

My way is the way of love and free will. Only by letting go of control could the church experience an epiphany: instead it walks the streets with whores.

Man was given the keys to a Rolls Royce, but he has settled for a wheel barrow.

Chapter 18
Verses 1–24

After these things, I saw another angel coming down out of the sky, having great authority. The earth was illuminated with his glory. ²He cried with a mighty voice, saying, "Fallen, fallen is Babylon the great and she has become a habitation of demons, a prison of every unclean spirit and a prison of every unclean and hateful bird!

³For all the nations have drunk of the wine of the wrath of her sexual immorality, the kings of the earth committed sexual immorality with her and the merchants of the earth grew rich from the abundance of her luxury."

⁴I heard another voice from heaven, saying, "Come out of her my people, that you have no participation in her sins and that you don't receive of her plagues ⁵for her sins have reached to the sky and God has remembered her iniquities.

⁶Return to her just as she returned, and repay her double as she did and according to her works. In the cup which she mixed, mix to her double. ⁷However much she glorified herself and grew wanton, so much give her of torment and mourning; for she says in her heart, 'I sit a Queen as I am no widow and will in no way see mourning.'

⁸Therefore in one day her plagues will come: death, mourning and famine, and she will be utterly burned with fire for the Lord God who has judged her is strong. ⁹The kings of the earth, who committed sexual immorality and lived wantonly with her, will weep and wail over her when they look at the smoke of her burning, ¹⁰standing far away for the fear of her torment, saying, 'Woe, woe, the great city, Babylon, the strong city! For your judgment has come in one hour.'

¹¹The merchants of the earth weep and mourn over her, for no one buys their merchandise any more; ¹²merchandise of gold, silver, precious stones, pearls, fine linen, purple, silk, scarlet, all expensive wood, every vessel of ivory, every vessel made of most precious wood, and of brass, and iron, and marble; ¹³and cinnamon, incense, perfume, frankincense, wine, olive oil, fine flour, wheat, sheep, horses, chariots, and people's bodies and souls.

¹⁴The fruits which your soul lusted after have been lost to you and all things that were dainty and sumptuous have perished from you and you will find them no more at all. ¹⁵The merchants of these things, who were made rich by her, will stand far away for the fear of her torment, weeping and mourning; ¹⁶saying, 'Woe, woe, the great city, she who was dressed in fine linen, purple, and scarlet, and decked with gold and precious stones and pearls! ¹⁷For in an hour such great riches are made desolate.'

Every shipmaster and everyone who sails anywhere, mariners and as many as gain their living by sea, stood far away ¹⁸and cried out as they looked at the smoke of her burning, saying, 'What is like the great city?' [19]They cast dust on their heads and cried, weeping and mourning, saying, 'Woe, woe, the great city, in which all who had their ships in the sea were made rich by reason of her great wealth for in one hour is she made desolate.'

[20]"Rejoice over her, O heaven, you saints, apostles and prophets; for God has judged your judgment on her." [21]A mighty angel took up a stone like a great mill-stone and cast it into the sea, saying, "Thus with violence will Babylon, the great city, be thrown down and will be found no more at all.

[22]The voice of harpists, minstrels, flute players and trumpeters will be heard no more at all in you. No craftsman of whatever craft, will be found any more at all in you. The sound of a mill will be heard no more at all in you. [23]The light of a lamp will shine no more at all in you. The voice of the bridegroom and of the bride will be heard no more at all in you; your merchants were the princes of the earth; for with your sorcery all the nations were deceived. [24]In her was found the blood of prophets and of saints—and of all who have been slain on the earth."

<u>Prophecy</u>

Chapter 18 describes the aftermath of the fall of the church/state federation.

<u>Parody</u>

Again, all the main players are portrayed as allegorical characters and having come this far however, the characters are thinly disguised.

<u>Process</u>

This is another of the bridge chapters used to move the story along. The church/state federation has fallen. The Remnants are called out from the masses and are given an opportunity to minister to the remainder of humanity who still seek to awaken.

<u>Progression</u>

The end times have progressed away from the battle for control of the earth by church and state and have entered a final healing ministry that will be provided by the Remnant. For a brief time the Beast of prophecy, the Church State Federation, has reigned and world government shall have existed under the rule of one man. This man was NOT "the" "Antichrist"—for notice the word Antichrist does not appear in Revelation. Rather he was a pawn, a dupe, placed there by the federation of banks, merchants and the mob of organized crime. Like those before him, he spouted religious platitudes to lull the sleeping masses into an even deeper sleep.

Oh Man, how you love your religions; how easily you cede your conscience to their comforting word. I, Jesus, leave you for but a moment to prepare a place for you and return to find you asleep. You fight to the death to protect your comfort, yet will not spend one hour with my Word to learn the truth.

In these last moments you look through watery eyes trying to spot the false prophets of the end times. Yet right before your eyes your elected leaders fulfill that role and you do not recognize them. They lead you to break every Commandment of Moses, yet you bless them and elevate them as they commit fornication with the merchants of the world.

You think yourself righteous because you belong to this or that Christian sect and let your elders teach you situational ethics. Your church groups perform feel-good acts of "Christian kindness" intended to recruit new members. Like foolish children, you cling to the pap of tribal wisdom, doing as you are told and sleeping in the comfort of numbers. You kill those, even as the Son of God, who bear the Truth; yet praise and rewards you heap on the political puppets groomed to lead you astray.

Oh modern day Scribes and Pharisees, you too turn your Father's house into a den of thieves and in these last moments I call to you!

Oh Roman Catholic Church and your Protestant spawn Babylon the Great— your tents have become the habitation of devils and of every foul spirit; a cage of every unclean and hateful birds. All nations have drunk of the wine of the wrath of your fornication; the kings and presidents of the earth commit fornication with you and the merchants of the earth are made rich through the abundance of your delicacies.

While time still exists, come out from the churches. Hear my Word as it is written in the gospels.

Awaken! Awaken and throw off your "spiritual" rulers. Have no master other than "The All That Is." Put aside your egos and recognize the truth of whom and what you are. Leave your ego-life and follow the words that I, Jesus, provided you so that you might live life more abundantly. Turn fear into love; live the Ten Commandments of Moses and keep them in your heart. Obey none but the Father.

A church by any other name remains a church. Look how the Christian church has glorified "herself" and lived deliciously. She says: "Behold the queen with no master, I rule as I see fit." Yet, in the space of one day, will the so called "Christian" church be laid low through its own deceit.

Look upon the rotten and burning remains of the Catholic Church; view the bloated, stinking bodies of the Christian Fundamentalist sects as they follow the Church of Rome into the fornication beds of the politicians.

Look upon WW III and the glutinous eyes of the world merchants as they ride upon the coattails of the Christian Church to World government. All too soon, what appeared to be a good thing will turn sour as the true nature of the Church becomes evident to all!

The merchants and bankers shall weep and mourn over man's release from the tyranny of religion—for no man will buy her merchandise any more. No merchandise of gold and silver, of precious stones or pearls; neither fine linens of purple, silk or scarlet; precious woods and all manner of vessels of ivory; nor of brass, iron or marble. No more will the churches of the West and the churches of the East wield power over the minds of men. In one hour will the power of the church state come to naught—but the *first* to fall will be the church.

Your churches do not understand the Book of Revelation, which is why it has survived into modern time. The Christian churches interpret Revelation as God's divine judgment against all who do not enter the tent of *their* particular religio-political belief system. Yet this I tell you: in the last moments it will not be MY supernatural judgment, but rather the good judgment of an awakening mankind that shall condemn the man-made church of Christ and cast it like a millstone into the sea.

There resides among you a portion of the Remnant who agreed to return to earth at these end times to help the sleeping to awaken. It is not a matter of being "saved by the blood of the lamb," rather it is a matter of offering as many as possible the experience of fully experiencing God living in human form. Those who awaken will come to Eden to live with me as God in physical form. Those who do not will return to the Universal Soul. Neither heaven nor hell exists, but my Word prevails.

Chapter 19
A Digression

My beloved Remnant, now I speak to you. Revelation is my book and is about you whom I called to listen to my words. I am not the only one who has come from the Father to speak to the populations of the World, for many have come before and after. Their words too have been ignored; their teachings corrupted by ego and their followers led astray by fear, greed and the search for control.

Among the Jews, the Christians, the Moslems—all the myriad religions of the World, exists a Remnant who have heard and followed the common Truth in the teachings of the Masters. Yet mass populations, lost in the hypnotism of religion and led by power mongers, continue to prostitute the truth. *Know this Christianity: you are no better than the terrorists, since before God, you are one and the same.*

I came to call my people forth from the world; My message being: "love God above all earthly delicacies, above all beings, above physical life itself and "love your brother as yourself"—***FOR YOU ARE ONE AND THE SAME!***

Only by separating yourself from the illusion of the world while living in it could you realize your true potential as God/Man. Many choose to follow me and their spirits shall inhabit new bodies and be strengthened during the one thousand years of renewal to come. They shall see clearly who and what they are and shall possess no ego.

This is not about a fight between good and evil or about retribution. It is about *your* soul participating in the development of a perfect physical vehicle in which to experience *your* material creations.

At the end of the one thousand years, the new physical models shall have their full creativity restored to them in a new "Eden"—a place where no hatred or fear exists. Those physical forms that fall back into the trap of ego will then be weeded out, the same as a dysfunctional car would be replaced by a more efficient model. The universal soul will abandon those dysfunctional vehicles and return the soul to itself—and the bodies will dissolve into the earth. I am telling you these things at this time so that you may see and hear the truth and will withdraw from the victim mentality of your race.

Versus 1–6

After these things I heard something like a loud voice of a great multitude in heaven, saying, "Hallelujah! Salvation, power, and glory belong to our God: ²for true and righteous are his judgments. For he has judged the great prostitute who corrupted the earth with her sexual immorality and he has avenged the blood of his servants at her hand."

³A second said, "Hallelujah! Her smoke goes up forever and ever." ⁴The twenty-four elders and the four living creatures fell down and worshiped God who sits on the throne, saying, "Amen! Hallelujah!"⁵A voice came forth from the throne, saying, "Give praise to our God, all you his servants, you who fear him, the small and the great!

"⁶I heard something like the voice of a great multitude, like the voice of many waters and like the voice of mighty thunders, saying, "Hallelujah! For the Lord our God, the Almighty, reigns!

Prophecy

Revelation now moves from what was at the end times to what will be in eternity. The wheat becomes separated from the chaff and the chaff is burned and made into compost for the next generation of wheat.

Parody

The allegory turns away from the evil wrong-doers and begins to focus on rejoicing in the "Kingdom of heaven."

Process

The process of reclamation and re-seeding of creation begins with unification of the souls of the living and dead—which of course are all one soul to begin with. The physical earthly experience has completed and some physical forms lend themselves to spiritual growth and maturity more than others. The ripened or better prepared physical forms are evaluated for further opportunities to mature in Eden.

Progression

The progression turns from physical progression to spiritual growth and evolution in preparation for further experiments in producing physical bodies capable of maintaining a balanced existence between the material and spiritual dimensions.

By now you see that man mistakenly awaits a great reckoning that will never come since you and your brother are one at the soul level. Instead of thousands of souls, there exists only one and collectively *you* are that one, the All That Is—or at least part of it—along with everything else that exists in the Universe. Neither heaven nor hell exists and neither good nor evil exists: rather only "love and fear." I came to teach love, but the majority of the human race has clung to fear.

"Fear" formed a church in my name and has mislead the majority of the population for generations; creating illusions and tricking church followers into breaking every one of the Ten Commandments of Moses to suit the illusion of the moment…even murdering those who tried to bring forth the Truth I had taught.

Yes, the whole man-made illusion of the Church of Christ is about to fall. Do not sit about in your holy garments singing self-righteous hymns while carrying on your televised ministries lest you be among those to fall.

No joy exists in disposing of an airplane that fails to fly and this alleluia is not about the Universal Soul judging itself and finding it deficient; rather it is about the Universal Soul analyzing physical vehicles and finding some not suited to its needs.

The first Alleluia represents dispensing with the man-made Church of Christ—and other man-made religions will experience similar fates at the same time.

Verses 7–10

7Let us rejoice and be exceedingly glad, and let us give the glory to him. For the marriage of the Lamb has come and his wife has made herself ready." 8It was given to her that she would array herself in bright, pure, fine linen: for the fine linen is the righteous acts of the saints.9He said to me, "Write: 'Blessed are those who are invited to the marriage supper of the Lamb.'" He said to me, "These are true words of God."

10I fell down before his feet to worship him. He said to me, "Look! Don't do it! I am a fellow bondservant with you and with your brothers who hold the testimony of Jesus. Worship God, for the testimony of Jesus is the Spirit of Prophecy."

The second Alleluia recognizes the Remnant and calls upon you to recognize who and what you really are: God existing in human form.

Verses 11–16

11I saw the heaven opened and beheld a white horse and he who sat on it is called Faithful and True. In righteousness he judges and makes war. 12His eyes are a flame of fire and on his head are many crowns. He has names written and a name written which no one knows but he himself. 13He is clothed in a garment sprinkled with blood. His name is called "The Word of God."

14The armies which are in heaven followed him on white horses, clothed in white; pure, fine linen. 15Out of his mouth proceeds a sharp, double-edged sword that with it he should strike the nations. He will rule them with an iron rod. He treads the winepress of the fierceness of the wrath of God, the Almighty. 16He has on his garment and on his thigh a name written: "KING OF KINGS, AND LORD OF LORDS."

This represents the coming together of the Remnant as you recognize one another and as you prepare to join me for the one thousand years of purification prior to testing the new physical model you are about to inhabit. At this point you will become fully awakened and knowledgeable of the Word of God.

Verses 17–21

[17] I saw an angel standing in the sun. He cried with a loud voice, saying to all the birds that fly in the sky, "Come! Be gathered together to the great supper of God [18] that you may eat the flesh of kings, the flesh of captains, the flesh of mighty men; the flesh of horses and of those who sit on them and the flesh of all men, both free and slave and small and great."

[19] I saw the beast and the kings of the earth and their armies gathered together to make war against him who sat on the horse and against his army. [20] The beast was taken and with him the false prophet who worked the signs in his sight, with which he deceived those who had received the mark of the beast and those who worshiped his image. These two were thrown alive into the lake of fire that burns with sulfur.

[21] The rest were killed with the sword of him who sat on the horse, the sword which came forth out of his mouth. All the birds were filled with their flesh.

Will the earth be "destroyed?" That rhetorical question accompanies this one: What do you think the chances are of armies dissolving, of Christians putting down their tanks, planes and weapons of mass destruction and trusting in "The All That Is" to bring about peace?

Wormwood, your tenth planet, has already emerged in the sky and The Beast of Earth and Sea have merged, yet you do not see them for what they are yet—for they are YOU.

Come out from your Churches, your Synagogues and all forms of man-made illusions, while time still exists for you to be among the Remnant (those now living and those who went before) who will participate in the thousand year re-creation of the "new" heaven and the "new" earth. The forces of natural re-creation and cleansing are now in motion—above, below and upon the face of the earth.

What about the beast and his army being sent to "Hell" to burn? If by now you are still looking for a false prophet and his army of people with a mark on their head fighting the angels, go back and re-read Chapters 1–18.

When the hidden world government shows its true face, the Christian church (which once seemed delectably good and wholesome) will be seen for what it is: an "abomination" and will be rejected by mankind. Those henchmen who still hang as did Hitler's Gestapo, will serve as "Wise Guys" for organized crime—World Government. Many of the remaining population will go along with them, just as many Germans continued to follow Hitler. Hypnotized by prejudice and fear, those bodies will perish and their souls will return to the All That Is.

Sorry, all of you self-righteous who hoped to be rewarded, while others among you burned in hell. No hell, no fire nor brimstone either—other than the tilting of the earth on its axis and the shifting of its landmasses and oceans—and, no souls suffering eternal agony.

Those of you who deliberately choose to awaken will come with me to help create the final physical model for a renewed earth. Those who choose to live in ego will return to God to come back at a later time or go on to another experience.

Disappointed oh Modern Day Scribes and Pharisees? Well…freewill truly exists, always has, always will. You and your ilk however, will not!

Chapter 20
Background Information

As I told you, the end of the present civilization is imminent as witnessed by the accelerated extinction of animal/plant species, changes in climate at your poles and the reappearance of the planet Wormwood in the heavens. Had you awakened at an earlier stage, all the "end time" signifiers could have been controlled and eliminated. Unfortunately you spent more time fighting among yourselves than you did learning to live as God.

The effects of fear on man thus far were very predictable **BECAUSE IT HAS ALL HAPPENED MANY TIMES BEFORE.** Fortunately, enough souls have "Awakened" in present and past civilizations to produce a perfected model capable for allowing the Universal Soul to walk the earth as God/Man. Chapter 20 addresses this "first resurrection."

In this first resurrection, all those fully awakened aspects of the Universal Soul who "lived, and live not, but will live in the future," are about to join me in a place that I prepared for you, called Eden. Why Eden and not earth? Why only those portions of the Universal Soul that have lived fully awakened lives in the past?

The answer is that the Universal Soul evolves and increases in knowledge and wisdom with each new experience.

In the beginning I simply WAS. I experienced neither love nor fear prior to creating myself in physical form. In the lower evolved beings, fear worked as a survival mechanism to keep me alive long enough to evolve into a more interesting physical form capable of thinking and controlling its environment…in other words: YOU, for You and I are one. The difference between you and the plants and animals preceding you, is that you are part of my growing consciousness of who I am.

With previous civilizations on earth and elsewhere in the Universe, you and I—"WE"—experimented with introducing various balances between love and fear. "Pure love" resulted in a return to my primitive state and "Pure fear" self-destructed. In the creation of free will, we developed a complex overlay where "fear of the unknown" could be enlightened with love to form an internal combustion engine capable of cosmic self-exploration. Without me, you are nothing and without you, I remain static—but together, we continue to evolve.

Prophecy

Although this chapter appears to forecast the ultimate victory of good over evil and casting Satan into hell, it's not. Remember that the modern bible comes from Greek and Roman translations and interpretations. In my time the words for "good" and "evil" translated roughly as "ripe" and "unripe." Hell and eternal damnation were not even in my vocabulary.

This Chapter actually forecasts taking the "good' seed, the "ripe" seed, and replanting it while the "unripe" or "poorly developed" seed is eaten, burned or turned to compost for the next generation of life.

Parody

The parody of this chapter follows the idea of how a good gardener keeps the ripe seed and burns the unripe. The "ripe" physical forms will dwell with me in Eden where the process of winnowing the ripe from the unripe will continue. Eventually the best of the best will be retained for a time when God will exist simultaneously in physical/spiritual form to enjoy the fruits of His (our) labor.

Process

The process of breeding a new animal or plant involves producing many generations, winnowing the best, re-populating, etc. This process has gone on in THIS universe for <u>billions</u> of years. With each generation, the physical beings are able to see and understand more about the many dimensions of God. Imagine yourself a fish in a pond. All you have ever seen or experienced is water. Suddenly a dolphin jumps in and out of your pond. One minute he is in your dimension, the next he's gone. Gone where? You just had a visit from a being from another dimension: So too with God.

Progression

Why would Satan be freed for a short time after the new breed of physical forms live with Jesus for a span of time?

Well first, Satan does not exist as an evil tempter/entity. Satan is that word used for the opposing force that helps a child experience and overcome obstacles on the way to maturity. Man came into this three-dimensional earth as a dependent spiritual child and then experienced the opportunity to grow into a self-actualized spiritual adult.

In Eden, the physical form experiences an opportunity to develop and grow in the 4th through 10th dimensions. The return of the opposing force merely indicates the opportunity provided to the more highly evolved species to test itself for spiritual fitness prior to the physical reign of God/Man.

Verses 1–6

I saw an angel coming down out of heaven having the key of the abyss and a great chain in his hand. 2He seized the dragon, the old serpent which is the devil and Satan who deceives the whole inhabited earth, and bound him for a thousand years; [3]cast him into the abyss, shut it and sealed it over him, that he should deceive the nations no more until the thousand years were finished. After this, he must be freed for a short time.

[4]I saw thrones and they sat on them, and judgment was given to them. I saw the souls of those who had been beheaded for the testimony of Jesus and for the word of God, and such as didn't worship the beast nor his image and didn't receive the mark on their forehead and on their hand. They lived, and reigned with Christ for a thousand years.

[5]The rest of the dead didn't live until the thousand years were finished. This is the first resurrection. [6]Blessed and holy is he who has part in the first resurrection. Over these the second death has no power, but they will be priests of God and of Christ and will reign with him one thousand years.

The above words of prophecy from the Book of Revelation may come as a surprise to many of you—particularly those who used the name of my franchise (Christianity) without following the franchise contract—The Ten Commandments. As far as we (the Universal Soul) presently understand, these Commandments (business operating systems) work best in terms of developing a harmonious, creative society that allows forward evolution. We gave you the Ten Commandments of Moses based upon *eons* of experience, both on Earth and elsewhere in the Universe. I, Jesus, then came and interpreted conditions of the contract for you.

In earth terms, you have breached the contract and the head office is about to pull the contract from you. Of course I am speaking in a modern metaphor, but one I know you can understand. Allow me to continue.

We, the Universal Soul, are in the Business of Evolution. We exist to grow in consciousness of whom and what we are and to enjoy the fruits of our labor. As part of the Universal Soul in human form, you perform as both management and workforce for the physical department of the business. You have not yet written a business plan because you do not know your market nor your strengths and weaknesses—or the potential for creative growth, as yet. Your Department of the Evolution Business does, however, possess well-tested bylaws—the Ten Commandments.

The human race (and many other beings throughout the Universe) has attended the University of Physical Existence for eons. Some of you have graduated at the top of your class, although many have failed miserably, preferring to party or to second guess your instructors. In just a few months, school will be out, your grades will be in, and those of you who graduate will go on with me to write the business plan.

The story of Satan being thrown into a pit and bound for one thousand years is, of course, John's metaphor for my taking my "graduates" out of the world and over to a conference center where we will draft and test our business plan. During the "one thousand years" you and I will be perfecting a physical model capable of holding, but not restraining, the "All That Is" as the Universal Soul pushes the frontiers of physical existence. Through experimentation, we know a balance must exist between spiritual ease and spiritual dis-ease in order to promote forward movement.

Verses 7–10

And after the thousand years, Satan will be released from his prison ^{8}and he will come out to deceive the nations which are in the four corners of the earth, Gog and Magog, to gather them together to the war; the number of whom is as the sand of the sea.

^{9}They went up over the breadth of the earth and surrounded the camp of the saints and the beloved city. Fire came down out of heaven from God, and devoured them. ^{10}The devil who deceived them was thrown into the lake of fire and sulfur, where the beast and the false prophet are also. They will be tormented day and night forever and ever.

Sounds pretty ominous, doesn't it? Hallelujah, at last, Fire and Brimstone, the Christian fundamentalist win! Sorry, but you hypocrites make me laugh. Will the ego (the need to be separate, to control and to be right) undergo eternal fire and brimstone? You bet—but not the way you think!

For the next one thousand years all of us involved with the first resurrection, will be removing the ego-function from human form in order to harness the energy of internal combustion and translate it into progress. Nuclear fission can be used to destroy the earth with an atomic bomb (reminiscent of your present human ego) or—it can be harnessed to generate light power. At the end of the one thousand years, the improved ego-function will be re-installed, complete with fire and brimstone, encased in a modern engine capable of moving the Universal Soul through rapid evolution.

Verses 11–15

^{11}I saw a great white throne and him who sat on it from whose face the earth and the heaven fled away. There was found no place for them. ^{12}I saw the dead, the great and the small, standing before the throne and they opened books. Another book was opened, which is the book of life. The dead were judged out of the things which were written in the books, according to their works.

13The Sea gave up the dead who were in it. Death and Hades gave up the dead who were in them. They were judged, each one according to his works. 14Death and Hades13 were thrown into the lake of fire. This is the second death, the lake of fire. 15If anyone was not found written in the book of life, he was cast into the lake of fire.

Notice something here: "every man is judged according to his works!" Once the Father created life and found a way to place pieces of Himself into that life, He, the Universal Soul, began to experience himself. The combinations of the Universal Soul that achieved full awakening have already been busy during the one-thousand years creating a perfected body/mind/ego capable of existing as God/Man. Those combinations of God's soul that can operate in this new vehicle will now have the opportunity to enter physical form and go on. Death (and the notion of Hell) no longer serve a purpose and will be eliminated.

This is the second death and whosoever was not found written in the book of life was cast into the lake of fire.

Now we come to the most difficult verse in Revelation. Hell fire and brimstone at last and now SOMEBODY'S going to suffer! Fundamentalism served some purpose after all! Yeah right…you guys never give up do you! Who other, in the man-made religion of Christ, hates, snipes and eats away at the soul of mankind—than the fundamentalists of any religion of man? Remember this: each and every one of you volunteered to come here into mortal form, so sorry fellows, NO soul will be cast into flames, but guess which aspect of man's nature is about to be eliminated—forever!

---

13 20:14 or, Hell

Chapter 21
The seven new things: the new heaven and the new earth.

By now, most of you realize that this entire book is about *you*, a piece of God, attempting to become more and more conscious of yourself. Each one of you came to earth voluntarily as a piece of the Eternal Soul experiencing itself in human form. The Jewish peoples received the Ten Commandments—your operating orders. I, Jesus, came among you and told you the Truth. My Apostles remained behind to help grow the mystic school intended to quicken your awakening. Why then, would you think that when the earth renewed itself you would go to "The Emerald City" to live stagnantly ever after with the "Wizard of Oz?"

Verses 1–8

I saw a new heaven and a new earth: for the first heaven and the first earth have passed away and the sea is no more. 2I saw the holy city, New Jerusalem, coming down out of heaven from God, made ready like a bride adorned for her husband. 3I heard a loud voice out of heaven saying, "Behold, God's dwelling is with people and he will dwell with them and they will be his people and God himself will be with them as their God.

4He will wipe away from them every tear from their eyes. Death will be no more; neither will there be mourning, nor crying, nor pain any more. The first things have passed away." 5He who sits on the throne said, "Behold, I am making all things new." He said, "Write, for these words of God are faithful and true."

6He said to me, "It is done! I am the Alpha and the Omega, the Beginning and the End. I will give freely to him who is thirsty from the spring of the water of life. 7He who overcomes, I will give him these things. I will be his God and he will be my son. 8But for the cowardly, unbelieving, sinners, abominable, murderers, sexually immoral, sorcerers,14 idolaters and all liars, their part is in the lake that burns with fire and sulfur, which is the second death."

Yes, earth as you know it, will pass away (for the time being) then at that point the sea of human mass consciousness will exist no more. The human experiment is over—for it has been successful. God came in conscious human form; God experienced fear of the unknown and God conquered that Fear. Now the "New Jerusalem" descends, not as the "Emerald City" a place, but rather as a new level of God-Consciousness.

Now God wipes the slate clean. He has found in the Remnant the ability to dwell in form minus death, sorrow or pain. God—and all conscious form—stand

---

14 21:8 The word for "sorcerers" here also includes users of potions and drugs.

on the brink of renewal. God is Man and Man is God; the Environment is God and Man is part of His Environment.

The Remnant has learned to transcend death by fully awakening to their Godhood. In the process God learned more about Himself and created all things new. Indeed the Father *is* the Alpha and Omega, but the Omega does not remain stagnant. It grows and recreates itself from nanosecond to nanosecond. The second death does not refer to souls burning in hell; rather it heralds the end of the old experiment and the beginning of the new.

Verses 9–13

⁹One of the seven angels who had the seven bowls, loaded with the seven last plagues, came and he spoke with me, saying, "Come here, I will show you the wife, the Lamb's bride." ¹⁰He carried me away in the Spirit to a great and high mountain and showed me the holy city Jerusalem coming down out of heaven from God, ¹¹having the glory of God.

Her light was like a most precious stone, as if it was a jasper stone, clear as crystal; ¹²having a great and high wall; having twelve gates and at the gates twelve angels; and names written on them, which are the names of the twelve tribes of the children of Israel. ¹³On the east were three gates; and on the north three gates; and on the south three gates; and on the west three gates.

Notice three things about the New Jerusalem: 1) It descends out of All That Is, carrying the full glory of God; 2) It possesses a light like jasper stone that is crystal clear; 3) It has a high wall with twelve gates named after the twelve tribes of Israel. This is not a city at all, but rather the new experience of God in physical form. The new form glows like a precious stone, an individual element that glows with crystal clarity of who and what it is. The high walls represent the ability of God to exist physically in many diverse forms. The twelve gates honor the tribes of Israel that voluntarily took part in the Earth experiment and brought you the Ten Commandments.

Verses 14-18

¹⁴The wall of the city had twelve foundations and in them the names of the twelve apostles of the Lamb. ¹⁵He that talked with me had a golden reed (rod) *to measure the city, the gates and the walls thereof. ¹⁶The city lies foursquare: the length as large as the breath and he measured the city with a reed of twelve thousand furlongs.* (One furlong equals 660 feet. Twelve thousand furlongs equals 792,000,000 feet divided by 5280 equals 150,000 miles.)

¹⁷The wall measured a hundred and forty four cubits, according to the measure of the angel. (Each cubit is equal to approximately 22 inches, therefore the wall measured close to being 5 miles thick.) *18The building of the wall was jasper and the city was pure gold, like clear glass.*

The foundations for the new physical form honor the Twelve Apostles who understood and spread my word. Notice that Judas *is* included in the foundation, for of all the Apostles; he did his job the best and suffered the most. The gates are made of pure white pearl and remain open at all times, allowing the soul of the new form to come and go between being pure God and pure form. The streets of gold represent the pure God-consciousness within the physical form.

Versus 19–27

19The foundations of the city's wall were adorned with all kinds of precious stones. The first foundation was jasper; the second, sapphire[15]; the third, chalcedony; the fourth, emerald; 20the fifth, sardonyx; the sixth, sardius; the seventh, chrysolite; the eighth, beryl; the ninth, topaz; the tenth, chrysoprasus; the eleventh, jacinth; and the twelfth, amethyst.

21The twelve gates were twelve pearls. Each one of the gates was made of one pearl. The street of the city was pure gold, like transparent glass. 22I saw no temple in it, for the Lord God, the Almighty, and the Lamb are its temple. 23The city has no need for the sun, neither of the moon, to shine, for the very glory of God illuminated it—and its lamp is the Lamb.

24The nations will walk in its light. The kings of the earth bring the glory and honor of the nations into it. 25Its gates will in no way be shut by day (for there will be no night there) 26and they shall bring the glory and the honor of the nations into it so that they may enter. 27There will in no way enter into it anything profane or one who causes an abomination or a lie, but only those who are written in the Lamb's book of life.

The new form shall exist with no need of a church, for God dwells in full consciousness within. In Eden, no strife exists for God has chosen to live in full consciousness, full harmony and full love. The new adventure begins.

---

15 21:19 or, lapis lazuli

Chapter 22
The new Paradise and its' river of the water of life
Verses 1–6

He showed me a river of water of life clear as crystal, preceding out of the throne of God and of the Lamb, 2in the middle of its street. On this side of the river and on that was the tree of life, bearing twelve kinds of fruits, yielding its fruit every month. The leaves of the tree were for the healing of the nations. 3There will be no curse any more.

The throne of God and of the Lamb will be in it and his servants serve him. 4They will see his face and his name will be on their foreheads. 5There will be no night and they need no lamp light; for the Lord God will illuminate them. They will reign forever and ever. 6He said to me, "These words are faithful and true. The Lord God of the spirits of the prophets sent his angel to show to his bondservants the things which must happen soon."

The river of the pure water of life refers to full consciousness of whom and what you are. That knowledge comes directly from your connection to the Universal soul for the Tree of Life *is* the Universal soul. The twelve fruits refer to the twelve tribes of Israel and to the twelve Apostles, of which form the new body is built. The leaves of the tree refer to each individual person who comes forth from the Tree of Life. The soul of God shall inhabit every new physical form and all physical form shall possess God-consciousness *(…and his name will be on their forehead.)* There will be no fear of the unknown because the new bodies (physical forms) will be enlightened with full God-consciousness.

Verses 7–15

7"Behold, I come quickly. Blessed is he who keeps the words of the prophecy of this book." Now I, John, am the one who heard and saw these things. When I heard and saw, I fell down to worship before the feet of the angel who had shown me these things. 9He said to me, "See you don't do it! I am a fellow bondservant with you and with your brothers, the prophets and with those who keep the words of this book—worship God."

10He said to me, "Don't seal up the words of the prophecy of this book, for the time is at hand. 11He who acts unjustly let him act unjustly still. He who is filthy let him be filthy still. He who is righteous let him do righteousness still. He who is holy let him be holy still." 12"Behold, I come quickly. My reward is with me, to repay to each man according to his work.

13I am the Alpha and the Omega, the First and the Last, the Beginning and the End. 14Blessed are those who do his commandments that they may have the right to the tree of life and may enter in by the gates into the city. 15Outside are the dogs, the sorcerers, the sexually immoral, the murderers, the idolaters, and everyone who loves and practices falsehood

These verses attests to the truth: that the old paradigm will pass away and those who were able to awaken during this lifetime will reign with me in Eden for one thousand years as we prepare for the new body with its fully enlightened soul. Outside of Eden, in other places in the Universe, other bodies will continue to evolve with various levels of God-Consciousness.

Verses 16-18

16I, Jesus, have sent my angel to testify these things to you for the assemblies. "I am the root and the offspring of David; the Bright and Morning Star." 17The Spirit and the bride say, "Come!" He who hears, let him say, "Come!" He who is thirsty, let him come. He who desires, let him take the water of life freely. 18I testify to everyone who hears the words of the prophecy of this book, if anyone adds to them, may God add to him the plagues which are written in this book.

The Truth about your creation and mission on Earth lies directly in front of you. My words have borne witness to the truth, as have the prophecies in this book. Your job is to seek after the Truth with your whole mind, body and soul.

Verse 19

19If anyone takes away from the words of the book of this prophecy, may God take away his part from the tree of life and out of the holy city, which are written in this book. 20He who testifies these things says, "Yes, I come quickly."

Revelations survived for two reasons: 1) The man-made church did not understand its meaning and 2) The man-made church was afraid to change its words.

In this book is everything you need to know in order to fully awaken.

The last promise and the last prayer of the Bible

The Final Summation

Verses 20–21

20He who testifies these things says, "Yes, I come quickly. Amen! Yes, come, Lord Jesus. 21The grace of the Lord Jesus Christ be with all the saints." Amen.

The body and the mind of Men are vehicles and some vehicles are physically deficient—also some of the experimental models came through morally deficient. That is not held against the soul, it is just that some physical models worked and some did not. I have built the New Jerusalem upon the physical/spiritual models (from Earth and from other places in the universe) capable of full awakening to God-consciousness.

Eden will not be a place of struggle. You will be able to pursue your interests, explore your new environment and all of the possibilities therein. It will be joyful for there will be no pain as there will be nothing to harm you.

The reason that life on this planet has been so difficult is because few humans heeded the call to awaken to full God-consciousness. Instead they struggled under the burden of "*man-made*" churches. The various religions told you that you will do it their way or go to Hell; as a result people have forgotten who they are—and they live in fear and darkness. That is coming to end for the awakened souls will come with me to Eden. After one thousand years, the New Jerusalem— a fully awakened model of God Consciousness in physical form—will be prepared, tested and ready for habitation by all aspects of the Universal Soul. At that point, "The Second Coming," all defective *physical* models will be destroyed and only the New Jerusalem will exist.

The "All-That-Is" loves diversity and continues to evolve in self-understanding forever.

Amen.

DIVINE SECRETS REVEALED

THE CHAKRAS

The Chakra System

The Chakras

Divine Secrets Revealed

Have you ever heard the term "Chakra?" Well hold on to your seatbelts. *"The Truth About Christianity"* explains them as you have never heard them explained before. So, what are the Chakras?

In Eastern mythology they are a set of seven energy centers located along the spine and up into the cranium. These energy centers both radiate and absorb energy pertinent to your life history, thoughts, use of energy, relationships and those things that pertain to your health and spiritual growth.

Each energy center controls—and is controlled by—nerve centers located along the spine. Modern day mystics use the Chakra centers to diagnose and ameliorate illness and to raise spiritual consciousness. Interestingly enough, generalized nerve centers do exist, along the spine and up into the cranium, that enervate the various levels assigned to the Chakras.

So what is <u>different</u> about the information in *"Divine Secrets Revealed?"* Now—for the first time—you are about to learn the original meanings of the Seven Chakras as developed over 4,000 years ago in the Kabbalah and later incorporated into Eastern mysticism. You will also learn about how the Seven Chakras pertain to prophecy's about the Seven Churches in *"The Book of Revelation."*

Introduction by Jesus Christ

I grew up as the son of a carpenter, in the dwindling middle class Jewish society under the rule of Rome. My father, Joseph and my Uncle Joseph of Arimathea, both held high offices in the mysticism of the White Brotherhood. They saw to it that I received an advanced education in the religious heritage of the Kabbalah and Torah, as well as the mysticism of the Essenes, the Druids, the Egyptians, Greeks and Indians.

My native language, Aramaic, contained no concept of heaven or hell or eternal punishment. Rather, in its own poetic nature, Aramaic carried connotations of an all-inclusive God of Unity, of man "resonating" to the higher dimensions of God and his fellow man. We believed that by coming into unity with all the diverse part of ourselves we could live a rich, abundant life right here on earth and that as part of nature we automatically lived an eternal life of ongoing creation.

It is too bad that the poetic nature of Aramaic became lost in the black and white mathematical language of the Greeks. Interestingly enough, the left-brained mathematical approach has now come full circle in demonstrating the ten dimensions of God, foretold over 4,000 years ago in the Kabbalah.

According to the ancient wisdom, given to Father Abraham in the Kabbalah, man comes into this world as a spiritual/physical infant. This baby man is:

- Created by his parents.
- Controlled by his parents.
- A blind absorber of knowledge.
- A taker.

In order to mature, the baby needs obstacles against which to test his skills and we call that obstacle: Satan. Satan is neither good nor bad. Satan's influence grows as we grow and requires greater obstacles against which to pit ourselves. Eventually however, we mature into:

- The creator/cause of our own earthly experience.
- The controller of the outcome.
- A skeptic and tester of all he is told.
- The giver of love and sustenance to our brothers.

In the process of spiritual maturity, man moves from wondering who he is to full knowledge of his place as a part of the universal soul—the creator God. Now let's relate that to the Chakra's and the seven Churches.

Origins of the Seven Chakras in the Kabbalah

We tend to think about ancient people as being primitive. Nonsense! Over 4,000 years ago Abraham commissioned the books of the Zohar. The mysticism of the Kabbalah came from the teachings of the Zohar—teachings which influenced major Western scientists throughout the ages; even playing out in the modern day "String Theory" of Hyperspace. The profound teachings of the Kabbalah spread as well to the East where they became incorporated in Chakra mysticism.

The teachings of the Kabbalah are this: each of us is born a spiritual infant from which we grow by physical/physiological stages into spiritual maturity. Each of those stages is represented by one of the seven Chakras.

As each individual man proceeds through the seven stages of development from infant to sage, so does mankind. The Chakra's speak to individual "Man's" spiritual development, and the seven churches of the Book of Revelation speak to "Mankind's" spiritual development.

The information below, received from Jesus, flows with the rich Aramaic mysticism of God as an all inclusive-source of unity and of man's growing "ripeness" for understanding his place *right here in the present* in the "Kingdom of Heaven."

The First Chakra

This Chakra manifests itself as a ball of red flame at the base of the spine.

The first or "base Chakra," located at the base of your spine, glows with red, very hot cosmic energy, reminiscent of the energy of fusion that creates all things new.

Picture being ripped away from your spiritual godhead and dropped into a tribe of strangers. Remember the story of Joseph in the Bible; how he was ripped from his family and sold into slavery? The emotional/physical/spiritual experience of birth is much the same. You arrive on earth (with amnesia) in the presence of complete strangers, who may or may not want you. Eventually you learn about your true membership in the royal family of God, but for many years you roam the earth seeking acceptance from mankind.

The first Chakra represents a balancing act between remembering your true identity as God/Man and gaining acceptance from your human family/tribe for you arrive on earth with *no memory* of God. If Mom, Dad and/or the tribe fail to welcome you to earth, your base Chakra flashes: *"Danger! Danger!"* Immediately the ego, acting through fear, begins separating you from everyone else, making you "special." It tells you that you have only yourself to trust. Over time, fear and alienation erode your connection to your brother resulting in physical/mental illness.

Your existential journey on this planet involves 1) realizing you are more than just a body, 2) remembering your spiritual identity and 3) balancing the two so that you can exist like me, Jesus, as Man and God. If society tells you the truth and teaches you to collaborate with your brother to live in your God-given role as co-creator and protector of the planet, then you feel safe in the arms of your family/tribe as you begin your spiritual journey. But what happens when society lies to you? What about the symptoms of *spiritual* abandonment?

THAT is the story of the first church at Ephesus. In the beginning the church taught about your priceless inheritance, but as the Apostles died off and ego-ruled men usurped my leadership, the church taught that you were basically evil, born in sin and susceptible to temptation by some outside spiritual force called Satan;

only redeemed by my death and in need of spiritual guidance by the church fathers.

Nothing could be farther from the truth! The churches took advantage of your trust to portray you as an undeserving, evil stranger in a strange land ruled by corrupt spiritual despots and a horrific God—talk about the dark night of the soul! Only love and the truth bring light into your life for everything is the "dark night" until you begin to question and eventually overthrow the oppression started by the Church of Ephesus.

Are you fearful and worried all the time? Do you suffer from obsessions or compulsions? Must you control everything? Do you feel alienated from your family and society? Do you have a "Type 'A' Personality," and find yourself working all the time? Is it impossible to trust that all will turn out alright without your having to DO anything? Must you play the white knight and take care of everyone around you? Do you have problems standing up for yourself? Do you fear God? Do you "not believe in" God? Does a dark cloud follow you wherever you go? Is there no peace in your life? Do you fear abandonment?

These symptoms of fear and alienation come from distortions of the energy of the first Chakra and reflect a lack of knowledge of your spiritual royalty. What can you do to attain spiritual alignment and peace? Clear your spiritual slate; throw off everything you have ever been told about who you are, where you came from and the nature of God. Learn from John's letter to Ephesus. Do what you must to take the candle (authority) out of the hands of your church (Ephesus). Come directly to me in prayer and trust and learn from me.

You were *born* into a physical family; but remember this: **You are a spirit with a body—not the other way around.** Your human tribe may or may not accept you, but that's *their* problem. They may even kill the body, but the body is only a temporary vehicle in which you reside. Your true identity is that of a spirit that is part of God and part of every other human being in the universe. You are never alone, nor can you be abandoned. You **are** God; and you came to earth with the full authority and responsibility of God.

To find out what it means to be God/Man, read the scriptures for yourself; let me, the Christ, help you understand the true meaning of my words through meditation. Then you will learn to ground yourself in the powerful loving force that binds this universe together. Once grounded in the Father, branch out and learn to enjoy the fruits of the Universe by using your body/mind to prepare yourself to live with me in Eden.

A sample prayer for centering based upon the prayer that I gave you: first in *Aramaic;* then the **Greek** translation and then in <u>Modern</u> vernacular.

The Lords Prayer Translated from Aramaic

*O cosmic Birther of all radiance and vibration. Soften the ground of our being
and carve out a space within us where your Presence can abide.
Fill us with your creativity so that we may be empowered to bear the fruit
of your mission.
Let each of our actions bear fruit in accordance with our desire.
Endow us with the wisdom to produce and share what each being needs to grow
and flourish.
Untie the tangled threads of destiny that bind us, as we release others from the
entanglement of past mistakes.
Do not let us be seduced by that which would divert us from our true purpose, but
illuminate the opportunities of the present moment.
For you are the ground and the fruitful vision, the birth, power and fulfillment,
as all is gathered and made whole once again.
(Retrieved on 8/25/04 from http://www.thenazareneway.com/lords_prayer.htm)*

A Translation of "Our Father" from Greek into English

**Our Father who are in heaven, hallowed be Thy name.
Thy Kingdom come, Thy will be done, on earth as it is in heaven.
Give us this day our daily bread and forgive us our debts as we forgive our
debtors.
Lead us not into temptation, but deliver us from evil, For thine is the king-
dom, the power and glory forever.
Amen.**

A Translation of "Our Father" into Contemporary English

Greetings to you, Oh Highest Source of all creation and to Jesus Christ our example, friend and mentor, it is: (enter names) that stands humbled in your presence and honored to be called to your service.

We ask in Jesus' name that you prepare us and empower us to *Center* our thoughts within *You* in order that we might know and accomplish *Your* divine bidding. We ask this relying on your promise that whatsoever we ask in Jesus' name shall be granted to those who honor and follow in his footsteps. We make this request and thank You in advance for granting our plea.

As we approach you in prayer and meditation, we ask that you help us to attain an ever-deepening understanding and active obedience to your will. We trust in you to provide for our daily needs as we consecrate ourselves fully to your service. Correct us when we go astray and help us to return immediately to our *centeredness in you.* Teach us to live in peace and lead us ever closer to a more profound participation in Your Divine Love.

We ask that you bring together all people and groups of like minds to pray for peace and unity; for a world community that collaborates to live in harmony, in order to bring about harmonious relationships where you, Father, can experience yourself.

Keep our ego needs from distracting others from their paths as you keep others from distracting us from ours. We pray that we be given the truth about everyone and everything, as seen through your eyes.

We surrender completely to you so that you may return us to our full knowingness. May we stand steadfast in your service in perfect health, free from all fear, doubt and distraction; for we have heard your call; your kingdom is near and we know that the time to call in your flock is now at hand.

[1]Be our friend God, help us to live in harmony with our universe. Help us to know who we really are so that you may experience yourself in us. We ask this in your name and we ask it in our name. We ask this for our society and all societies in the universe. [1](Cited from "Love and Beyond" By David Kessler, singupPublishing, www.SingUpPub.com)

Amen—for this is my true and heartfelt wish.

Summary

Influence of the Church of Ephesus

* I, Jesus, did not come to be worshiped as God. I came to tell you the truth about whom and what you are and your relationship to the Cosmos. Read MY words and you will find the key to traveling your own path.

* I did not come to "save" you. You must "save" yourself by seeking the truth and living your own path from spiritual childhood to spiritual maturity.

* Soon after my death and the death of the original apostles, the mythology of the Greeks, Romans and Egyptians began to pervade Christian belief. Consequently, the original intent of my teachings became entangled in Gentile beliefs.

* Each writer of the four Gospels put his own slant on whom and what I was. For the most part they stripped away my role as your teacher and guide and

made me into the only Son of God, an object of worship. In truth, you too are God, as is taught in the Kabbalah.

- For the most part, my actual words remained intact—particularly in the lost Gospel of Thomas. Go directly to my words for the truth.

- Although you can get the gist of my sayings from the Greek translation, in order to understand the *intent* of my words, go to direct translation from the Aramaic.

Teachings of Jesus

- The same as the Kabbalah.

Influence of the Kabbalah

- God, the Infinite Soul, is the cause of man's creation; man is the effect of God's will. God is the creator, controller, giver. Man is the created, controlled, receiver.

- Man's mission on earth is to find out who and what he is so that he becomes the cause, the creator, the controller and the giver, i.e. he assumes his place as God in human form, completely united with everything else in the universe.

- In spiritual infancy other people control you and tell you who you are and what parts of your physical/mental processes are acceptable. In order to spiritually mature, this man must find, accept and bring all his divergent parts back into unity so he becomes at peace with himself and his creator.

- Don't believe a thing you are told. Search and experience for yourself until you find the Divine Light within you.

Influence of Eastern Mythology about the Chakras

- Follows the essence of the Kabbalah in terms of unity of all things with the Divine.

- Identifies the birthing process with the first Chakra, a set of nervous tissue located near the base of the spine, an "energy center."

- The first Chakra retains memories of the wrenching away from the Divine during the birth process, the acceptance or non acceptance by our earthly caregivers, and our early experiences as the created, the controlled, the helpless effect of Divine creation now dependent upon an earthly environment for survival.

- The first Chakra nervous tissue controls the health of the support structures (lower limbs, hips, lower colon, and intestine) throughout our life.

- The first Chakra spiritual energy controls our spiritual ability to experience—and later outgrows—our need for spiritual dependency. Getting "stuck" at first Chakra spiritual dependency leaves you forever at the mercy of the churches and false spiritual leaders.

- Getting "stuck" or emotionally/spiritually blocked at the First Chakra can result in physical/physic of the supporting lower limbs of the body and internal organs. It can also result in a sense of separation from God, your brother and the Universe, and to complete dependency on a church or cult for spiritual sustenance. In effect, you remain a spiritual moron.

- To clear these disabilities, you must "clear" the root Chakra and move on in your journey towards spiritual maturity.

The Second Chakra

*This Chakra manifests itself as a ball of orange flame just below the navel
at the level of the sexual organs.*

The first Chakra represents your spirit being wrenched from its cosmic home and being placed, completely helpless, into the hands of earthly caregivers—who may or may not accept you. Conversely, the second Chakra represents the second step on your spiritual journey as you learn to attract and accept other people. Not to just accept other people, but come to the realization that the spirit that inhabits your brother inhabits you as well.

What are we made up of? What is at the core of being? What is the major driving force behind everything we think and do? According to the Kabbalah, that essence of our being boils down to desire. We desire to be perfectly happy at all times. In infancy we desire to be warm, snuggled, dry, safe and well fed. All these things (and more as we grow in consciousness) the Kabbalah defines as "light." The ultimate makeup of our body and soul seeks to find the ultimate light—God.

Why are we not born just *knowing* we are God? Two reasons: (1) We are stuck into a physically immature body that takes 13 to 14 years to become fully functional physically and sexually and (2) The early experiments with being brought forth fully conscious of our Divine nature (The story of Adam and Eve) didn't work out to our satisfaction. Accordingly, in order to appreciate being God, we chose to EARN our God nature. Therefore we asked to be "born again" as infants who could learn how to become God and, in order for us to have time to mature spiritually, a curtain was drawn at birth.

Our all-knowing "God soul" entered a physical body capable of comprehending only four dimensions: length, width, height and time. The other six dimensions postulated (and in modern day confirmed by physicists) remain unknown to us. In Kabalistic thinking one percent of our spirit is known to us and 99% remains hidden.

In infancy (first Chakra) either we get enough physical sustenance or we don't, and if we don't a floating anxiety develops for we can't trust other people to create, control and give us what we need.

In the second Chakra we physically mature enough to begin interacting with other people and if we succeed in attracting other people to us so that we have our physical/emotional needs met, then we learn to trust. Otherwise fear grows and we begin to act on our feelings of separation.

The second Chakra nerve tissue enervates the sex organs, kidneys and part of the bowel. If we become locked in the second Chakra, unable to trust, unable to give to others, we develop physical/physic ailments in those areas. We also become mental/spiritual sociopaths, unable to experience our relationship with the "other" and unable to grow into our ultimate role as God, the giver/sharer.

What happens at exactly the time that we start to speak and share ideas? The so-called "Christian" church tells you that you are sinners: no no, don't do this, don't do that, don't touch yourself there, don't take things without asking, don't don't don't. Also that I, Jesus, sacrificed my life to rescue you; that you are separate from God, your brother, the universe and even your own nature.

My brother, those words and concepts did not even EXIST in my native Aramaic language and culture. I could not possibly have thought or taught such concepts! So where did they come from? The church at Smyrna!

The Church at Smyrna represents the culmination of a grand scheme initiated by gentile usurpers. The Constantine (Catholic) church separated man from God and instituted an authoritarian Pope and his henchmen (the church) to interpret my words and decide the eternal fate of man...and the temporal fate of the Roman Empire. Instead of teaching "Love thy brother," the church taught: "Love some of thy brothers...but only the ones that love and obey Christian (Church) Doctrine." Witness the Crusades and the ongoing Wars in the Middle East.

How does separating you from God and from your brother impact your second Chakra? It extinguishes the light. Instead of collaboration and harmonious creation, the selective dogma of the church teaches: "It's us and them! Love God (as interpreted by the church) With Thy Whole Heart and (some of) Your Brothers As Yourself." Put that together with the unholy trinity: church, politics and big business and you have: "Get yours before someone takes it away from you."

The letter to the Church at Smyrna foretold the coming of a quasi political/religious church that would separate you from God and your fellow man; and, the second Chakra regulates how your body/soul reacts to such separation. Symptoms of second Chakra dysfunction are: fear of other people, paranoia, obsession with money and power, sexual dysfunction, physical ailments involving the kidneys, hips, and pelvis radiating to the lower extremities; greed, hostility, ruthlessness, dishonesty, lack of ethics/morals, hatred, anger, grudges and retribution, lack of self-confidence, lack of creativity.

So what can you do, how can you remember your true identity, truly love your brother and find the peace I gave you?

- **Develop Courage:** First off, you must develop courage. My life represented a life of courage. I can tell you that if I came to earth today, I would be crucified all over again—only quicker.

- **Read:** Sit down with the five gospels and especially sit down with the Gospel of Thomas. Read them in light of what I have told you: You ARE God. The body is merely a vehicle in which the spirit temporarily resides while creating a prototype vehicle that will allow you to live with me in Eden as God and Man. What an eye opener, for suddenly everything makes sense and knowing your identity provides the key to opening the gospels.

- **Meditate:** It won't be long before you begin waking up around 4 AM every night. Get up. Read my words and meditate on their meaning.

- **Open to new possibilities:** Let the weight of my words sink in. Let go of what the churches have taught you. If you want to belong to a fellowship that celebrates my Truth, pick out a group with *no* leader, *no* doctrine and *no* organization.

- **Beware and Be Aware:** Beware of anyone who tries to pressure you into submitting to their doctrine; be aware of the atrocities wrecked in my name— and who really is behind war and hate.

Being accepted by others as being part of them and by accepting other people as being part of you is a two way street. Yet this delicate balance between the first and the second Chakra will determine whether you are with me or choose to be left behind.

Once the First Chakra balances, you begin to feel more at home away from home. You know your true parents (the Universal Soul), but you also accept your earthly family. You know who you are—the Universal Soul inhabiting a body— but you are not quite sure who everyone else is or how to act towards them.

The Second Chakra is about understanding that you and your brother are one; that you and the universe are one. This differs from the Christian teaching of "Seeing Christ in your brother" which *still* denotes separation. You and your brother truly *are* one just as two fingers on the same hand are one with the hand.

If the church/state in America truly saw Christ in their brother, why did they bomb Iraq? Bloody, forceful "conversions" didn't work in the time of Constantine, nor do they work now since brotherly love comes from soul work, not from combat. The second seal represents your earthly journey to reconcile and reunite with your brother.

Summary

Influence of the Church at Smyrna

- The Emperor Constantine hurried to solidify his empire. The Greek translation of my message distorted and concretized my message and mixed it with Gentile traditions to make it convenient for promotion as Constantine's new mandatory State Religion.

- For those brought up in the West, your earliest memories are those of separation, sinfulness, hell and damnation. The Western Christian church portrays creation as something accomplished in the past with God and Man as separate from each other, and locked in a battle between Good and evil. In other words, Christianity after Smyrna taught **the exact opposite of my words, thus making your journey towards wholeness and brotherly love practically impossible.**

Teachings of Jesus

- I never taught—nor even thought—in terms of the apocalypse, hell and damnation. For me and my constituents, change was the only constant. Each day man started from where he was at in that moment and moved forward. Our tradition called for respect for those who went before, brotherhood with those in our midst and a sense of conservation for those to come.

- In all my sayings—and particularly in the Beatitudes—I spoke of man becoming "ripe" to receive the Wisdom of the Cosmos, of softening those ridged places with and accepting all the scattered parts of yourself.

Influence of the Kabbalah

- Because man needs time to mature and because he desires an opportunity to "earn" his Godhood, a curtain drops at the time of conception when the spirit entered human form so that it became cognoscente of only 1% of its cosmic ability. The other 99% remains hidden for him to find as he matures physically and spiritually.

- In order to motivate him on his cosmic journey, man's main driving force is a desire for complete happiness. The Kabbalah uses the word "Light" as a codeword for man's instinctive search for his own Godhood.

- Because of his desire for the Light, man instinctively begins the quest to find his true identity from earliest consciousness.

Influence of Eastern Mythology about the Chakras

This mythology identified the sense of being able to take care of self and to successfully interact with your brother at a level of the spine just above the genitals. It commenced the process of "giving and receiving," as opposed to receiving alone.

A belief in separateness from yourself, your brother and God results in various physic/physical problems in the genitals, kidneys, small intestine and endocrine glands.

Clearing this Chakra (see above) assists with physical healing and with the beginning stages of taking control of your life, creating your future and of feeling at peace with your place in the Cosmos.

The Third Chakra

Represented by a yellow flame between the navel and the chest cavity.

The third Chakra represents accepting your own Godhood, for on the journey you may surrender your will to that of a number of churches, political groups, etc., hoping one of them will take charge and make you happy. Indeed it seems that the whole human race participates in an eternal journey of looking for someone to think for them or to find someone to lead them. I tell you this: "stop waiting for me, anyone or anything else to take charge of your affairs." You ARE God. Take on the responsibility for manifesting your own life for that is what you came here to do. If you came to live my life, why would the Father need you?

You came to live and fully experience your own life as God and Man. Failure to accept those responsibilities results in numerous body ailments of the stomach, spleen, gall bladder, intestine, transverse colon, adrenals—all of the organs in the upper abdomen. It also results in insecurity, feelings of unworthiness, low self-esteem, a need to keep up with your neighbors and a fear of going against the wishes of society.

When you go through the dark night of the soul and come to accept your own Godhood, you establish your own living space (boundaries); set your own code of ethics, develop your own sense of honor. Yes, you and your brother are one at the soul level; however you have been given a body and mind to allow you a space of your own in which to co-create the universe with God and your brother creators. What can you do to open and strengthen the third Chakra?

Take charge of your life: You ARE God. Why do you need to rely on anyone else to make important decisions, about who you are, what you want to do, who you want to marry or where you want to live. Accept "mistakes" as normal and make lots of them because mistakes help you explore new avenues to success. The only caveat is this: accept the Ten Commandments/Attitudes as your guide.

Take charge of your abundance: Accept yourself as an idea generator, a creator of abundance. Share your abundance out of love, rather than out of a sense of obligation. If you need money, then create it through your own divine ability to generate ideas.

Take charge of your career: Instead of creating yourself in the image and likeness of job advertisements in the paper, define your own bliss. Decide what allows you passion and follow that road. Create your own business opportunities.

Take charge of your body: Some things about your body you can regulate and some you cannot, but take care of your health and appearance. You yourself selected the form you are in prior to coming to earth. Your form possesses unique abilities and opportunities for you to create and experience your role as God/Man. Take pride in yourself.

Take charge of your spirit: Remember that the underground church has been persecuted by both the political and religious forces throughout time. None-the-less the ONLY way you can have freedom to accomplish your mission here on earth is to take responsibility for your *own* spiritual growth. At some point, you have to re-assess your attachment to whatever faith or belief system dominated your youth—and this may result in a split from your family/tribe. Have the courage to do as you must in order to fully awaken. Meditate one hour each day and don't worry if you fall asleep; all you need to do is to <u>set</u> <u>your intent</u> to meditate. Meditation reunites you with your true spirit and provides guidance and wisdom…even in sleep.

Ask how love would handle each situation: It may sound strange to take charge of your life but surrender to God; however, when you conduct your life from your heart and act in love, no discrepancy exists. You have surrendered to God/Love and you walk in the light.

The third Chakra represents a time of further separation from your tribal teachings, of setting your boundaries and of establishing a strong code of ethics: yet another balancing act…for how do you separate, yet remain connected? I told you this: "Live in the world, but not of it."

Your tribes live in an illusion of fear and separation. Do not separate from your brother, rather separate from his fears, delusional ideation and false perceptions of life. Make sense? Establishing boundaries does not mean putting up walls of fear and resentment between you and your brother. It means reading my words, going into your heart, listening to what those words mean to you and making decisions based upon your *own* truth.

Summary

The Church at Pergamos:

Babies don't know that someone else controls their lives. If anything they think they control the adults who come when the baby cries. But young people come to realize that guardians, society, politics and religion very closely control everything they do and think. At some point, the young person rebels against their guardians, the church included.

This phase we refer to as the "Dark night of the soul." The adolescent is neither child nor man, same thing with the adolescent spirit (regardless of age.) Look upon the struggle to release yourself from your church heritage the same as you look upon the Satan/Opponent. In venturing out on your own to find your spiritual truth, dark days loom ahead. Everyone in your old culture is angry with you; you search for answers, but find none.

Eventually you retreat into yourself, but answers do not come. Then one day you release all your old ideas. Wonder of wonders, understanding begins to fill the void. Maybe you return to your heritage, maybe you don't. Regardless you remain forever changed. When I was a child I thought and acted like a child. When I became a man I put away childish things…sound familiar?

Teachings of Jesus

When reading through the Thomas Gospel you come to a saying that goes like this: "If a man desires to kill a prominent man he will first draw forth his sword and thrust it into the wall to test his hand. Then he will kill the prominent man." Strange as that saying may sound, it has nothing to do with murdering anyone.

Rather it has to do with testing your mind, spirit and body until you gain the self-confidence to begin functioning as an intern God. The Kabbalah tells you not to believe a word you read, but rather test everything for yourself. In my sayings you will find the same wisdom. Test me and test God. Seek the truth until you find it. Only in that way can you grow into spiritual maturity.

Influence of the Kabbalah

The Kabbalah calls for each man to search his heart in order to experience his Godhood. In order to grow and perfect his skill, however, man must have an opposing force. This opposing force the Kabbalah refers to as Satan. Satan is neither good nor bad, merely an opposing force sufficient to allow man to test and perfect his skills. At the level of the third Chakra man acts as "apprentice God."

Influence of Eastern Mythology about the Chakras

Eastern mythology calls this adolescent spiritual stage, the third Chakra. Located at about the level of the belly button, the nervous tissue along the spinal cord controls the major organs of the gut, the stomach, pancreas, liver and your belief in yourself as a whole person. One who is able to function on his own as an adult, starts here. You get "Butterflies" in your stomach at the approach of danger. Yet the more you learn to listen to your "gut instincts" the faster you mature in the skills needed for survival.

Clearing the Third Chakra means having the courage to take charge of your own life; it's the first significant step in becoming the creator/controller/giver of your TRUE heritage as Son of God.

The Fourth Chakra

*This Chakra represents your complete surrender to God and taking charge
of your own earthly experience as God/Man; it manifests itself as a ball of green
flame at the level of the heart.*

The Fourth Chakra represents a time of wandering in the desert and, in entering the fourth Chakra energy, we are passing through the dark night of the soul; throwing off false beliefs; assuming responsibility for ourselves and finally reaching a balance between body and soul. When we have truly entered the Fourth Chakra, we throw off all fear and replace it with an understanding of our rightful inheritance as a physical manifestation of the mass soul. No separation exists between us and our brother other than the cloak of illusion drawn when we enter a body.

Remember in the Lord's Prayer I suggested: "Forgive us our trespasses as we forgive those who trespass against us?" What did that really mean? It meant there was never anything to forgive. Bodies try out various modes of behavior, depending on the degree to which they are caught up in their ego/fear or in their heart love/light. Bodies make mistakes, but the soul can never make a mistake. See past your own body (and that of your brother) to the soul and you see only love.

Your brother's actions towards you mirrors back your own perception of him; let go of all judgment against your brother and Center in the Father, "The All That Is." Let go of all fear and act as if the abundance of the universe is yours and as if the Universe wishes to bestow blessings on you and your brother alike. Be generous towards those in need—without any judgment; for it is not what you give to them that increase your love, but rather the trust with which you give it.

When the black cloud of fear seems to be gaining on you, do what you can, then hand over the reins to me and let go. I alone change your perception and the results that you bring upon yourself through your actions when you release fear—and trust in me. You truly bring about your own "Heart-attack" by closing down the center of your spiritual power and allowing ego to attack your physical center.

All these years society has told you that the Father is a God of Wrath; **nothing could be farther from the truth since God knows only love!** You can not pass through the Fourth Chakra until you accept your Godly responsibility to rule through love—and this is the hardest lesson of all. I said: "it is easier for a camel to pass through the eye of a needle than to enter the kingdom of heaven." How else could the camel make the journey other than to let go of physical form and pass through as a puff of smoke (spirit)? You can only pass through the eye of the Fourth Chakra when you let go of all sense of human need and learn to walk in perfect trust in the Father and love of your brother.

So far you have learned to feel at home between heaven and earth; to accept that we are all one and to remain centered against the storms of life. The fourth Chakra opens the door to becoming Man/God. Not only are you a stranger in a strange land (God in human form) but now you must take your place as Emperor elect—apprentice God, if you will.

What one gift, my young apprentice would you choose to rule yourself and to co-create the universe? Solomon chose well. When the pale horse of death—false teaching and war—rides forth all before him quake with fear. Why did good Christian Germans murder Jews and why do good Christian Americans hold dissidents in Cuban, American and Iraq prison camps?

Summary

The Church at Thyatira:

In the period of Thyatira the Catholic Church broke into the mother institution with multiple protestant offspring's. The population began to rebel and try to return to what they thought were the basics of my sayings.

Breaking away and—most significantly—throwing off all that you have been told about yourself so that you can come to know your own true nature represent the work of the Fourth Chakra. This is your time for exploration of new ideas, new ways of doing things.

Remember, the religious mentality that produced the problem of self-alienation is not capable of solving the problem. Therefore don't settle for replicating what you have been taught; the Protestant Churches did that. Instead, leave behind the Greek translations of my words. <u>Seek out the lost Gospels and read my words as directly translated from the Aramaic</u>. Then the rejuvenation of your soul shall become complete.

Teachings of Jesus

Love God above all things and your brother as yourself, the rest is window dressing. But how do you come to love yourself, much less God or your brother?

When you read the Aramaic you will see that the word for "bad" is "unripe;" the word for "good" is "ripe." You are neither bad nor good in the Greek sense of being, but rather you are ripe for the word of God or unripe—still tied up in your ego.

In my native Aramaic, the word for God means "all inclusive." The words for "Love your enemy" translate: "Find that place inside of you that resonates to your brother and slowly find common ground from there." The key to opening your fourth Chakra is to cast away the Greek translations of my words and cast away everything the churches have told you. Go in search of my Aramaic sayings.

Influence of the Kabbalah

I, Jesus, knew the Kabbalah well. The mysticism of one soul, unity, returning to your spiritual child and then learning to create, take charge and give from abundance—all comes from the Kabbalah.

The key to learning to love God above all things and your brother as yourself, also come from the Kabbalah teachings. Here is the key, instead of reacting in your old tired out emotional way:

- **Stop:** Your old reactive ways. Take a deep breath and learn a new mentality.

- **Think:** "What response would solve the problem with the least chaos?"

- **Pro-act:** Take action devised by a cool and loving mind.

Influence of Eastern Mythology about the Chakras

Located at the heart level, the fourth or Heart Chakra, represents the ripening of your spirit, your readiness to accept unity as a way of life. Here you cast aside judgmental thinking about others and turn your thoughts to how to bring about unity and peace. You accept yourself with all your warts and your brother with all his. Now a profound peace settles upon you.

Experiencing chest pains, having trouble breathing; dizziness and/or tightness across the chest? All these symptoms represent pent up anxiety that comes from feeling separate and alienated from your environment. BECOME your environment, and then peace and freedom from pain will find you.

The Fifth Chakra

This Chakra manifests itself as a ball of blue flame at the level of the throat.

Remember I told you that the third Chakra was a time to hold your own counsel? Well the Fifth **Chakra** represents time to speak your truth; but without wisdom, a true understanding of your God nature and practice in "management by love," (MBL) how could you speak your truth? The Elders ask: "When will we share a place with you on Earth or in Eden?" I reply, "Wait a bit longer and allow the mass consciousness time to grow."

Notice that the Fifth Chakra occurs *after* the dark night of the soul; *after* you have awakened to who you are; *after* you realize your responsibility for becoming God on earth—and ACTING the part. How appropriate that the blue flame occurs at the level of the throat and affects all physical aspects of speaking and breathing.

The Fifth Chakra is about speaking and living your role as God/Man right here on earth. It is about faith in the mass soul. It's about LIVING your divine nature and doing the right thing no matter what anyone else says or thinks, and trusting that all the power of the universe is acting in alliance with you.

Sound like you lost your marbles? You are in good company for they thought I had too! In fact they were so afraid of breaking away from the paradigm of separation and tribalism that they crucified me—and it might yet happen to you too.

The question is: "What really matters? The answer: Nothing! "No-thing" matters because you are *not* your body, you have come to earth to: (1) learn your true identity (2) live your true identity and (3) to help your brother awaken. THAT was the true message of the crucifixion.

I knew who I was; I lived who I was and I did my best to pass the message to you—in full realization that it might cost me my body to do so, therefore the crucifixion is all about the Fifth Chakra and of speaking our own truth.

Remember, I told you: "The Kingdom of Heaven is all about you, but you do not see it." By that I mean that the Kingdom surrounds you and that it literally is about your journey. At the level of the Fifth Chakra you DO see the Truth. But…there is still that element of doubt, that "what if" voice of the ego that tells you that you are separate and in danger from your brother. If your spirituality were threatened, you might work at strengthening it, but instead your spirituality is lulled to sleep; yet the mind can not stand a vacuum. So what happens?

Your mind turns from thoughts of God to thoughts of fear and when they come to crucify you, you run away. Then you experience physical problems with your voice, thyroid, etc. You become Jonah, swallowed by your own whale and are not released until you speak and act as you know you must.

Speak up. Ask "How would love handle this?" Accept, understand and act in accordance with the Ten Commandments/Attitudes. Then and only then are you free.

Summary

The Church at Sardis

The Church at Sardis represented a time of stagnation and bickering among the various Christian Churches. For you, this may be a stage of stagnation; also you have broken with mainline Christianity and have explored various religions. Now you have to admit to yourself that no religion or any other institution will get you where you need to be in order to experience your own Godhood. The dark night of the soul has passed, but nothing has yet come to fill the void.

Teachings of Jesus

I told you that it is not what goes into a man's mouth, but what comes out of it that affects the soul. By this I meant first you must learn to speak your own truth, not someone else's and secondly, you must learn to speak it in such a way as to bring about unity with your brother, even though you may believe differently.

Influence of the Kabbalah

Passing through the fourth Chakra you learned to stop, think and pro-act. Now in the fifth Chakra you learn to become initiator of new thoughts, the creator of new actions and the giver of grace. In other words you grow up.

Influence of Eastern Mythology about the Chakras

At the level of the fifth Chakra you learn to go into your heart for answers and then to speak your own truth; even when it makes no logical sense to you or anyone else at the time. Speaking an unpopular truth can get you into big trouble. Blockages at this Chakra will cause diseases of the neck including sore throat, laryngitis, thyroid problems and tongue and mouth problems. You will recognize fifth Chakra people by their calm demeanor, their silence and solitude, and by their compulsion to speak the truth, even when no on wants to hear it.

The Sixth Chakra

This Chakra manifests itself as a ball of deep indigo flame, the color of the midnight sky in the center of the forehead just above the eyes.

This is the Chakra of full Spiritual Awakening accompanied by fully enlightened participation in the universal soul. The Sixth Chakra represents the archetype of the mature King who rules with wisdom and grace; this is the first stage of experiencing God Consciousness. You are no longer caught up in the events of the world and when someone says: "Come here and see what your brother has done to hurt you," panic no longer sets in since you have already undergone the crucifixion of your ego for now you stand in a place where you can see the truth.

Others may injure your body, but they have no control over your soul. In point of fact, your soul and theirs are the same soul. Their power over you is no more than that of men dressed in red underwear rattling chains to frighten you. Your power to enlighten them and lead them to their true nature far overshadows their weak attempts at frightening you.

Your emotions, as you enter the Sixth Chakra, will be those of wonderment and puzzlement. You will *know* you can heal others (or whatever your gift happens to be) yet you will still want physical manifestation to prove to yourself that you are right. On your journey to become God/Man, you are presently Man/God. The doubt will pass as you mature in spirit and grow in faith. Learning the extent of your gifts and how to use them with discretion takes time.

Be patient with yourself: If ever there were a time when your ego will rise again, this is it. Remember that ego wants power and control—it's sneaky that way. Whenever you ask for anything, make sure to ask for it to manifest for the good of all that is. Your ego won't like that and will try to convince you it's a cop out, but it's not. Allow time for discernment to mature. That will happen in the next, the Seventh Chakra.

Meditate: This is how you maintain and grow your connection with the universal soul.

Persevere: As it is always darkest just before the dawn; so too is this a time of continuing to do what you know is correct—even without physical manifestation. Remember those old fashioned pumps where you had to pour water in before any came out? First you "primed" the pump, then you pumped and you pumped and you pumped and nothing happened. Finally you gave it one last pump and BINGO the water started to flow.

The Sixth Chakra is like that. You are "charging" your spiritual center by putting in faith and continuing to do the work until finally the water flows.

Summary

The Church at Philadelphia

The Church at Philadelphia represents that period in your life when you begin dabbling in mysticism and the paranormal. You join self-help groups. You go to psychics for Tarot readings. You KNOW an integrated energy source exists, but you don't know how to attain it.

After a while, you don't need psychics or anyone else. The searching from church to church and from metaphysical experience to metaphysical experience is simply part of your journey to awakening. Once you realize that only one soul exists and you are part of it—as is everything else in the universe—you no longer need an intermediary. Your journey is about planting the seed and then letting it ripen inside of you.

Teachings of Jesus

I told you right along that I will give you life and give it to you more abundantly. Did you think I meant when you died? Nonsense, you were designed to live a full and abundant life right here on this planet. You were NOT designed to get up in the morning, stick your head in the newspaper, drive to work on your cell phone, spend the day on the computer, drive home on your cell phone and spend the evening in front of a television set.

If that is how you live your life then no wonder you feel empty and stressed. You are meant to begin your day in quiet meditation where you let your soul do the talking, followed by time fully present with your family/friends, a drive to work fully aware of the world about you, time at work focused on doing what is appropriate—like doing your job and helping others to do theirs. When you drive home, notice your environment and be fully present with those about you. Come home to your family/pets fully aware of their beauty and essence. In that way you live life abundantly PLUS you tap into the eternal life of the soul.

Influence of the Kabbalah

In the Kabbalah, heaven is attained by learning to stop, think and act in a way that solves the problem while creating harmony. Spiritual maturity involves changing from the created to the creator; from the receiver to the giver of good things. How many people do you know who hurt and feel empty because for them life is all about "me, me, me?" If you want to find fulfillment, have life become about what you can do to help others awaken.

Influence of Eastern Mythology about the Chakras

The sixth Chakra can be found in the center of your forehead just above eye level. It represents your "sixth sense," your ability to just "know" the truth about yourself and others. The reason you visit Psychics is because you think they know something you don't. Not true! You came equipped with a sense of the truth that is just as perfect as that of birds flying north for the summer or butterflies making their first voyage to the exact spot of their ancestors. The sixth Chakra is about learning how to operate your "Third Eye."

The Seventh Chakra

This Chakra manifests itself as a ball of violet flame at the crown of the head.

This Chakra represents the transition from Man/God to God/Man. It represents a cataclysmic awakening of your soul to its rights and duties in the Universe *and* it serves as the yeast for the grand awakening of mankind. When the critical mass of humanity awakens, a sudden shift will occur in mass consciousness that will allow all to awaken who choose to do so.

How will you know when awakening has occurred for you? The existential fear of separation will vanish and be replaced by a love for all things. You will no longer just love, rather you will **become** love.

You will see yourself, the earth and all around you for what it is—an illusion to be enjoyed and recreated in the image of love.

You will meditate, listen to your inner voice and trust more in the unknown than the known.

You will seek the path of your bliss, rather than the path of safety in choosing your career, your mate, your lifestyle.

To other people you are delusional because you return good for evil; raise your hand against not man, beast or any part of the environment.

You give from bounty you do not appear to have.

You keep your own counsel, explaining yourself to no one. You remain independent of needing the good will of other people.

You recognize the inherent goodness in all people and speak ill of no one.

You teach by example, stories, questions and non-interference. You force your ideas on no one.

Goods and earthly "things" no longer matter to you. You make use of what you need and give the rest away. No one can steal from you because you willingly give your goods to them.

You laugh often and live in joy and in peace.

These actions come from inside your nature—and *are* who you truly are.

Summary

The Seventh Level

Notice there are no churches mentioned after the Church at Philadelphia. The reason: you don't need them. By the time you reach the seventh level of spiritual maturity you fully accept that you are God—as is everything else in the universe. This truth no longer presents itself as a matter of faith, it manifests as certainty.

Teachings of Jesus

I told you in the Gospel of John 14:20: "I am in the Father as He is in me and I am in you." At the level of the seventh Chakra, no one has to tell you, you already know.

Influence of the Kabbalah

According to the Kabbalah, a curtain is drawn when you come to earth. Therefore you have two sides to your understanding of God. The 1% side you can see with your five senses and the 99% side you can eventually predict and feel, but not experience with your five senses.

The Kabbalah predicted ten dimensions of physical existence. We see three and experience time. That leaves six not experienced by the human body. Yet modern physics now confirms that these additional six dimensions must exist, and man's deepest desire is to attain the spiritual light contained in all ten dimensions.

Reaching the Seventh Chakra represents reaching the moment of transformation where you come into contact with the 99% realm. At this level we easily resist our negative impulses and use obstacles as opportunities to connect to Divine Light. Once you access Divine Light you love God above all things and your neighbor as yourself—all else is just window dressing.

Influence of Eastern Mythology about the Chakras

Attaining the seventh Chakra and opening to the Light of the 99% realm of reality are virtually inseparable.

Amen.

Epilogue

Upon the re-inauguration of the current President of the United States, the final events will have taken place, for this action will inaugurate the beginning of the end of times; setting in place the events forecast.

When the President believes he is doing God's work, he is correct because after all, someone needs to work for the "dark side" in order to enable the escalation of Armageddon. Remember—*"we are all one"* and this task is a difficult one. As you have read in the text, Armageddon is the "final battle" preceding the Apocalypse. Insofar as he (the President) is concerned, his mindset is that God speaks directly to him and that he has a mandate from God to wage holy wars. Forgive him, bless him and thank him for his courage, and keep him always in your prayers.

As for your own actions, avoid those who disagree with your knowledge. Do not go forth, postulate and/or "preach" to anyone; let them come to you. Only relate to those who agree with you, eliminate those who disagree from your beingness.

Keep the faith and God Bless You One and All!

Finis.

Recommended Readings/Listening

POWER OF KABALLA—Secrets of the Universe and the meaning of our lives, by Yehuda Berg, Kabbalah Centre International, Inc. *(ISBN 1-57189-180-3)*

GNOSIS—by Todd Settimo, as referred to on page 59. Available at: tsettimo@mind.net

LOVE AND BEYOND—Your journey on Earth with God, By David Kessler—Sing Up Publishing, PO Box 505, Bettendorf, IA 52722 www.SingUpPub.com

ORIGINAL PRAYER—Teachings and Meditations on the Aramaic Words of Jesus, By Neil Douglas Klotz—Sounds True, PO. Box 8010, Boulder, Co. 80306 www.soundstrue.com

THE COURSE IN MIRACLES—Pu*blished by the Foundation for Inner Peace.* *(ISBN 0-9606388-8-1)*

THE TRUTH ABOUT CREATION—The Book of Genesis Deciphered. (Due in the fall of the year, 2005.)

0-595-33043-6

Lightning Source UK Ltd.
Milton Keynes UK
UKHW041018060521
383240UK00001B/13